"WHEN THE LAMP IS SHATTERED"

Desire and Narrative in Catullus

Micaela Janan

Southern Illinois University Press
Carbondale and Edwardsville

Library of Congress Cataloging-in-Publication Data

Janan, Micaela Wakil.
    "When the lamp is shattered": desire and narrative in Catullus /
Micaela Janan.
    p.   cm.
    Includes bibliographical references and index.
    1. Catullus, Gaius Valerius—Criticism and interpretation.
    2. Love poetry, Latin—History and criticism. 3. Psychoanalysis and
literature. 4. Desire in literature. 5. Narration (Rhetoric)
6. Rome in literature. 7. Rhetoric, Ancient. I. Title.
PA6276.J36   1994
874'.01—dc20   92-43064
ISBN 0-8093-1765-6   CIP

"For Once, Then, Something" by Robert Frost. From *The Poetry of Robert Frost*, edited by Edward Connery Lathem. Copyright 1923, © 1969 by Holt, Rinehart and Winston. Copyright 1951 by Robert Frost. Reprinted by permission of Henry Holt and Company, Inc.

"From a Letter from Lesbia," from *The Portable Dorothy Parker* by Dorothy Parker, Introduction by Brendan Gill. Copyright 1928, renewed © 1956 by Dorothy Parker. Used by permission of Viking Penguin, a division of Penguin Books USA Inc.

To Viola and Leonard Dalton
Parentibus optimis dulcissimisque

When the lamp is shattered
The light in the dust lies dead—
When the cloud is scattered
The rainbow's glory is shed.
    When the lute is broken,
Sweet tones are remembered not;
    When the lips have spoken,
Loved accents are soon forgot.
                    —Shelley

. . . Then all the charm
Is broken—all that phantom world so fair
Vanishes, and a thousand circlets spread,
And each misshapes the other. Stay awhile,
Poor youth! who scarcely dar'st lift up thine eyes—
The stream will soon renew its smoothness, soon
The visions will return! And lo, he stays,
And soon the fragments dim of lovely forms
Come trembling back, unite, and now once more
The pool becomes a mirror.
                    —Coleridge

Contents

Preface

... the life and writings of Catullus, that imbroglio of problems where dogma and ingenuity have their habitation, where argument moves in circles, and no new passage in or out.

—R. Syme[1]

CATULLUS IS A POET about whom everything is difficult. First, there are the manuscript problems: rarely has an author survived to the modern age by so slender a thread—a single manuscript in a state of wretched confusion. The text as we have it is neither the author's autograph nor an *editio princeps,* with form, order, and content authorized by the writer—and only a few extremists argue that what we have reflects Catullus' intentions closely.[2] As a result, we as readers are not sure of the most basic characteristics of our text: Where does one poem end, and another poem begin? Which poems are complete, and which are mere fragments? What is the governing order of reading—which poem are we supposed to read first, and which next?[3]

Beyond the single point of ordinal clarity—poem 1, the dedicatory poem to a poetry book, whatever poems in whatever order that may have encompassed—the reader is left to piece together a narrative from the poems of the corpus. The text solicits the reader's desire for narrative closure and completeness, a desire ultimately doomed (like all desire) to frustration: the clues within the text will support any number of orders of reading and thus any number of "plots", none clearly predominant. And the bait within the text is also desire—chiefly, the fragmentary history of a love affair between Catullus and a woman he calls Lesbia. Thus the Catullan text demands that we align its mechanics of reading with its subject matter along the same axis: desire. I seek to describe just exactly how this works—how the Catullan text addresses the reader, and how it represents the subjects who speak, act, and love within it—from a point of view informed by modern and ancient theoretical discourses on desire.

I draw principally upon Plato, Freud, and Lacan to flesh out a poetics of desire suited to the Catullan corpus. These three theoreticians of the erotic all draw an explicit connection between *erōs* and the creative arts (including poetry); but more importantly, they all conceive of human consciousness as itself fragmentary and incomplete, radically divided from itself. All consequently craft methodologies designed to recover knowledge only imperfectly available to consciousness (knowledge of the Beautiful, for Plato; of unconscious desire, for Freud and Lacan).

The theory of divided consciousness shared by Plato, Freud, and Lacan allows us to displace the comparatively narrow and monolithic terms in which Catullan consciousness has traditionally been discussed—for example, *person/persona, individual,* and *self*—with a more comprehensive and flexible concept. The traditional terms imply a consciousness completely self-aware, self-controlled, and autonomous. They thus resist accounting for the effects of forces that someone neither originates nor controls. I propose to supplement these with the concept of the *subject*—conceived, not as a substance (like a stone), but as a site through which social, cultural, institutional and unconscious forces move. The model is the grammatical subject, governed from outside itself by rules of grammar and syntax making up a linguistic structure—rules that grant the "I" its meaning. The subject is thus the vector product of all the forces in play at the site of consciousness at any one time.[4] Thinking in these terms wins for the Catullan corpus a flexibility in constructing the text's agents and speakers equal to the flexibility of constructing the orders of reading invited by the corpus itself. I shall argue that neither the Catullan subject nor the Catullan text is a reified determinate given, but a polymorphous and continuing production of meanings.

Expanding the conceptualization of text and subject in this fashion allows me to align questions of the subject's construction with questions of knowledge, as both are dramatized by the Catullan text. What we can know—and, even more insistently, what we can*not* know—about this seductively mysterious body of poetry, is a question that conditions our reading. Not by accident does the question haunt poems chiefly concerned with desire: I shall argue that for Catullus, no less than for Plato, the soul flies toward knowledge on the wings of desire. But what Freud and Lacan make visible in Catullus is the degree to which both the shape of the wings and of the goal are gender-specific—though I shall also contend that

x

"masculine" and "feminine" in Catullus have nothing to do with anatomy and everything to do with epistemology.

I see in Catullus' fascination and identification with women in his poetry[5] a determined interrogation of the institutions Man and Woman, as fictions erected by culture. Catullus' poems rest the opposition between the two positions on knowledge, not biology. Determinate, transmissable meaning and epistemological certainty—the satisfying closure the reader desires to extract from the text—align with the sign of "masculine" authority: the phallus. But against this transparent ruse, the text deploys with equal vigor the forces of skepticism, logical fracture, "gaps" in meaning, and a knowledge that exceeds rationality—all subsumed under the "feminine" concepts of *jouissance* and *mania,* the gifts of saints and sibyls.

Seeing the text in this light changes the questions we ask of Catullus, but also of Lesbia. She has been reified not only as the source of all Catullus' woes but as a symptom of all the Late Roman Republic's ills: greed, aristocratic pride, deception, and profligacy. But by treating so implausibly evil a figure as a transparent reflection of reality, we elide certain questions before we have properly faced them—questions such as, Why does Lesbia (much more so than Mamurra or Vatinius or even Caesar) bear the burden of history in this text? Why is a *woman* the "right man for the job?" To answer this and other questions aimed at elucidating Lesbia's exact function in the text, I shall examine her appearances less as a particular woman who gave the poet trouble than as an instance of the overarching, misogynistic construction of Woman—a fictive symptom of what is repressed and disowned in cultural discourse.

Acknowledgments

THIS BOOK HAS LEFT behind a trail of happy debts in its wake—
happy for me, at least, the grateful debtor. More people have contributed
to its existence than I could possibly mention on this page, or thank
adequately: if they do not see their names here, they should know I am
perplexed by an embarrassment of riches rather than ungrateful.

I owe my principal acknowledgment to the one who introduced me
to the ancients and their literature: Mary-Kay Gamel, at the University of
California-Santa Cruz. She brought to her classes the comprehensive wis-
dom of Minerva and the infectious verve of Bacchus. Her example inspired
me to study the classics and unwittingly set me on this long journey to
Catullus.

I also wish to thank Mary Elisabeth McDavid-Rivetti, who first saw
in the *disiecta membra* of my sketches on Catullus the possibility of a
coherent approach. At a critical early moment, she suggested the overall
plan and order of this study, which has made all the rest possible. I owe
much, also, to Graham Hammill and Leigh DeNeef of Duke University's
English department, who gave generously of themselves and their time to
further my education in Lacan. My colleagues at Duke's Department of
Classical Studies have provided the help, advice, and atmosphere of learned
camaraderie necessary for me to finish this book. In particular, Peter Burian,
Diskin Clay, and Francis Newton read more versions of the manuscript
than should reasonably be expected of any mortals. I have benefited immea-
surably from their suggestions and corrections, which account for many
of the book's felicities; its errors, of course, are wholly my own.

I am grateful to David Konstan and the late J. P. Sullivan, who
kindly consented to be Southern Illinois University Press's readers for the
manuscript. I hope this ultimate version mirrors my deep engagement
with their readings.

Acknowledgments

Teresa White of SIU Press edited the manuscript with an ingenious mixture of tact and firmness. Jane Bullock and Ann Wood staunchly battled computer insubordination to produce the final version. The Research Council of Duke University generously paid for research assistance, which Denise McCoskey executed with her customary shrewd intelligence and gift for scholarly sleuthing.

Finally, loving thanks to my friends Kären Wigen and Martin Lewis for tea, laughter, and Catullus in the kitchen.

A Note on Citation

IN MY TEXT, I have cited both ancient and modern works according to the conventions of classical philology (and provided my own translations, unless otherwise noted). The abbreviations for ancient texts are taken from *The Oxford Classical Dictionary;* those for journals, from *L'Année Philologique*. My text for Catullus is that of D. F. S. Thomson (*Catullus: A Critical Edition;* Chapel Hill, NC, 1978); for Plato, John Burnet (*Platonis Opera,* Oxford, 1901); for Freud, *The Standard Edition of the Complete Psychological Works of Sigmund Freud,* ed. and trans. James Strachey. I have, as is customary, abbreviated the Latin word for poem (*carmen*) as "c."—"cc." for "poems"—followed by the appropriate number from the Catullan corpus. Accordingly, "c.7" = "poem 7"; "cc.5–8" = "poems 5 through 8." References to Plato are keyed to the page, section, and line number(s) of the Renaissance edition by Stephanus, standard for all serious editions. Citations from the *Standard Edition* of Freud appear as "*SE,*" then the volume number, followed by a colon, then page numbers: thus, "*SE* 23:209" = "Standard Edition, volume 23, page 209."

Citing the works of Jacques Lacan presents peculiar problems: first, there is the difficulty of the Lacanian corpus itself. The bulk of Lacan's work was transmitted orally, in his *Séminaires* given between 1953 and 1980; the texts of these seminars are being slowly edited from student notes and tape recordings of the sessions by Lacan's son-in-law, Jacques-Alain Miller. Yet at this writing, out of almost thirty seminars, only some six have been definitively edited. The rest enjoy a precarious twilight existence: some are partially recorded in the journal *Ornicar?*; some circulate in "pirate" texts established unofficially by the members of *École Freudienne de Paris;* some have, as yet, no public written redaction at all. Citing pages from the unpublished works that constitute the substance of

Lacan's work would be unhelpful, given that such texts and their pagination will eventually be rendered obsolete by Miller's definitive editions.

But more importantly, Lacan is next to impossible to quote, or cite, in exemplary fashion. Seldom can a concept of his be pinned down to a sentence, paragraph, or page of a specific composition. Lacan requires the reader to keep so many conceptual balls in the air at one time that she needs almost the whole of his work as context to interpret any part of it. I would be doing the reader a disservice to pretend otherwise, and to cite narrowly, as though understanding Lacan were a matter to be solved by a casual glance here and there in his oeuvre.

For both these reasons, I have followed a somewhat different procedure from the customary scholarly reference to exact pages in particular works. My notes generally cite *in toto* seminars and essays especially relevant to a concept, rather than select pages. If any section of a seminar is unusually rich in references, I single it out for special notice. However, Lacan's concepts evolved continually, and many make their advent long before being given substantial theoretical shape. *Jouissance,* for example, appears briefly in the 1953 *Discours de Rome* but must wait over twenty years before being fleshed out in the 1974 *Séminaire* XX *(Encore)*. I have not cited early glimmers of a term where it would serve no purpose to do so.

Lacan's surrealist style and the breadth of his conceptual antecedents together make the task of broaching his thought formidable indeed. Fortunately several excellent guides to his work have been published in the last few years, which can offer help to the reader wishing to delve further. I have derived inestimable aid and comfort from the following:

Mikkel Borch-Jacobsen, *Lacan: The Absolute Master* (Stanford, CA: Stanford University Press, 1991).

Malcolm Bowie, *Lacan* (Cambridge, MA: Harvard University Press, 1991).

Juliet Mitchell and Jacqueline Rose, eds., *Feminine Sexuality: Jacques Lacan and the école freudienne* (New York: W. W. Norton, 1982).

Ellie Ragland-Sullivan *Lacan and the Philosophy of Psychoanalysis* (Urbana, IL: University of Illinois Press, 1986).

Ellie Ragland-Sullivan, and Mark Bracher, eds., *Lacan and the Subject of Language* (New York: Routledge, 1991).

To avoid cumbersome citations in the text, I list below in full the works of Lacan I have used; only brief citations will be given in my discussion. "S" followed by a Roman numeral refers to the *Séminaires:* if published, I refer to the page numbers of the published edition; if unpublished, to the date of the particular session in question. A page citation alone refers to the pages of the essay collection, *Écrits;* a double-page citation refers to the original French edition of *Écrits* and to the corresponding passage in Sheridan's English translation of selected essays from *Écrits* (or, in the case of *Séminaires* I and II, to the translations by Forrester and Tomaselli, respectively).

Séminaires

  I: *Les écrits techniques de Freud* (Paris, 1975); translated as *Book I: Freud's papers on Technique, 1953–54*, trans. John Forrester (New York, 1988).

  II: *Le moi dans la théorie de Freud et dans la technique de la psychanalyse* (Paris, 1978); translated as *Book II: The Ego in Freud's Theory and in the Technique of Psychoanalysis*, trans. Sylvana Tomaselli (New York, 1988).

  III: *Les psychoses* (Paris, 1981).

  IV: *La relation d'objet et les structures freudiennes* (unpublished) (1956–57).

  V: *Les formations de l'inconscient* (unpublished) (1957–58).

  VII: *L'éthique de la psychanalyse* (Paris, 1986).

  VIII: *Le transfert* (unpublished) (1960–61).

  X: *L'angoisse* (unpublished) (1962–63).

  XI: *Les quatres concepts fondamentaux de la psychanalyse* (Paris, 1973).

  XIV: *La logique du fantasme* (unpublished) (1966–67).

  XX: *Encore* (Paris, 1975).

  XXII: *R.S.I.* Published in *Ornicar?* (1975), ed. J.-A. Miller.

  XXIV: *L'insu-que-sait de l'Une-bévue s'aile à mourre.* Published in *Ornicar?* (1977–79), ed. J.-A. Miller.

Écrits (Seuil, 1966); *Écrits: A Selection*, trans. Alan Sheridan (New York, 1977)

  "Le stade du miroir comme formateur de la fonction du Je" [The mirror stage as formative of the function of the I] 93–100/1–7.

  "L'aggressivité en psychanalyse" [Aggressivity in psychoanalysis] 101–24/8–29.

  "Le temps logique" [Logical time] 197–213.

  "Fonction et champ de la parole et du langage en psychanalyse" [The function and field of speech and language in psychoanalysis] 237–322/30–113.

"L'instance de la lettre dans l'inconscient ou la raison depuis Freud" [The agency of the letter in the unconscious or reason since Freud] 493–528/146–78.

"La direction de la cure et les principes de son pouvoir" [The direction of the treatment and the principles of its power] 585–645/226–80.

"La signification du phallus" [The meaning of the phallus] 685–95/281–91.

"Propos directif pour un congres sur la sexualité féminine" [Guiding remarks for a congress on feminine sexuality] 725–36.

"Subversion du sujet et dialectique du désir dans l'inconscient freudien" [The subversion of the subject and the dialectic of desire in the Freudian unconscious] 793–827/292–325.

In the following pages, works that have been translated into English will be cited by the pagination in the French edition, followed by a slash, then the corresponding pages in the English edition.

Other Abbreviations

Pf. (or "Pfeiffer") = R. Pfeiffer, ed., *Callimachus* (Oxford, 1949–53).
LP (or "Lobel-Page") = E. Lobel and D. Page, eds., *Poetarum Lesbiorum Fragmenta* (Oxford, 1955).

1

From Plato to Freud to Lacan: A History of the Subject

Theoretical Framework

IN THE BRIEF BIOGRAPHY prefacing his widely circulated 1893 edition of Catullus' poems, E. T. Merrill dismisses history with Olympian unconcern:

> It is possible to know [Catullus] personally as only now and then an ancient writer can be known to us, and yet he gives us but few definite biographical facts concerning himself, while still fewer are given by other authors of his own and later ages. But the little body of poems that constitute his extant works is so replete with his intense personality, and shows forth so unreservedly his every emotion, that the man stands out before us as does no other man of the age with the exception of two or three of its political leaders. And all this is true, even though we acknowledge, as we are bound to do, that in many questions of importance concerning his life we must be content with a working hypothesis instead of a series of established facts, and that the biographer, as the interpreter of the poems of Catullus, must be understood to be presenting probabilities, and not certainties.[1]

Merrill's serene summation of the mystery and faith necessary to Catullan criticism articulates perfectly the tension I wish to fret in the Catullan text: the pull between the fragmentary nature of the data on the one hand (chiefly the poems themselves, with a few biographical notes of dubious merit from other hands) and the need to construct a meaningful whole from it on the other (which Merrill translates as the need for a biography). The naïve assumptions of biographical criticism have long been discredited,[2] but I strive to retain a kernel of perspicacity about to be discarded with unfashionable chaff. Whatever the merits of Merrill's assumptions, he at least saw that questions basic to interpretation—"who is speaking? to whom is he speaking? what is he telling us?"—are all functionally interrelated. When Merrill emphasizes Catullus' poems over any other evidence of his life, when he glosses "the biographer" as "the interpreter of the poems of Catullus," he attends closely (*malgré lui*, perhaps) to the way in which Catullus' "I", the necessary fiction of identity, rests upon a purely textual function.

The conceptual connection Merrill's statement crystallizes importantly insists upon seeing the problems of the Catullan poems—the exiguous and confusing evidence of the text; the uncertainty of the narratives it supports; the vivid contradictions of its personalities—as intimately interrelated. Because the manuscript that preserved the "little body of poems" did not thoughtfully provide us with an authoritative sequence as well, "what he is telling us" adds up to a troubled narrative (indeed, more than one). Though obviously the Catullus who speaks in this poetry fell in love with Lesbia and found his love troubled; learned his brother died, went to Bithynia, visited his brother's grave and returned—when, where, and how is this supposed to have happened? Were there many fallings out between him and Lesbia, or just one great, final rift? Why is he certain his family line ends with his brother's death—why won't Catullus marry and have children? And does his decision bear upon Lesbia?

The problems with narrative affect our construction of the poems' speaker. Catullus is regularly regarded as unstable in basic categories of the self[3]—such as gender.[4] Because he so often compares himself to women, he is said to have "a strong dash of the feminine" about himself.[5] Nor can he keep a firm hold on his identity: often he splits into Catullus the admonisher and Catullus the admonished in a single poem or schizophrenically spits hatred and warbles love at the same object in poems mutually referenced by meter, diction, and subject matter.[6]

Returning full circle, the dramatic contradictions of the speaker are drawn into the arguments over reconstructing the *Ur*-text and the sensible order to be drawn from it. Readers justify dividing a poem because they find its emotional vicissitudes psychologically implausible; or they make Catullus' emotions describe the history of his love affair in a naïve, simplistic trajectory from love to hate but not back again.[7] Read vituperation after adoration;[8] disillusionment after wonder; despair after hope.

Yes, we know Catullus—but both too much, and too little, ever to produce certainties from the plethora of contradictory data his poems generate. We have too much that tempts us into speculation and too little ever to replace speculation with certainty. Our problems arise (as I shall argue) from acknowledging insufficiently the play between these two poles—from imposing certainty with a textual coherence that naïvely parallels psychic coherence. Catullus flatly contradicts us with his testimony against himself: "odi et amo," "I hate *and* I love" (c.85).

As I have defined the problems of the Catullan corpus above, two things become obvious. First, every category affects every other. Deciding that a poem is a unity or a disunity will affect the order of reading; the order of reading will affect the narrative; the narrative, the shape of the speaker that emerges from it; the shape of the speaker, the construction of the narrative. Each chain of meaning connects to every other: touch one and you touch them all.

Second, the basic conceptual terms around which our investigation revolves are *boundary* and *transgression,* concepts that govern the problems of

a. The borders of the individual poems—where they begin and end
b. The borders of the order(s) of reading—where it (or they) begin(s) and end(s)
c. The borders of the personae produced by the text—how and where they are divided up among such categories of the person as male/female; self/ other; mad/sane.

The key terms are not accidental but are suggested by a concinnity between aesthetics and subject matter—between, respectively, the Callimachean poetics Catullus espoused and the predominant subject matter of his poetry, desire.

Callimachus and the Poetics of Limit

Callimachean poetics hinges upon the concepts of boundary and transgression, insofar as it is a poetics of discrimination and exclusion. Strait is the gate and narrow is the way that Callimachus would have limit the scope of the poet's ambition and the size of his audience to an exquisite minimum; his own aesthetics effectively remove him from the sphere of the Homeric epic tradition (a tradition, Wendell Clausen argues, too great to be imitable and therefore designedly given a wide berth by Callimachus).[9]

Callimachus' most notorious aesthetic statement is that "a big book

3

is a big evil."[10] Yet his own poetic practice makes it clear that size alone is not the issue: though he quotes his critics as lambasting him for not writing a continuous poem in thousands of lines,[11] his *Aetia*, by most estimates, comprised four thousand to six thousand verses. But the episodic arrangement of the *Aetia* detaches the poem from the necessity of describing a continuous narrative, unlike the cyclic epics[12] that carried on the Homeric tradition. The poet is thus free to evidence his discrimination in the choice of material selected for his compartmentalized frame and to invite the reader to grant each modest subunit a correspondingly more intense attention. By contrast, Callimachus' pungent expressions of distaste for cyclic poetry imagistically suggest that its ambition to be comprehensive entails lack of selectivity: cyclic poetry is as bad as a public fountain or a promiscuous lover.[13]

Yet if size is not per se the central consideration in poetry, Callimachus nonetheless deploys it metonymically as a common token of discriminatory criteria. When Apollo, the god of poetry, gives Callimachus metaphorical standards by which to shape his poems, he cautions his follower to "keep the Muse *slender* (*leptaleēn*)" and "drive your chariot . . . on unworn paths, even if your path is *narrower*."[14]

The narrowness of the "road" Callimachus' poetry must travel limits traffic to the few; this elitist poetry rejects catholic participation in favor of a small, but select, group. Ruthless editing keeps the Muse slender: exiguous verses betoken discrimination. Accordingly, Callimachus praises the *Phaenomena* of Aratus as the result of winnowing and many sleepless nights of effort: "not to the very end of his songs, but only the most honey-sweet of his verses has the Solian poet copied. Hail, *slender* (*leptai*) discourse, token of Aratus' sleeplessness!"[15] Callimachus himself also eschews inflated style: "Don't look for me to bring forth a great noisy song; *thundering* belongs to Zeus, not to me."[16]

These images all adduce limit as a criterion applied to the poets, the audience, and the verses themselves of "good" poetry—but upon what basis is such discrimination made? The only positive value Callimachus clearly espouses is learning—not unexpected for a man so long connected with the great Library at Alexandria. Erudition, recherché reference, the display of knowledge for its own sake, are intrinsic to the Callimachean aesthetic. He admires Aratus precisely as "the most *widely learned* (*polumathēs*) and excellent poet possible"[17]—and his own notoriously obscure allusions make the epithet equally applicable to Callimachus himself (and to his readers).[18] But he is no sour pedant (strange if he were, and Catullus, "tenderest of Roman poets," were his admirer): his scholarly subtlety often

4

shades off into something less august and more wickedly playful. He regularly challenges his audience to exercise their wits upon how to take what he says: is he speaking comedy? tragedy? or that maddeningly ungraspable mediate entity, irony? Callimachus' poetry deploys the always-just-possible gap between "what he says" and "what he means" to fascinate his audience.

Catullus and a few of his contemporary fellow poets[19] inherited this aesthetic. Catullus' own introductory poem to his corpus announces, in an offhand way, the compositional aesthetic that governs his poetry. He writes "trifles" (*nugae*), which he can fit into a "booklet" (*libellus*); but this *libellus* is nonetheless "witty" (*lepidus*) and "polished" (*expolitus*). He views his poetry as physically delimited, yet the focus of the elaborate care Hellenistic aesthetics prescribes.

But any poetics whose governing ideology can be expressed as "stop here" must, to be meaningful, imply the opposite, "don't stop here."[20] Boundary *ipso facto* implies transgression as its antithesis. And the same paradoxical conceptual poles govern erotic desire: *erōs* arrays an impressive cultural machinery (in legal codes, in religion, in custom, in mythology, etc.) to say "we two are as one"—even though it exists precisely because a conceptual and physical boundary separates "I" from "thou."

But even granting this parallel, what has this to do with Catullan textual problems? How is it possible to compare the random accidents of manuscript transmission with considered choices of aesthetic allegiance and material? It is possible because I wish to trouble the easy apportionment of the text's problems between choice and chance—between the "conscious" and the "unconscious" of the text. As we examine the Catullan corpus, we will grapple with the problem Merrill's statement threw into relief: how we, as readers, constitute a text—an enterprise riddled with ideology, largely unguessed, concerning the coherence of individual poems, of narrative, of personae, and so on. I do not claim that my investigation proceeds from some Archimedean point free from such preconceptions; rather, I shall show that an expanded theory of agency and narrative in the Catullan corpus can save us from "rectifying" every apparent incoherence in a troubled manuscript tradition before we've plumbed its import.

From Person to Subject

The conceptual paradox shared by the formal principles of the Catullan corpus and its subject matter, desire, hints at a new way of approaching the corpus—but first we need to rethink the categories of text, personae,

5

and narrative along more flexible lines. If these obey both "stop here" and "don't stop here," they can hardly be monoliths: already the problems in locating the poems' speaker, as I have outlined them above, have put pressure upon the term *persona* (as well as the *self* implied behind it). The idea of masks (*personae*) assumed by the artist seems initially an appealing way to deal with inconsistencies in Catullus' self-portrayal; we have already implied that such a gap between the poet and his self-presentation inheres in the aesthetic Catullus received from Callimachus, when we spoke of Callimachean irony. Perhaps Catullus simply assumes a number of contradictory roles. But that formulation breaks down logically in interesting ways. First, it assumes that, behind these various masks produced by the text, there is nonetheless an entity unified enough to be called simply "Catullus the author," whose agency accounts for what we read. Even though we know nothing of him beyond the text, we can tell when he is assuming a mask.

But the fact that readers cannot agree on precisely when this happens contradicts such an assumption. Consider: long-standing debates exist over whether this or that Catullan poem is "humorous" or "serious," with impressive reasoning ranged on both sides of the question.[21] Arguing either side hinges on gauging the relationship between what the speaker says and what he "really means" (and, by extension, who he "really is"). That formulation curiously posits "Catullus" as a numinous unity and consistency implied by the words on the page but either contradicting what they say, or needed *in addition* to ratify their meaning, by what he thinks. If that is true, we need, not a text, but a spiritualist; and if not true, we want a better formulation of textual agency and consciousness to ground our discussion of the Catullan corpus, if we are to account rigorously for its phenomena without simply reconfiguring the biographical fallacy as an authorial fallacy.

As I said in the preface, I propose to set alongside the terms I have been using to describe agents and speakers in the corpus—*person/persona, individual,* and *self*—the more comprehensive and flexible concept of the *subject.* As noted, *person* and its synonyms register badly, if at all, the effects of forces that exceed any particular agent. These forces particularly interest us, since we are accounting for an agent entirely produced by language (the "words on a page" *and* our reading of them)—an institution shared by speaker and reader, but exceeding their individual mastery. When I mentioned the advantages of subject over more individualizing terms, I cited its flexibility of construction as matching the variable construction of the Catullan corpus. As an analytic term, *subject* has the additional

6

advantage of making explicit the fact that any one construction of "I," to whatever degree perceived as stable, continuous, and authentic, is nonetheless a function of who or what constructs that "I." Thus not only can "subject" better embrace all the "Catulluses" we have arrayed in our brief conspectus of Catullan debate, but it draws in the reader and *her* own provisional unity as an integral part of making each Catullus. The apparent stability of the perceiver, as well as the perceived, turns out to be governed by the slippery paradox of "stop here"/"don't stop here."

Despite the apparent modernity of the term "subject," the conceptualization of consciousness to which it points has a long history in discourse on desire. Three theoreticians of desire of the ancient and modern worlds are particularly suited to fleshing out an erotic poetics suited to Catullus' text, narrative, and subjectivity. Plato, Freud,[22] and Lacan all explicitly theorize a connection between desire and creative art. Plato draws the connection in the *Symposium* (and, more loosely, in the *Phaedrus*); Freud, in his various literary-critical essays; Lacan, in his own literary-critical essays, and in defining poetry as the sole instrument adequate to an investigation of love.[23] These links not only match the Catullan corpus' solicitation of the reader's desire with an enigmatically incomplete love story but also parallel Catullus' metaphorical equation between writing and desire. For example, he consistently uses such words as *ludus/ludere* ("play") to mean both "make love" and "write (in the Callimachean aesthetic mode)" as part of a considerable vocabulary that leans upon erotic and literary-aesthetic connotations for its effect.[24]

All three (as earlier remarked) conceive of human consciousness as radically divided from itself—a model suited to the contradictory subject of the Catullan text. Plato's, Freud's, and Lacan's particular models roughly coincide: the theory of the tripartite soul in Plato (divided amongst the domains of reason, spirit, and appetite) resembles the tripartite psyche mapped by Freud (divided in Freud's earlier writings amongst Unconscious/Preconscious/Conscious, upon which the Id/Ego/Superego schema is later superimposed). Lacan expands the model to encompass social and cultural effects that exceed the subject but retains the tripartite division and the broad conceptual features of the Platonic and Freudian models.

As a logical consequence, all three locate knowledge crucial to the subject elsewhere than in the forefront of her awareness. They treat this knowledge as a fragmented text, presumed once to have been complete but now imperfectly represented. Plato seeks, through anamnesis, to rescue precorporal knowledge of the Forms, through exposing the inadequate, contradictory and partial nature of common opinions about the Good.

Freud and Lacan, on the other hand, analyze the fragmentary and riddling "texts" of dreams, parapraxes and symptoms, to put together the narrative of trauma and desire that generated these records. Consequently all their methodologies offer ideal tools with which to handle the fragmentary Catullan text—and by "fragmentary" I refer not only to the present troubled state of the Catullus manuscript and its relation to the author's imagined pristine autograph but also to the relation of the poems in that ideal, vanished autograph to the mythical train of events they purport to record. My purpose, however, is not to generate yet another speculative version of the *Ur*-text or of Catullus' biography. Rather, I wish to examine the ways in which "wholeness" is constructed, to expose the psychic underpinnings of what we consider narrative and history. The reconstitution either of a text or of "events" deduced from their alleged record can tell us much about our preconceptions not only behind reading and writing but behind truth and fiction.

Central Questions

Exploring the usefulness of Plato, Freud, and Lacan, I have obviously moved among different aspects of the poems—narrative order, personae, poetics—though I focus broadly on desire. My inquiry necessarily fractures into different registers with the questions, "*whose* desire—the reader's or the text's? And where, how and through what is it expressed?" I shall use desire as an interrogative tool to map the experience of these poems intersubjectively between reader and text (since the author's desire is, apart from the text, virtually unknowable). Yes, there *is* a text in this classroom, but it is emphatically text-as-textual-production,[25] so that the reader and her role in constructing it will be as crucial to our investigation as the subject represented within it. "Where, how, and through what?" will be filtered through, "*for* whom and *by* whom is desire staged in and around these poems?"

At the beginning of this chapter, I troubled much that seemed a "given" in Catullan criticism. I cast doubt upon the conceptual rigor of addressing plot, personae, and textual boundaries in isolation, pointing out that all are mutually implicated, and none has a purchase outside the system. But it would hardly be useful simply to construct a new excuse for hand-wringing over Catullus: What, then, does my methodology hope to accomplish positively? I propose a set of questions, here at the beginning of this journey through the enabling constructs of my chosen theorists, to which I shall have answers by the end.

8

1. What is the system of time, and of causality, suited to the Catullan corpus? When we read contradictory data in the corpus, do we have to choose one over the other, or separate them in time, as anchoring points in a rationalized "progression"? Or is there another way that allows us both to preserve and to push the contradictions to their limits until they yield new information?

2. Is there more than one order of signification in the Catullan text? How do we read what "speaks besides" in the textual lacunae, gaps in logic, breaks in sequence, and so on?

3. How is the subject constructed in Catullus? How exactly do we track the eddying currents of knowledge, desire, and language flowing through those who speak, act, and love in these poems? And does this make any coherency meaningless, or can we adjust the notion of dramatis personae to make it useful to us as we read?

These questions and the method behind such a reading program begin in Plato, who, importantly, emphasizes the knowledge the subject "has," but not at her conscious command, as the key to her being—a knowledge she can recover only by reading the logical gaps in what she thinks she knows. But we shall need the full theoretical exposition of unconscious knowledge and its link to desire available to us from Freud and Lacan before we can begin to find specific answers to these questions applicable to the Catullan text. For that reason, I shall in the main defer indicating exemplary applications to Catullus until we have a critical mass of theory behind us, toward the end of this chapter.

The schematic array I sketched above of Platonic, Freudian, and Lacanian consonance scants key points of tension both among these three and within their own theories. I shall spend some time in the following pages arraying the points of tension crucial to my project; I shall show how deficiencies and problems in various formulations of the desiring subject are themselves springboards for provocative reformulations. Sometimes the theorist himself rethinks an earlier solution (as when Plato returns in the *Phaedrus* to the problem of an ecstatic knowledge beyond rationality he deferred in the *Symposium*); sometimes another of the "fellow travelers" I have assembled for this journey does so (as when Freud refines Plato's explanation of object-choice to account for socialization; or when Lacan escapes Freud's conceptual impasse over femininity by relocating sexual difference in language). I shall exploit tensions, as well as consonances, among these three, in order to shed light on the contradictions of the Catullan corpus.

I divided the useful resemblances among Plato, Freud, and Lacan into

9

three headings above, saying that they share belief in (1) desire as a motive force for creativity, (2) a divided, desiring subject, (3) a technique for recuperating the whole precursor of a fragmented text. The desiring subject shall concern us first, as the anchor point of all three theories. Agency, though problematized, is the focus of all three theorists; even divine *erōs* is legible only in and through those who desire; thus our other two headings can best be approached through subjectivity.

From Plato to Freud

Plato's animadversions on the desiring subject are chiefly contained in the *Symposium* and the *Phaedrus*. I concentrate on the *Symposium* because, in most of the points that impinge upon our present discussion, the *Phaedrus* simply recapitulates the earlier dialogue's tenets. There are some important differences, to be sure, and I shall revert to the *Phaedrus* wherever its divergence with the *Symposium* illuminates our discussion and broaches an important subject the *Symposium* eschews. My focus within the *Symposium* narrows further to concentrate on the versions of *erōs* and the lover posed by Aristophanes and Diotima alone. Their two speeches—two of the longest in the dialogue, which underlines their centrality—subsume most of the points advanced by earlier speakers, whom it would be tedious and repetitive to recognize specifically. (Aristophanes and Diotima also precede a *very* long soliloquy from Alcibiades; but as his is an autobiographical account of his amorous pursuit of Socrates, not a thesis per se, it adds nothing material to our present discussion.)

The Subject of Desire

The questions asked by Diotima and Aristophanes chiefly come down to Who *is* the lover? What does she want, and why does she want it? And what happens to her when she loves? Their accounts are similar, yet they differ in key points.

To Aristophanes, the lover is a remnant, half of a former double-bodied species divided by Zeus for its arrogance. The god relented a little when species members began dying off out of futile longing for their other halves; he had their anatomy reengineered, and invented sex as a substitute for reunification. Remnants of double women are attracted to women, of double men to men, and of half-male, half-female *androgunoi* to members of the opposite sex. The pleasure they all obtain in sex distracts them from reunification long enough to make them productive members of society: sexual satisfaction, though palliative, is always temporary.

10

To Diotima, the lover is pregnant either in body or soul and desires to "give birth and procreate in the beautiful."[26] In the ideal philosophical ascent of *erōs* she then sketches out, the philosopher-lover (pregnant, of course, in *soul*) begins by loving a beautiful body and engendering philosophic discourse with its owner; then moves on to loving a beautiful soul; then laws and institutions; and finally the Beautiful Itself, where he engenders true virtue. Each step on the *scala amoris* involves a consolidation of, and diminution of one's attachment to, the beauty instantiated at the previous level (so that, e.g., one comes to love a beautiful soul by noticing that the beauty in all beautiful bodies is much the same, and thus unworthy of a particularized attachment).[27]

The similarities between the two accounts are striking: when we ask our first question, What does the lover want? the answer in both cases is "something that sex cannot give her." As David Halperin has shown,[28] erotic desire in both cases is mediated by something about which the desiring subject consciously knows nothing and cannot attain by any of the customary cultural pathways laid down for *erōs:* sex, marriage, ordinary pederasty (as opposed to philosophically guided pederasty), reproduction, parenting, and so on. In Aristophanes' case, the "something" lovers seek is "wholeness" (*tou holou epithumia,* 192e10) or more loosely, "kinship" (*oikeiotēs,* 192c1); in Diotima's case, immortality through "birth and procreation in the beautiful." Both Diotima and Aristophanes agree in lifting *erōs* out of the realm of satisfiable appetite and into the realm of unsatisfiable desire.

But the differences between the two accounts are also crucial. For Aristophanes, erotic desire is intrinsically, structurally unsatisfiable (even if temporarily assuageable)—two half-bodies cannot grow together again. For Diotima, however, erotic longing is only unsatisfiable below the top rung of her ladder. The hardy few who *do* make it into the presence of the Beautiful Itself will be lost in rapt contemplation of it, with nothing left to desire. And the structure of Diotima's and Aristophanes' aetiologies of *erōs* differ in important ways also: Aristophanes roots *erōs* firmly in the body and traces its origins in the past. Diotima is chiefly interested in *erōs* (i.e., "pregnancy") of the soul and sets its face firmly toward the future, ultimately equating it to a longing for immortality.

Diotima and Aristophanes differ chiefly in the degree of their optimism (whether *erōs* is ultimately satisfiable or not) and in their chief points of orientation (body/past versus soul/future). These differences now split our second question—"what does the lover want, and why does she want it?"—into two parts: the proximate focus and the ultimate goal of desire.

11

We can anticipate our discussion of Freud and Lacan by using the terms *object* (proximate focus) and *aim*[29] (goal) without violence to Plato. Plato has moved the discussion of desire in a direction to which the psychoanalytic distinction between these factors in the drive—the pressure that moves us toward an aim—is crucial. The Platonic desiring subject does not know (is unconscious of) what truly motivates her longing: she knows the object, but not the aim, unless and until she is philosophically enlightened. But at this point also, holes start to appear in the two Platonic accounts of *erōs* and in the subjects they construct—holes that necessitate moving our discussion in a direction only psychoanalysis can take it.

Though both Diotima and Aristophanes can account (differently) for the aim of *erōs* only Aristophanes has an explanation for its object:[30] the sex of one's beloved will be dictated by the sex of one's ancestral "other half." And there is a promise of a more specific fit than appropriate gender, though exactly what is unclear. Some lucky few find their complements in a fuller sense, as Aristophanes briefly, tantalizingly hints at the end of his speech. But that is a grace entirely in the gift of the gods (*Symp.* 193b3–c5). Diotima, by contrast, in her manifest distaste for "mortal trash," would prefer to explain away the details of object choice as a blind and fumbling grope toward the pellucidly unspecific Beautiful Itself. Something crucial is elided in her hasty dismissal of "the way things are" in favor of "the way they ought to be." But on the other hand, Diotima's view importantly focuses upon an area of desire that cries out for explication: the felt continuity between passion for another human being and passion for poetry, art, philosophy, and so forth.[31] Mercifully (unlike Epicurus, Lucretius, or the Stoics), Diotima allows passion to cohabit with philosophy.

If we now stand back and survey our juxtaposition of the two *Symposium* accounts, we will be able to tot up gains and losses. On the positive side, the complete lack of adequation between the vehicle (sex) and the goal ("wholeness"; the Beautiful Itself) of erotic longing has raised the entire investigation of *erōs* out of the realm of pure satisfiable appetite, on the level of hunger and thirst, into a fundamental reconceptualization of it as profoundly conditioning all levels of human subjectivity. *Erōs* has becomes *the* mystical humanizing force.

Yet we still lack an adequately refined explanation of the here-and-now of *erōs'* specific expression in sexual activity: Aristophanes supplies an explanation for some human object choice, but how would he explain bisexuals? How would either he or Diotima explain fetishists? And what about activities other than genital or anal sex (e.g., sadomasochism)?

This tale of the ledger sheet lands us firmly in the problematic of desire and the desiring subject taken up by Freud, and by Lacan in Freud's footsteps. Both may be said to bridge some of the stark dichotomies posed by Diotima's and Aristophanes' models, by taking account of both body and psyche, past and future, in the construction of adult sexuality. Yet more importantly, the key link between Plato's inquiry and Freud's and Lacan's is their refusal to take anything at face value. To Freud and Lacan, as to Plato, every aspect of human behavior poses the question "why?" Their answers—especially in this case—fundamentally shift prevailing cultural paradigms, by demanding a rigorous explanation of what seems "just natural." They all three join in thought realms of human activity previously seen as separate, in a way that illuminates the operation of each.

Plato anticipates Freud when he poses the question, "What is it to be a desiring subject?" in a way that cannily separates object from aim and transforms the question into "What is it to be fully human?" That same transformation marks Freud's inquiries into the human subject: his investigations of desire (as in *Three Essays on Sexuality*)[32] lead him to map out the creation of the human in all its aspects. Contemplating the transformation of the child's "polymorphous perversity" into a sexuality referenced to social norms, Freud eventually hypothesized that the intrafamily rivalries and attachments subsumed by the Oedipus were resolved by the castration complex—by the boy's fear or the girl's resentful "observance" of castration. But as Juliet Mitchell observes, the Oedipus and the castration complex confer upon the subject not just gender and object choice but the concept of Law itself as it founds the human order (where "Law" refers to *all* social restraints, even those not formally embodied in legal codes).[33] By instituting the censorious superego as the representative of the castration complex—and thereby the internal representative of Law—the Oedipus resolved *makes* us human. Like Law, and as a foundation for Law, the castration complex intervenes between desire and fulfillment; positions the subject within a hierarchy of relations of power and desire (mother, father, child); and leaves behind internal surveillance of this prohibition and this order in the form of the superego.

Both Freud's intimate intertwining of desire with Law and culture and Plato's anticipation of it, in seeing *erōs* as attempted recollection of the Good-Beautiful, strive to rehabilitate a reprobate energy. Plato combats the weight of social indulgence that places the lover outside the Law (*Symp.* 183b2–c2); Freud, the nineteenth-century's narrowing of sexuality to pure carnality and pure sin. We need their ennobling schemata to understand Catullus' view of his affair with someone else's woman as an honorable and fully humanizing process. All that is painful and degrading in the

13

present moment changes, upon Catullus' recollection, into a crucible of virtue. When memory allows him time to match carefully his pursuit of Lesbia against the traditional Roman merits of *fides, amicitia, pietas,*[34] and so on, he finds himself oddly aligned with his culture's highest ideals by a path it did not suspect capable of good.

The Object of Desire

Culture makes but a modest entrance in Freud's initial thoughts on sexuality. The early correspondence between Freud and Wilhelm Fliess grants culture only as much weight as biology in producing the human subject—but that evenhandedness quickly changes. Freud originally subscribed to Fliess' notion of a "natural," biologically based bisexuality, which the intervention of culture merely modified to produce a being predominantly masculine or predominantly feminine. But the farther Freud delves into his investigations of sexuality, the less his own discoveries will support such a theory. The first of the *Three Essays,* analyzing sexual "aberrations," expressly shows that neither the aim nor the object of the sexual drive is fixed: early childhood experiences coordinate the one and the other imperceptibly but do not guarantee their alignment with social norms. Thus in accounting for the fetishists and sadomasochists whom the *Symposium* overlooked, Freud partially bridges Diotima's and Aristophanes' divergences.[35] Freud sides with Aristophanes in seeking an explanation in the past; yet he moves erotic longing much further into the realm of psyche and culture, as opposed to body—which is Diotima's triumph. Freud's analysis proceeds logically from his own evolving notions about the drive (*Trieb*). The drive is a mere psychic representative of biological need: no physical motive force can be directly read out of any human action. How, then, to account *exactly* for sexual positioning, normative or otherwise?

Freud's thoughts on gender, sexuality, and their relation to humanization had passed through early versions of the Oedipus in which it simply seemed to dissolve on its own, to culminate in his final formulation, where the castration complex ends it. Mitchell has well emphasized Freud's final concept of the Oedipus' resolution as an *event:* a hypothetical moment in which, under the threat or the "fact" of castration, the child renounces its original, culturally forbidden love object (the mother) and begins the long process of transferring its love to culturally approved objects.[36] Such a formulation emphasizes the subject as historically constructed, precipitated by an intervention in the child's life. The adult subject thus does not "evolve" out of some natural, biological process that comes about of its own accord and develops inexorably along predetermined pathways.

14

Rather, given that accession to gender is also accession to Law as embodied in the castration complex, the Oedipus and its outcome bequeath to the child the essence of its cultural inheritance, the whole history of being human shrunk to the compass of a few childhood years.

Moreover, this inheritance functions as a narrative. The castration complex—like the Oedipus—is foundational for Freud, which means that other, earlier separations in the child's life (from the womb, from the breast, from excreta, etc.) are interpreted in its light. The gendered, socialized human subject is thus constructed retrospectively, as an effect of narrative. More importantly, this story of the irretrievably lacking subject proceeds from the human order of symbolization intervening in the child's life. Nothing is seen as either "missing" or "present" in the body until culture makes that body signify:

> When a little boy first catches sight of a girl's genital region, he begins by showing irresolution and lack of interest; *he sees nothing* or disavows what he has seen, he softens it down or looks about for expedients for bringing it into line with his expectations. *It is not until later,* when some threat of castration has obtained a hold upon him, that the observation becomes important to him: if he then *recollects or repeats it,* it arouses a terrible storm of emotion in him and forces him to believe in the reality of the threat which he has hitherto laughed at.[37]

Thus the Oedipus resolved—interposed between desiring subject and desired object, the separation that sweeps the child into the human order— is entirely an effect of signification, of reading the body as corroboration of social distinctions and prohibitions. The Freudian subject is the effect of a story she tells unknown to herself, inscribed on her own body as the mark of a history that never happened.

To Lacan to Plato

Freud's focus on signification in his work predates developments in linguistics and other humanist disciplines that Freud would have needed to develop it fully. As a result, Freud never really resolved his thinking on the Oedipus or castration complex so as to exploit fully their revolutionary implications for the social order's role in human sexuality. He remained unhappily stymied, for example, in conceptualizing "penis envy" as the neurosis foundational to femininity[38] without being able to push to its limits the question of why and how the little girl comes to read her body as "lacking," the penis as desirable. Lacan's self-styled "return to Freud" is a fitting extension of inquiries that Freud initiated, in the light of post-Freudian developments in linguistics, anthropology, sociology, and philosophy, for the purpose of clarifying and corroborating Freud's thought and expanding its implications. Lacan's theories share with Freud's a focus on:

a. Desire alone, explored and defined independently of its objects (the austere basis of Freud's middle-to-late works on sexuality)[39]—a concentration that emphasizes the "constructedness" of sexuality

b. The divided subject (implied since Freud's formulation of the Unconscious, but a concept that increasingly held his attention)[40]—a focus that emphasizes desire's unsatisfiability, since something will *always* be "missing" from its subject

Lacan, like Freud, sees desire and the subject as effects of culture and as virtually synonymous: to be a subject is to desire and vice versa. But Lacan's inspiration was to expand the understanding of "culture" in this formula, bringing the discoveries of the structuralists to bear on psychoanalysis. He, like the structuralists, mapped culture as a set of interlocking signifying systems, whose operations are paradigmatically represented by language.

In the following sketch of Lacan's psychoanalytic theory, I have ranged broadly in his thought. A curtailed summation would falsify and distort the profundity of Lacan's project, because he demands from us that we discard everything we think we know in favor of the radically counterintuitive. In this, he does not differ from Plato and Freud—except that their revolutions have passed (often, alas, in ill-understood popularized versions) into intellectual lingua franca; they no longer shock us. Lacan particularly felt the injustice of psychoanalysis' ersatz domestication and sought to recuperate its true radicality. As Shoshana Felman has put it, "for Lacan, psychoanalysis is an invention that, in its practice, *teaches people to think beyond their means.*"[41] Much of the infamous difficulty of Lacan's thought derives from his adherence to this precept, which dictated that popular conceptions could not be challenged in their own idiom, nor "common sense" gainsayed by an appeal to common sense. But our reward for struggling with his conceptual and stylistic difficulties is to begin to see what our complacent assumptions previously obscured, both in the text and in ourselves.

The Real, the Symbolic, and the Imaginary

Lacan divided the registers of the subject's experience into the "orders" of Imaginary, Symbolic, and Real.[42] The tripartite division echoes, as I have said above, the tripartite schemata of the psyche formulated by Plato and Freud. But whereas the anthropomorphic rhetoric employed by Plato and Freud had the unfortunate (if vivid) effect of setting squabbling homunculi at each other's throats in the soul of the human subject—the long-suffering ego battling both the savage superego and the consummately selfish id;[43] the master, Reason, trying to control his Ariel and his Caliban, Spirit and Appetite[44]—Lacan adapts these insights to a nonanthropomorphic model. His vision carries Plato's and Freud's troubling of the discrete, integral "person" to the ultimate extreme: whereas the Platonic and Freudian models suggest the question, Which one of those homunculi is *me?* Lacan's model makes the question virtually unaskable. The three orders cannot be located intrasubjectively but subsume all social and cultural phenomena that intersect the subject.

The Real, in Lacan's explication of it, is *not* "reality" as we conventionally conceive of it.[45] The Lacanian definitions of the Real proceed (maddeningly) *per viam negativam* to specify what the Real is *not,* without particularly clarifying what it *is.* The Real is the "nonhuman," the "undifferentiated,"[46] "without fissure."[47] But these gestures of cunning aporia follow logically from Lacan's precept that the Real is that which cannot be signified—how, then, to make it clear in signification? The Real can only be defined by an awkward combination of negation, and of stalking its specific intrusions into the Symbolic and the Imaginary orders. Hallucinations belong to the Real, though few would think of them as reality. Traumas are of the Real: they give rise to significations in symptoms, dreams, parapraxes, and so on, but are not themselves signifiable. The Real is anything and everything upon which human signifying systems cannot gain a foothold, and because of that implacable resistance, the Real "always comes back to the same place."[48]

The last definition gives some hint of the Real's connection to repetition: it motivates repeated, futile attempts to reduce it to signification. For example, the analysand's symptoms clothe a traumatic kernel of the Real in signification. She produces a message with a specific addressee—the analyst who, by the mechanism of transference, stands in for other important figures in the analysand's life.[49] But the messages are themselves produced around an unsignifiable core; were the case otherwise, deciphering the message would mean unravelling the trauma itself. Not only that specific symptom but all future symptoms resulting from the trauma would disappear, and analysis would take days, not months and years. But patients often continue to produce symptoms around a single traumatic event, even after they have wrapped the originating "wound" in narrative.

17

Clearly, something that cannot be reduced to signs persists above and beyond the symptom's message: that "something," in Lacan's account, is the Real. Why human beings cling to this kernel of the Real is an explanation we must defer until an account of the complementary terms *Imaginary* and *Symbolic* can properly found our discussion.

Lacan's formulation of the Imaginary emphasizes his concept of the subject's genesis as rooted in representation. The name of the Imaginary points to its status as the realm of ego identifications, metaphorically summed up in a mirror's reflections—thus Imaginary means "the realm of images," not "illusory." To understand this, we must return to one of his earliest essays, "The Mirror Stage as Formative of the Function of the 'I,' "[50] the first inkling of the Imaginary order. Building upon the infant's fascination with mirrors, Lacan postulated that the reflection grants the child her concept of a unified self—her "ego-function," that which allows her to operate as "I." Almost anything can reflect back to the child a self-image—her mother, for example. In Lacan's analysis, the mirror functions purely as a convenient metaphor. But by granting that image, the reflector immediately involves it in paradox. The concept of self as "autonomous" and "whole" is structurally split between a site of perception and a site of reflection. Thus the intimate concept of "I" always refers the self to an external order, in a movement analogous to the perpetually referential relationship between signifier and signified in language.

And the image does more: it precipitates the subject into desire, rivalry, and "misrecognition" (*méconnaissance,* in Lacan's terminology). "The Mirror Stage" ought to be read in the light of another early essay, "Aggressivity in Psychoanalysis."[51] The conjunction points up Lacan's early and enduring fascination with Hegel's dialectic of the Master and the Slave, sparked by his formative involvement with Alexandre Kojève's seminars on Hegel at the *École des Hautes Études.* Lacan plots the Hegelian "struggle to the death" for "recognition" (*Anerkennung*) between two mutually dependent, mutually defining antagonists onto the child's hypothetical moment of self-conception. The mirror presents the child with an image more coordinated and more unified than her infantile difficulties in negotiating the world would seem to warrant. The image simultaneously provokes jubilation, emulation, and jealousy: jubilation insofar as the image is "misrecognized" as truly representing the self ("that's me!"); emulation and jealousy insofar as the image is perceived to exceed the child in power and majesty ("that's not me, but it ought to be, and that other is taking my place!").

The consequences of a self-concept precipitated in misrecognition and

18

rivalry deeply affect Lacan's optimism concerning interpersonal relations—most especially relations between the sexes, as we shall presently see. Suffice it to say for now that Lacan's concept of desire as *rooted* in oscillations between hatred and narcissistic adoration illuminates Catullus' frequent *volte-face* in his relationship to Lesbia. The Imaginary particularly clarifies those moments when desire and despite *both* arise from seeing her as his mirror image. If she publicly rails against him, for example, she plays the same game of dissimulating love that *he* plays (cc.83, 92). But facing that reflected deceit, he can never be sure of what she means, even when she flatters him (cc.70, 72). Tellingly, Catullus perceives his contradictory emotions as a self agonizingly wrenched apart: "my mind . . . has destroyed itself in doing what it must" (c.75.1–2); "I hate and I love"; "I am laid on the cross" (c.85.1, 2).[52]

Revolving thus around a split and alienated self-concept, the Imaginary is conceptually homologous to the realm of signification that Lacan calls the Symbolic. Language, like the image in the mirror, represents the subject, but extrinsically and in a distorted fashion: hence Lacan's economical coinage *parlêtre*, the "subject-in-language," to designate the alienated subject produced by language. Lacan (borrowing from Emile Benveniste)[53] illustrates the *parlêtre* by resolving the apparent paradox of the statement "I am lying."[54] This is only a paradox, he remarks, if one does not realize that there are two "I's" involved: the "I" who speaks and the "I" of the speech—and only one of these is lying.[55]

The noncoincidence of the speaking subject and the subject of the speech is useful to us in that it offers a context in which the flat contradictions of the Catullan corpus begin to make sense. If Catullus denies he spoke ill of Lesbia (c.104), while a host of other poems attest his extravagant insults to her, Lacan's analysis of "I am lying" can sustain both moments. Lacan raises Freud's observation that the Unconscious knows no contradiction into a principle that organizes our whole existence, and that proceeds from our status as subjects-in-language—and so saves us from explaining away Catullus' antitheses before we have properly trained our sights on them.

The Imaginary and the Symbolic share a structural principle based on schism; but whereas the subject caught in the Imaginary will attempt to deny the split, the subject in the Symbolic will embrace it. The Imaginary is Freud's "narcissism" magnified and projected onto the world at large. As Malcolm Bowie has written: "the Imaginary is the scene of a desperate delusional attempt to be and to remain 'what one is' by gathering to oneself ever more instances of sameness, resemblance and self-replication."[56]

19

The Symbolic, on the other hand, is determinedly intersubjective and social, a realm of signifying differences that retain their otherness. The Symbolic encompasses movement and intermittence, as opposed to Imaginary fixity and (false) consistency—which nonetheless has its uses. The Imaginary grants the subject the fiction of a smooth alignment among the different facets of subjectivity: body, being, gender, knowledge, and so forth. That consistency allows me to respond when someone calls my name or to sign legal documents, as if my name, as signifier, pointed to a coherent and persistent entity. Under the sign of the Imaginary, we can partially rehabilitate the notion of identity I questioned at the outset. Identity serves us as an innacurate, but wholly necessary, fiction—a fiction that allows us not to have to negotiate the world and its institutions as hopeless schizophrenics. The concept of identity, as distinct from the looser concept of subjectivity, is a useful *point de repère* from which to trace the odd melding of agents in the Catullan poems. The iconography of the *carmina maiora*, for example, makes Catullus' brother eerily similar to Lesbia; to Catullus' abandoned heroines, like Ariadne; and to Catullus himself. Without the sense of orientation identity affords us, we cannot read Catullus' intricate message in these instances—nor can we, if we ignore the ebb and flow that troubles its fixity.

In coupling a signifier (a name) and an illusory image ("identity"), my examples show that the Symbolic and the Imaginary are not successive stages. The Symbolic always operates simultaneously with the Imaginary, as stereophonic registers of perception and of being-in-the-world. This may strike the reader as odd: if the Symbolic is rooted in the workings of language, must its advent not wait until we master words? But for Lacan (as Mikkel Borch-Jacobsen has shown)[57] even so-called infancy participates in the structure of language.[58] Picture a hungry infant, crying to be fed. The preverbal cry is nonetheless language, according to Lacan's capacious definition of the term, in that it is a demand addressed to an other. Lacan analyzes this demand into two parts: (1) the expression of need (let us say for milk, in this instance), which can be satisfied; (2) the demand for love—but love of a very particular sort, love that is recognition by an autonomous subject, of the infant as autonomous *subject,* rather than as *object* (precisely the impossible demand Hegel's Master makes of the Slave).[59] That demand cannot possibly be satisfied, now or ever. Any object granted in response to the child's demands—the breast, candy, a toy, even a smile or gaze—ministers to real or putative needs, thus reducing the child to object, and consequently must be "annulled" for the child to retain its subjectivity. The term "annul" Lacan explicitly signposts as Hegel's

Aufheben—to negate but to retain the essential principles of the negated term in the negation. Lacan refers not to an outright refusal but to the elliptical structure of demand itself, which will annul the object by returning to the child the difference between satisfiable need and unsatisfiable demand as persistent desire.[60]

The Phallus: Oedipus Reconsidered

What does the child desire? What everybody desires—the phallus. And what is the phallus? What everybody desires.[61] The tautology illustrates the arbitrary, even "empty," nature of the phallus as signifier of desire: it is not the penis or indeed any *object*, as it names a desire to which an object is irrelevant (or more precisely, which demands that any and every object be negated)—the impossible desire to be recognized as Absolute Subject. Lacan translates this as the Desire of the Other. Capitalizing "Other" allows him to subsume in that term both the particular body caught in a dialectical relation with the subject and that dialectic's structuring principle: alterity, "otherness" (the whole basis of the Symbolic, which rests on difference). This telescoping gesture brings with it a thought-provoking tension: the "other persons" to whom we address ourselves always hover, in Lacan's thought, somewhere between particularity ("*an* other"), and the larger-than-life cultural ideals and roles that grant that particularity meaning ("*the* Other"). The Other's panoply of roles—Mother, Father, Man, Woman, and so on—also create *us*, their allocutors, as corollaries: Son, Daughter, Wife, Husband.

Already the territory covered by "the Desire of the Other" encroaches upon a new version of the Oedipus that emphasizes structure over substance. But when Lacan leans upon the ambiguity of the genitive in his phrase, he transforms Freud's into an overtly Hegelian Oedipus. The Desire of the Other as object, the desire to possess the Other, becomes, in Lacan's version, the desire to *be* the desire of the Other: to be desired *as* a subject, *by* a subject, purely and without condition. The phallus, signifier of this desire, resembles zero: nothing in itself, a "null set," but that which grants value to all other numbers in arithmetical notation. Lacan's choice of this particular term from the Freudian vocabulary as *the* key signifier of desire propels us into radically rethinking the Oedipus. Lacan's Oedipus is even more comprehensive than Freud's, because fundamentally defined and negotiated in language.

In Freud's analysis of sexuality, the phallus is the penis seen as separable;[62] he associates it quintessentially with the concept of castration. Lacan seizes upon this—the idea of (potential) division and loss—to develop a definition of castration that subsumes not just the outcome of the young child's "family romance" but the whole history of the subject as divided by the structure of the signifier, in both Imaginary and Symbolic registers.

In drawing upon Freud's writings to reconsider the Oedipus as a structuration of the subject, Lacan consistently bypasses the high dramas of the primal scene and primordial sons killing primordial fathers to concentrate on an enigmatic quiet game: the *fort/da* game from *Beyond the Pleasure Principle*.[63] The story concerns Freud's grandson, Ernst, and his play with a wooden reel:

> The child was not at all precocious in his intellectual development. At the age of one and a half he could say only a few comprehensible words; he could also make use of a number of sounds which expressed a meaning intelligible to those around him. He was, however, on good terms with his parents and their one servant-girl, and tributes were paid to his being a "good boy." He did not disturb his parents at night, he conscientiously obeyed orders not to touch certain things or go into certain rooms, and above all he never cried when his mother left him for a few hours. At the same time, he was greatly attached to his mother, who had not only fed him herself but had also looked after him without any outside help. This good little boy, however, had an occasional disturbing habit of taking any small object he could get hold of and throwing them away from him into a corner, under the bed, and so on, so that hunting for his toys and picking them up was often quite a business. As he did this he gave vent to a loud, long-drawn-out "o-o-o-o," accompanied by an expression of interest and satisfaction. His mother and the writer of the present account were agreed in thinking that this was not a mere interjection but represented the German word "fort" ["gone"]. I eventually realized that it was a game and that the only use he made of any of his toys was to play "gone" with them. One day I made an observation which confirmed my view. The child had a wooden reel with a piece of string tied round it. It never occurred to him to pull it along the floor behind him, for instance, and play at its being a carriage. What he did was to hold the reel by the string and very skilfully throw it over the edge of his curtained cot, so that it disappeared into it, at the same time uttering his expressive "o-o-o-o." He then pulled the reel out of the cot again by the string and hailed its reappearance with a joyful "da" ["there"]. This, then, was the complete game— disappearance and return. (*SE* 18:14–15)

What is Ernst doing as he alternately banishes the wooden reel from his sight and welcomes its return, accompanying this alternation with the rudiments of speech? To Lacan, the game crystallizes the only version of "castration" he will countenance. The little boy rehearses the split in the subject necessitated by being a subject-in-language—both an "I" who speaks, and another "I" represented by that speech.[64] We have already glanced at the broad foundation of this split in the Imaginary, where the concept of the subject is divided between perceiver and image. But the image in the mirror is also a signifier. As such, it models the publicly negotiated images of self that language—and the Symbolic realm in general—grants to the subject and, by that very fact, confers subjectivity upon her.

Ernst, then, creates a narrative of his own subjectification in and by language. Lacan reads the game as the child's exemplary grasp of signifying oppositions, but also as his paradigmatic self-narrative in which presence and plenitude (*da*) are posited as an Eden from which the child (as "I") has fallen into absence and loss (*fort*). Yet the temporal ordering of this tragedy-in-miniature is (like all narrative) retrospectively constructed, transforming what is merely logical priority into a claim to temporal priority.[65] *Da* has no meaning whatever until a second term, *fort*, opposes it; no sooner has *fort* appeared to grant meaning to *da*, than *da* becomes visible only *as lost*—a representative of a fictive bliss now construed as forever beyond recovery.

Lacan's insistence on logical priority over any fiction of temporal priority as organizing the Oedipus forces us to revise our thinking about the subject, narration, and the relation between the two. A Lacanian theory of narrative annuls in advance all attempts to construct a "master order" for the Catullan poems based on psychological plausibility, because the subject organized by the text, and the text organized by the subject, are interdependent. Any *points d'appui* they seem to offer are fictive.[66] But if we have to trade one order for multiple orders, Lacan's Oedipal model of narrative urges us to train close attention on what the *articulation* of each narrative order accomplishes that the narrative itself fails to account for.

If, as the *fort/da* game indicates, the specimen story of the subject tells of loss, what (or who), precisely, was lost? "The mother," says Freud; "the little boy," says Lacan.[67] Their answers in fact amount to the same thing, if we take thought for the Imaginary dyad formed by mother and child in Lacan's account: the concept of self arose from, and was instantly problematized by, the mother as Other. The fissure thus introduced into self-conception returns, arranged in a temporal relationship of origin and succession, as a narrative of a lost whole. This fissure serves as the basis for metaphoric substitutions—for the expansion of the Symbolic in the child's world to encompass a social system based on perceived lack, and thus on exchange and substitution. The divided self is figured by the absence of the Mother; her absence makes a place for the prohibition of the Father. What the Father forbids is Imaginary autonomy, the asocial delusion that the mirroring dyad is sufficient and nothing need be sought outside of it.

Moreover, "Father" must be broadly understood as a function, rather than any specific individual: hence Lacan's punning reference to the Father's "No!" (*Non*) as reducible to his Name (*Nom*). The Name-of-the-Father (*Nom-du-Père;* also known as the Paternal Metaphor) signifies a legislative and punitive power, but above all the power of want: without this third term enforcing both difference and (a curb on) desire, the human being has no reason either to master her culture's language or its laws. She need not, and cannot, grasp the system of differences that support language, cultural prohibitions, and cultural ideals, when she sees herself as complete and needing to ask for nothing. If the fundamental Paternal Metaphor fails in a person—or, in the terminology Lacan borrows from Freud, is "foreclosed" (*verworfen*)—she occupies the asocial position of the psychotic. The autistic, the catatonic, the schizophrenic, and other psychotics can master neither speech nor social norms, and both failings proceed from the same cause.

When Lacan turns his attention to Freud's Oedipus, then, its account and timing become a belated way of representing a self "castrated" *ab origine*—i.e., divided and made to want by the structure of the signifier. As the "residue" that escapes such figuration, the Real ensures the *fort/da* paradigm's endless, metonymic repetition. Rooted in the Real, desire continually presses forward for that fictive "whole" that remains forever in abeyance, and of which all intervening objects are merely metonymic tokens. Its repetition thus structures the entirety of our lives as subjects-in-language.

The Real, the Symptom, and Capitonnage

Lacan's interest in the repetitive aspect of desire led him to connect it with another effect of the Real: the symptom. Lacan's surprising association nonetheless fastens upon the drift of Freud's later writings (such as the already cited *Beyond the Pleasure Principle*), where Freud begins to divorce repetition from neurosis: the inventor of the *fort/da* game, is, after all, a perfectly normal child. For Lacan, too, repetition is not per se neurotic. If neurotics cling to their symptoms or invent new ones to enfold the same traumatic kernel, they simply dramatize in a particularly eye-catching fashion a structure that governs all our lives: the desire to place something unified between a Real void in being (the traumatic "castration" we all

24

sustain as subjects divided by language) and knowledge of that void. Repetition points to this Real void—*Kern unseres Wesen,* "the kernel of our being"[68]—and dissimulates it at the same time.

Lacan calls this void, when mythically construed as the marker of a "lost" whole, the Unary Signifier (*trait unaire*), repressed core of the primal Unconscious.[69] The Unary Signifier grants the subject an image of her own "lost wholeness," which she will perpetually seek through other signifiers, stringing them together into meaningful connection (or, in Lacan's expression, into "the signifying chain"). The process of forging the signifying chain under the pressure of the Unary Signifier resembles, and includes, connecting words to make sentences; yet Lacan's use of "signifier" extends far beyond the written or spoken word, to include images and ideas organized by language. The Unary signifier confers power upon certain other signifiers in the chain to organize a narrative that will retroactively grant the subject illusory wholeness. These "charged" signifiers Lacan calls *points de capiton*[70]—literally "upholstery buttons." In language, the *points de capiton* keep the continual metonymic movement of desire through the signifying chain "buttoned down" long enough to present a legible whole—a process Lacan calls *capitonnage* ("quilting"), exactly analogous to punctuating a string of words to create intelligible clauses, sentences, paragraphs. At the same time, Lacan's homely metaphor of quilting suggests a subject "stuffed" with amorphous and invisible "filler" (the various facets of subjectivity that intersect her), which must be "buttoned down" to grant her a particular, stable shape. *Fort* was a simple example of a *point de capiton* that, in its opposition to *da,* created a skeleton narrative of departure and return and thus produced its subject (Ernst) as an infant Adam. *Fort* thereby made *da* visible as an estranged point of the subject's paradisal unity, where he seemed to have been complete.

But other signifiers can also assume this function of promising unity, by anchoring the subject's self-narrative: we can construct our sense of self around the signifiers "Man," "Woman," "Father," "Daughter,"—and "Philosopher," too.[71] Lacan's model of desire as that which propels us to recover a blessed state we believe we once enjoyed so obviously parallels Plato's anamnesis that I have not troubled to mark the resemblances. However, in transposing both desire and its promised fulfillment into linguistic terms, Lacan matches the *Phaedrus'* restaging of the *erōs* question—Plato's refinement of the *Symposium.* The *Phaedrus,* like the *Symposium,* sees truth as its goal—but unlike the *Symposium,* the later dialogue makes language, in its relation to desire, a key issue in that pursuit. In the *Phaedrus,* Socrates emphasizes that language has the power to pin desire

25

to objects (exactly the power of *capitonnage*): our desire for anything depends upon the discourse we erect around it. This focuses a little more attentively on the varying subtleties of longing and on exactly how and why they may be influenced to change. By contrast, the *Symposium* depends upon fixed distinctions between "pregnancy in soul" versus "pregnancy in body" or among the natures of lost "other halves." At worst, this makes desire inflexible; at best, *erōs* must be managed by the philosopher-guide's sharp commands, to seek what it *ought* to seek.[72] But the *Phaedrus* grants language ambiguous and subtle power to shape desire: persuasion can invest unworthy objects with glittering attraction (the rhetorician's goal) and sway the philosopher from truth.[73] Or it can harness desire to the pursuit of truth alone and thus produce the "lover" as "philosopher." Either way describes Lacan's *capitonnage,* seen from a perspective confident there *are* truth-bearing *points de capiton.*

Moreover, the *Phaedrus,* unlike the *Symposium,* fashions a means to its goal conditioned from beginning to end by the particularity of a master signifier. Not the unspecific Beautiful, but each of the gods makes her or his mark on the lovers' souls: the trace so inscribed inspires the lovers with mutual attraction and refers them to the missing presence of their tutelary deity. By so doing, the god's mark tells the lovers who they should ideally be (*Phaedrus* 252c3–253c2). Thus does Plato recruit a form of "quilting" to help him explain a subject he had by and large avoided in the *Symposium:* the particularity of object-choice, beyond such crude dichotomies as "this sex or that one." The *Phaedrus'* model explains why we choose one *type* of person over another (though finer distinctions admittedly lie beyond the model's scope): our "types" are functions of divine "Unary Signifiers."

At this point, however, Plato would almost appear to have the better of Lacan in accounting for object choice: behind Plato's beloved stands the specificity of a tutelary god, whereas Lacan's object and its informing Unary Signifier screen the emphatically *non*specific, "empty" phallus. Granted that in our earlier discussion of the phallus, we stressed its radical failure qua object as fortuitous. Only perpetually dissatisfied beings will submit to cultural prohibitions in order to gain objects of exchange valued (albeit falsely) as assuaging dissatisfaction. Therein lies the only possibility of social bonds—but how to negotiate the seemingly impassable chasm Lacan's emphasis on the phallus as *non*object opens up between it and any particular object? Seemingly aware of this theoretical gap, Lacan developed the concept of *objet a* to supply it.

26

Objet a

Objet a (= objet a[utre], "other") is best understood as a *function*, rather than a discrete set of objects per se.[74] The term was Lacan's coinage, but its conceptual roots reach back to Freud's formulation of the object of the drive as entirely indifferent to the drive's operation (were the case otherwise, sublimation would be impossible, and wooden reels could not begin to compensate for mothers). Our previous discussion of the *fort/da* game shows that the drive revolves around the object *as lost:* it represents the object as a "hole" around which it (the drive) is organized.

Lacan seizes upon the referential relation between the drive and its (absent) object as a signifying relation. But just what does it signify? The subject divided by the signifier—whence arises the notion of *objet a(utre)*, a fleshly representation of the subject's self-alienation. The uneasy split exampled in the two "I's" of "I am lying" raises the specter of a stranger, an "other" who is yet myself; this *Doppelgänger* not only haunts my site of consciousness but makes that site meaningful through opposition. *Objet a*'s derivation from *objet autre* points to its ambiguous status as what is seen as a part of self nonetheless also estranged, "other." Lacan points to the objects regularly invested with erotogenic "charge" early in the history of the body, that shape the adult geography of desire. In his account of *objet a,* he analyzes the traditional psychoanalytic "part-objects" as instances of its function: feces, urine, the breast, the lips, the rim of the anus, the tip of the penis, are all graphic allegories of the function that creates them and that parallels the subject's genesis in division.[75] All are conditioned by the structure of autopartitioning. Excreta are portions of the self periodically "lost"; the breast is periodically gained and lost. Lips, anus, penis, represent in the flesh the loss and lack round which the subject himself is constructed, the "hole" of desire unanswerable by any object.

Thus motivated, Lacan's list can expand to include the "unthinkable" additions of the voice, the gaze, the phoneme, the nothing.[76] The phoneme as object we have already glimpsed in the *fort/da* game, where the child's pleasure derives in part from repeating these syllables. The voice and the gaze partake of the same structure of discontinuity as excreta and fleshly apertures: the voice cannot be heard unless it "separates" (is emitted) from the body; the eye sees without seeing itself, thus "loses" itself in the act of seeing; and the nothing is the ultimate, logical kenosis of *objet a:* the pure instantiation of lack as the precondition of desire.

Objet a thus provides Lacan a means of adequation between the theoretical operation of desire, in its sublime indifference to the object, and the observed fact that for any one individual, just *this* curve of the lip, *this* timbre of the voice, *this* term of endearment (or scorn) will excite desire.[77] (Even so pure an object as "the nothing" helps him out—the anorexic chooses the nothing.) *Objet a* supplements the function of the phallus as Master Signifier of desire, by giving that desire a name and local habitation, a bit of flesh and substance on which to fasten in a more-or-less predictable way for any one person.

Imaginary fantasy sustains *objet a* in play, keeping the game going over an unreachable prize—the fantasy of wholeness, founded by the Unary Signifier, that this or that object will complete the subject and grant her wish to be Absolute Subject. Yet the structure that creates *objet a* is a logical precondition to subjectivity: the subject desires insofar as she *is* a subject, and therefore lacking.[78] The impossible *objet a* that would eliminate that lack would eliminate the basis of subjectivity along with it. With the self-negating structure of *objet a* in mind, some of the extremity with which Catullus articulates his passion for Lesbia becomes legible. In c.51, he need only hear her "sweetly laughing" for her voice (as *objet a*) to undo him: he loses himself as subject, for that "snatches all my senses from me." The wonder of her auditor's godlike control—the impassive gentleman who "looks and gazes" upon her without turning a hair—Catullus measures by the contradiction the auditor sustains: he enjoys *objet a* and subjectivity at the same time.

Woman and Epistemology

Lacan's meditations on *objet a*, the phallus, and desire led him eventually to a fundamental reconceptualization of gender that oddly resembles Plato's project even more than Freud's. Desire is the vehicle of knowledge for Lacan as much as for Plato—and Lacan's articulation of knowledge, gender, and desire covers much of the same ground "divine madness" does in the *Phaedrus*. Jacques-Alain Miller and Ellie Ragland-Sullivan have both pointed out that for Lacan, Woman is a position outside clear meaning and grammatical language—she is *hors-sens*, "outside meaning/sense." As such, Woman signifies the antithesis of masculine certitude, based on identification with rules, order, Law. Thus the feminine is for Lacan an attitude toward knowledge and procedure, rather than a category defined strictly by gender, and occupies the same conceptual position as *mania* ("divine madness") in the *Phaedrus*.[79]

Lacan makes large claims in his account of Woman—yet all this quite logically develops from the fact that the phallus is *merely* a signifier and

28

bears no necessary or essential relation to any anatomical signifier, including the penis. Although the Symbolic order splits subjects into alignments with the signifiers "Man" and "Woman," these are for Lacan *only* functions of the signifier, of the phallus as the signifier of difference and desire. In this light, Catullus' easy transitions between one gender and the other in his poetry are understandable as mere changes in position with respect to an arbitrary signifier—and more, as driven by the same greed for something beyond the worn coin of "common sense" that propels Plato's philosopher-lover. But Plato concentrates more on *mania* as supplying a conceptual insufficiency in "rationality" and less on its implications for gender and relations between the sexes—areas crucial to our understanding of the relationship between Lesbia and Catullus. Plato thus takes a shortcut past much of what Lacan accomplishes in his elliptical meditations on gender and epistemology. We must therefore hold the *Phaedrus* temporarily in abeyance until we can rejoin its concerns from a trajectory traced through sexual antagonism.

Anyone can, in Lacan's view, take up the feminine or the masculine position with respect to the phallus—and many have. Those who do, have access to a knowledge impossible to comprehend within masculine "certainty." He points to the examples of (anatomically) male mystics, like St. John of the Cross, who touched upon knowledge banished to the side of Woman, as counterrational but true.[80]

Yet Lacan's astute skepticism about epistemology does nothing by itself to explain the historic difference in access to cultural privilege between bodies anatomically male versus those anatomically female. That, in his view, arises from a crude assimilation of penis to phallus[81]—an Imaginary strategem that tries to secure identity by interpreting as essence what is merely difference. Woman then becomes the subordinated guarantor of Man's identity qua Man, as the oppositional term in a (near-) binarism.[82] Here is Hegel's Master/Slave dialectic once more, where the Master is surprised to find himself dependent on the Slave for his identity *as* Master. Lack (as castration) is banished to her side of the opposition. She becomes *objet a* for Man, a collection of fetishized objects (breast, hair, lips, skin, etc.) that both figure castration for him (as division of the body) and deny it (insofar as he reads her body as his *complement,* his missing "other half").[83] Woman thus guarantees conceptual unity and wholeness to Man's side, underwriting his identity.[84]

But Woman so constructed is only a masquerade—a notion Lacan borrows from Joan Rivière, one of Freud's early followers. The feminine is a masquerade to the extent that Woman's entire definition rests on

29

difference: she is merely "what Man is not." Oddly, this makes her "identity" revolve around the phallus, as the signifier of pure difference—and inadequately so, since she is structured as pure negation, "not-Man." Femininity is thus nothing more than a simulacrum—a stunning blow to the Symbolic's claim to represent the world faithfully and exhaustively. Language and the various institutions that make up the Symbolic repeatedly stumble over Woman, who cannot be subsumed in the pure oppositions the phallus signifies. Lacan indicated the signifying system's failure with his phrase "the hole in the Other."[85] The phrase deliberately draws upon the most offensive representations of Woman as lacking and exposes them as attempts to inscribe the conceptual shortcomings of pure alterity onto Woman. "The hole in the Other" designates all the ways in which the Symbolic falls short of its claim to truth and totality, and repeatedly dissimulates such failures.

Yet a grim and disturbing ecstasy lurks around such failures. Lacan conceived the "hole in the Other"—the place where institutional sense fails—as the site of *jouissance*, punning upon dual senses of "enjoyment" and "orgasm." Lacan distinguished two types of *jouissance*, calling conventional sexual pleasure *jouissance phallique*[86]—ultimately, an effect of the erotic fiction "we two are as one,"[87] supported by the Unary Signifier. Yet he regarded this as a mere guardrail against the larger, more menacing conception of *jouissance féminine* (regularly shortened to *jouissance* when not specifically opposed to *jouissance phallique*).[88] The latter is *jouissance* as the drive beyond conventional pleasure into the disintegration of subjectivity (in "ek-stasy," being "beside oneself"); thus into the dissolution of self in pain and death. This is the very realm "beyond the pleasure principle" Freud investigated when he asked himself, Why do people unconsciously repeat acts, thoughts, dreams that give them pain? *Jouissance*, in its strange yoking of ecstasy, pain, and death, menaces the Symbolic as the symptom of what cannot enter into the logic of signification—and as such, it makes clear *Woman*'s threat to the Symbolic, insofar as *jouissance* is her conceptual corollary. If we take as *jouissance*'s peculiar territory "that which cannot be submitted to the logic of signification, that which is *hors-sens*," we can more easily see how Lacan ultimately sweeps not only Woman, but the concepts of mysticism and God Himself into his meditations on it. This triple alignment clarifies the way Catullus stages his persistent fascination with states of being that exceed the conventionally human. Catullus regularly dramatizes the loss of "normal" alignments of gender, identity, and psychic integrity as encounters with the divine. We have already noted

Lesbia's shattering effect on Catullus in c.51: she is the fulcrum upon which the auditor rises toward heaven, while Catullus sinks into incapacity, reft of any integrating "I." Some of the allegories of the *carmina maiora* restage and expand this *jouissance*-effect. In c.63, Attis, driven mad by Cybele, emasculates himself for the goddess, and slides dizzyingly between genders for the rest of the poem. C.64 articulates the same elements in a slightly different order: Ariadne, maddened by grief and rage at Theseus abandoning her, attracts the ardor of the god Dionysus. All three poems, however, see Woman, the divine, and the realm beyond rationality as concepts integrally related.

If we pause for a moment here and review the terms our discussion has clustered around the signifier "Woman"—the "hole in the Other"; "exceeding signification"; "guarantor of identity"; "repetition"—we will see that these same conceptual landmarks anchored our discussion of the symptom. The symptom dissimulates a "hole" in the subject's being that exceeds, and is the effect of, the signifier, by repeating certain acts, thoughts, dreams, and so on to create a semblance of identity. If the hysteric is nothing else, she "is" the one who has terrifying thoughts, strange dreams, uncanny accidents, and so on. This should smooth the way toward understanding the arresting apothegm of Lacan's late writings: "Woman is a symptom." She is a symptom insofar as her desire has not been, and cannot be, signified in a system constructed around the phallus as the central signifier of pure difference. The signifier of her desire is foreclosed (*verworfen*).

Lacan accounted for the effects of foreclosure with the following formulation: "what is foreclosed in the Symbolic returns in the Real" (as the psychotic's hallucinations and voices, for example). Thus Woman returns, persistently and repetitively, from the Real, as the effect of a central foreclosure in the Symbolic and the symptom, equally, of Man. Antagonistic relations between the sexes are but one manifestation of this lacuna, insofar as they undermine cultural myths of each sex's "natural" complementarity to the other. And whether that antagonism takes the form of misogyny or, more subtly, of idolatry, the motivation is the same: trying to explain the lack of natural complementarity as *Woman*'s fault, as either too impossibly bad, or impossibly good, for Man.

If we apply these reflections to the Catullan poems, we need no longer struggle to rationalize Lesbia's appearance in the corpus as both demon and goddess by constructing a specious history either of her "gradual deterioration," or Catullus' "slow enlightenment"; the cycle as a whole will support neither. Both Lesbia's unspeakable sordidness and her ineffable desirability are structurally overdetermined, always available simultaneously to cover over an embarrassing blind spot in the sexual *non*relation.

The idea of a conceptual insufficiency in the Symbolic, to which Lacan's theorization of Woman is addressed, brings us back, full circle, to Plato's worry over the same problem. Plato touched upon this inadequacy in the *Symposium* but deferred fully investigating his own question to the *Phaedrus*. In the *Symposium,* Diotima poses to Socrates the binarism "knowledge" versus "ignorance" and says, "Is this exhaustive? What if you just happen to be right without deductive proof?"[89]—whence is born the mediocrity "right opinion." Diotima thereby sidesteps a far more menacing category: the irrational that is nonetheless true, the *mania* of divine possession.

In the *Phaedrus,* Plato goes beyond her lukewarm category, to something that exceeds any orderly management of binary oppositions. In a fortuitous consonance between the dialogue's dramatic setting and its content, the *Phaedrus* ex-centrically lures Socrates outside the concentration of human symbolization systems located within Athens' city walls. He finds himself in a landscape irritatingly resistant to signification. He dismisses rationalizing logography as a waste of meaning on nonhuman objects[90] and later says, "I am a lover of learning; I can't learn anything from rocks and trees, only from people in the city."[91] But the marginal setting he initially contemns yields the lesson of *mania*—which, by definition, cannot be read by the light of Socrates' previous human experience. *Mania,* like *jouissance,* betrays what the Symbolic can*not* adequately represent—what it therefore prefers to marginalize and forget.

Conspectus

Having traveled so far in the erotic theory of Plato, Freud, and Lacan, we can now step back and see what we have in hand from our journey. First: all three stand firm upon the existence of an irrevocable fault line in the human subject, a split that apportions knowledge and desire into shifting configurations of what is "absent" or "present" to the subject at any one moment. Equally, all three lend as much or more weight to the "absent" realms of desire and knowledge in determining both what the subject is, and what she can become.

With this as background and paradigm, we are justified in shifting our focus as we investigate the subject of the Catullan text—in both senses, as "the one who speaks" and "what he speaks about"—to take in not only what seems logically "whole" in the text but also what does not. We shall then be engaged in listening to that crucial "other" discourse that splits both text and subject, and that evidences itself in the plethora of competing orders for the poems; the irreconcilable contradictions in the history they describe; the impossibly paradoxical agents who flicker in and out of that history; even the subtle failures of grammar and syntax. All these invite us to exchange common for uncommon sense.

All as well articulate a poetics of radical discontinuity, in the conceptual territory staked out by the Symbolic and *jouissance,* Conscious and Unconscious, reason and *mania.* However, we are interested in both sides of the divide, even if I have thus far emphasized the claims of "absent" knowledge as the more neglected terrain. Neither Plato nor Freud nor Lacan complacently abandoned human beings to hopeless schizophrenia. The notion of "identity" is still important to us, provided we always keep one eye on subjectivity as well. The "persons" organized by names and histories in the Catullan text are important coigns of vantage from which to measure those places where agents overlap and merge, as in the *carmina maiora.* Ideally, our attention continually divides, following the unceasing play between coherence and dissolution of the "person" conditioned by subjectivity.

So framed, our investigation of Catullus does not so much discard notions of "wholeness" as shift to a new perspective on "poetic unity." When we displace interest from, Where does this wholeness lie? to How is it constituted? we can focus closely upon the ideological threads used to suture over gaps in subject, text, and narrative *and* upon the nagging suspicion (pandemic to Catullus studies) that the sutures never quite "take." We can account for (if we cannot precisely pin down) the undecideable play between a shapely weave and a fluid unraveling.

An Outline of This Book

I do not offer this book as an exhaustive demonstration of its methodology's power to "explain" the entire Catullan corpus. Rather, I have concentrated on the Lesbia cycle alone as, for all its taciturnity, the most complete account of a love affair we have from the corpus; by comparison, Juventius, Camerius, Licinius, and others to whom Catullus addresses real or ironic desire are little more than brief images. I hope to demonstrate in my discussion the method's possibilities for other, more ambitious projects.

To make visible the sutures that hold together any reading of the text, I have used c.11 and c.51 as interpretive *points de repère* throughout the book (as well as objects of particular attention in chapter 3). The representations of Lesbia and Catullus encapsulated in these two poems succinctly summarize the extremes we have to bridge: demonized Whore and exalted Goddess; victim and devotee; putative "end" and "beginning" of the affair; *odi* and *amo*. These two poems thus anchor a dual problem of reading for the rest of the cycle. First, how do the other poems in the Lesbia cycle construe a relation between one tableau and the other? How do they reconcile the radical divisions between these two emotional moments and these two portraits of Lesbia vis-à-vis Catullus? Second, where such reconciliations logically conflict, how do these failings reveal the limits of representation described by this text?

The last question, stemming from failed unity, leads me to address gender representation particularly in the corpus, and gender's institutional supports, as insistent loci of gaps, dehiscence, and contradiction in the Lesbia cycle. Here I must keep two different orientations in mind: the phallus as joined to the penis, and as disjoined from it. I have presented the reader with two different aspects of Lacan's thought on gender and sexuality, arguing, on the one hand, that the phallus is not intrinsically a male symbol but only a cipher. On the other hand, I have unfolded the consequences of the Imaginary confusion of penis with phallus that characterizes patriarchy. Both versions aptly describe what the Catullan text does, in my opinion. I can hardly argue that Catullus occupied some coign of vantage free from all the misogyny of his cultural milieu, without gainsaying the model of the subject I have been at such pains to justify in this chapter. These attitudes are encoded in his cultural discourse—he cannot "stand outside" that system.

But neither need we read him as a "cultural dope,"[92] mindlessly reproducing Roman male prejudices. I see too many signs of deep cultural suspicion in Catullus' poetry—such as his fascination with gender mobility—to construe him simply as a male supremacist. In the pages that follow, I shall trace the clashes of dominant discourse with hermeneutic suspicion—clashes that oppose to Woman as natural complement, the vertiginous speculation that perhaps she does not exist at all.

In chapter 2, we shall read c.1 plus the Lesbia poems between cc.1 and 11 as an example in short compass of fragmented narrative. These poems narrate a brief, progressive history of the affair that introduces and develops the governing principles of the remaining cycle. In this chapter, I have used the concepts of metaphor and metonymy extensively as, on the one hand, the two basic tropes that control narrative and, on the other, as assimilable to the fundamental psychoanalytic functions of condensation and displacement. I can thereby reveal the ways in which the text solicits and frustrates the reader's desire to make legible "wholes" (metaphors, condensations) out of fragmentary and conflicting data (metonymies, displacements). These poems' jokes and irony, their jaundiced view of cultural icons, and their breezy rummaging through the costume closet of gender simultaneously reveal and paper over ruptures in the unifying fictions that govern the self, its gender, and its address to social ideals.

In chapter 3, we shall read cc.11 and 51 as constructing a purely repetitive oscillation between themselves, with clear formal connections but no clear causal or temporal relation. Once the interpretive field is so austerely limited, the functions of metaphor/condensation and metonymy/displacement recede to reveal the unconscious desire in which all are rooted—a desire subsumed under the concept of *jouissance. Jouissance* discloses another order of reading in the text, which fastens upon the subtle data easily overlooked or "explained away" in a purely "logical" reading: the hesitancies, the significant silences, and the anacolutha that trouble Catullus' two portraits of himself and Lesbia. What speaks "besides" in these poems transmits a message impossible to translate into the crude oppositions of the Symbolic. Accordingly, the Symbolic effects of language, rationality, and subjectivity break down before what Catullus' portrait of his lover reveals: the exclusions upon which he has based his own identity as Man.

In chapter 4, we shall read the epigrams as combining the reading patterns of cc.2–11 and cc.11 plus 51: both repetition and progressive refinement govern the epigrams. Metaphor reappears here as Lacanian *capitonnage,* with its link to identity as a unity constructed in narrative. *Capitonnage* addresses the epigrams' peculiar fascination with pinpointing the "truth" of Lesbia's speech as the obverse of constructing a (unified) Catullus—a Catullus whose reflection is sought in the fragmented and conflicting signs of his lover's spoken desire. Close scrutiny of *both* lovers' lies shows Catullus' project to be impossible—frustrated by the unbridgeable division in the subject paradigmatically represented in "I am lying."

In chapter 5, we apply the combined reading strategies and approaches to problems in the text developed in earlier chapters to the *carmina maiora* concerned with the Lesbia affair. We can thus see whether our responses apply equally when the received text, and not the reader, dictates the order of reading and the field of interpretation. The category of fantasy becomes important here as a way of (fictively) transcending the limits imposed on thought and experience by the Symbolic, without losing the ability to signify or be a subject. Fantasy raises the problem of constructing a (unified)

35

Catullus onto a new plane. In the figure of Hercules, Catullus imagines godlike "wholeness": a subjectivity not dependent upon an object and thus immune to loss in love. But he also depicts Hercules as a peculiar mix of metaphor and metonymy: a "transcendent" unity whose jointures are nonetheless obvious, so that its autonomy must be constantly renewed and reargued in narrative. Hercules is, in short, a perpetual narrative motor: he represents the constant renewal of desire in poetry.

2

Poems One Through Eleven: A Fragmentary History of the Affair

From a "Letter from Lesbia"

. . . So, praise the gods, at last he's away!
And let me tend you this advice, my dear:
Take any lover that you will, or may,
    Except a poet. All of them are queer.

It's just the same—a quarrel or a kiss
    Is but a tune to play upon his pipe.
He's always hymning that or wailing this;
    Myself, I much prefer the business type.

That thing he wrote, the time the sparrow died—
    (Oh, most unpleasant—gloomy, tedious words!)
I called it sweet, and made believe I cried;
    The stupid fool! I've always hated birds . . .
                                    —Dorothy Parker[1]

In this chapter, I propose to look first at c.1, considered as a prolegomenon to the original *libellus*; next, at the Lesbia poems from c.2 through c.11, seen as epitomizing the affair the Lesbia cycle putatively records. C.1, as an introductory poem, alerts the reader to the important concepts that inform the Catullan corpus—such as Catullus' allegiance to Callimachean aesthetics,[2] phrased as a concern with establishing (and undermining) boundaries. C.1 raises the problem of where one makes distinctions in the specific context of recording historical events by praising offhandedly Cornelius' ambitious history of the Italians. As such, the poem leads us into the problem of narrative selection and sequence raised by the corpus as a whole and by the Lesbia cycle in particular.

Obligingly, our one ancestral manuscript has staged this problem in the group of poems immediately following the dedicatory poem: cc.2–11 are the smallest group of poems that easily lend themselves to interpretation as a complete outline of the affair, and their manuscript order, happily, describes their narrative order. Consider the following common construction: cc.2 and 3 record first flirtations, while cc.5 and 7 progress to passionate infatuation; c.8 offers the first hint of disillusionment that leads to complete dismissal in c.11.[3]

But the amorous cycle these poems describe would be no more than mildly interesting, as a fortuitously orderly résumé, were it not that it raises most of the conceptual principles that govern the rest of the corpus. Just as Callimachean poetics unite in their scope levels of aesthetics stretching from the humble specifics of meter and form all the way up to the nature of the audience addressed and the attitude adopted toward literary tradition, so Catullus' aesthetic project links widely varying registers of human experience. Cc.2–11 examine limit and transgression as they govern poetic form but also gender, pleasure, and identity. These poems see boundaries of psyche and sexuality as determined by language, insofar as it reflects Law—even in mild forms, such as social decorum and gamesmanship—and imposes limits on desire. Catullus' subtle examination of where, how, and why in poetry one "draws the line," and crosses it, leads to an interrogation of the principle's operation in much of human existence.

Because questions of narrative will form our entrée to these other considerations, it will be useful, after examining c.1, to take up cc.2–11 approximately in numerical order. However, I shall also concern myself to elucidate the places where they strain against that linear construction. The poems demand cross-reference to other poems in the Lesbia cycle in order to be fully understood. Being attentive to these subtle eddies, our excursus through cc.2–11 will accordingly fetch a wide compass. To attempt to confine it strictly to linear exposition would be to pass over unseen those places where causality and progression are suspended and subverted in favor of undecideability and repetition—the places, in short, where the text itself interrogates the logic used to construct narrative.

38

Poems One Through Eleven

The History of the Piece

C.1, the introductory poem to the original *libellus*[4] posits several different types of limitation.

> Cui dono lepidum novum libellum
> arida modo pumice expolitum?
> Corneli, tibi: namque tu solebas
> meas esse aliquid putare nugas
> iam tum, cum ausus es unus Italorum
> omne aevum tribus explicare cartis
> doctis, Iuppiter, et laboriosis.
> quare habe tibi quidquid hoc libelli
> qualecumque quod, <o> patrona virgo,[5]
> plus uno maneat perenne saeclo.

To whom do I give the charming new booklet, polished just now with a dry pumice stone? Cornelius, to you: for you were accustomed to think my trifles worth something—even already in those days when you dared, alone of the Italians, to lay out all of time on three sheets, sheets learned and painfully worked out, by Jove. Wherefore, take for yourself this whadayacallit of a booklet; whatever it may be, oh patron maiden, let it remain, everlastingly, more than an age.

On the one hand, we have the poet affecting a trifling estimation of his own poetry—his poems are merely *nugae*. But that ironic diminution (worthy of Callimachus) is put into play directly following its own negation. Cornelius, his addressee, thinks that these "trifles" are actually "something." The litotes of Cornelius' estimation gains some force when we hear, in turn, Catullus summing up Cornelius' authorial career: Cornelius has undertaken to set out world history in a mere three volumes! As Kenneth Quinn remarks, this solicits "a visual image of 'the whole of time' laid out on three sheets of papyrus"[6]—and, one might add, by dint of the Herculean daring ("ausus es," 5) of just one man, the only one among the Italians ("unus Italorum," 5). Cornelius' unique courage is played off against the limited expectations one would naturally have of the lone scholar facing such a tremendous task—yet his taste as well as his courage are exhibited in his compressed accomplishment, a portable *Story of Civilization*. Such a calculatedly exiguous document merits the Callimachean stamp of approval: these volumes are "learned and show a lot of scrupulous work" ("doctis . . . et laboriosis," 7). Not that this necessarily constitutes

39

unqualified praise: once again, Callimachean irony dissimulates the poet's attitude. *Laboriosus* can mean "requiring much work" for the reader, as well as the writer.[7] The double-entendre leaves us guessing whether Catullus considered Nepos' *Chronica* a polished *chef-d'oeuvre* or a yawn. The latter gloss jars oddly against *doctus* ("learned"); in Catullus' poetry, *doctus* means much more than just educated or even scholarly. It implies the kind of wit and erudition necessary to write and/or to appreciate the subtleties of Callimachean aesthetics[8]—an aesthetic that would value a laconic but polished historian over a Roman Gibbon. But was Cornelius that polished historian? The poem refuses to resolve our dilemma, leaving it—and Cornelius—an open question.

Common aesthetic values motivate Cornelius and Catullus (even if we doubt that Cornelius can put *his* into practice)—aesthetics that link paradoxical concepts. Compression in space leads to expansion in time: small, painstakingly polished works win immortality. At least, that is what Catullus wishes for himself. He hopes that the Muse entertains the same notions about aesthetics as Cornelius does (and given that Catullus calls her and her sisters "learned maidens" ["doctis . . . virginibus," 65.2], she probably does). Let her think it worthwhile to let this diminutive book, a collection of mere trifles, last "more than an age" (1.10).

What c.1 sets in place is a positing of limit in several different dimensions of human experience—from a studied parsimony in written expression, to an assumed pose of modest accomplishment, all the way up to an insouciant confrontation with the biggest limit of all, mortality. Each of these the poem simultaneously undercuts, not only with the venerable Callimachean equation of tightly wrought poetry leading to an infinite *Nachleben* for its author, but with the strategic deployment of terms that strain against the confines of *nugae:* the immortals (Jupiter, the Muse); all the Italian races; all of time. The dimension of history leads us directly into the question of narrative and, even more directly, into our investigation of one particular branch of it—*fragmented* narrative. If "all of time" was reduced to three sheets of papyrus, what went missing in Cornelius' account?

Note that c.1 solicits the reader's desire to "fill in the gaps" in an uncertainly edited history, just as the question of selectivity—"what is *not* here?"—is one of the questions central to the Lesbia cycle and automatically solicits the reader's desire to answer it. The Lesbia-poems as a whole suggest a narrative, but a fragmented narrative—they describe points in time that both invite and resist ordering in meaningful temporal sequence. Take, as an example, poem 107:

Poems One Through Eleven

Si quicquam cupido optantique obtigit umquam
  insperanti, hoc est gratum animo proprie.
quare hoc est gratum nobisque hoc carius auro
  quod te restituis, Lesbia, mi cupido.
restituis cupido atque insperanti, ipsa refers te
  nobis. o lucem candidiore nota!
quis me uno vivit felicior, aut magis hac quid
  optandum vita dicere quis poterit?

If anything ever befell someone who wanted it and wished for it, but did
not expect it, this is especially pleasing to his heart. Wherefore this is pleasing
to me, and to me this is dearer than gold, that you restore yourself, Lesbia,
to me who desires you. You restore yourself to one who desires but does
not hope, when you yourself bring yourself back to me. O day with a whiter
mark! Who lives who is happier than I alone, or who shall have been able
to say that anything ought more to be wished for in this life?

The poem speaks of a loss and restoration not directly referred to in the
rest of the corpus. It invites the reader to construct a narrative sequence
of events in which to fit this piece of information.

> To Lesbia, who had returned unexpectedly after an absence. The poem implies
> a temporary reconciliation (Robinson Ellis, *Commentary on Catullus,* ad loc.)

> Felicità di Catullo per la riconciliazione con Lesbia. La poesiola sgorga fresca
> dal cuore in tumulto del poeta, senza artifici o lambiccature di stile. La
> situazione pare posteriore a quella del c.8: cfr. v.6 con 8,3. (Massimo Lenchan-
> tin de Gubernatis, *Il Libro di Catullo,* ad loc.)

> Lesbia has come back! After one of the *rara furta* of 68.136? Or a reconcilia-
> tion after Bithynia? (Kenneth Quinn, *Catullus: The Poems,* ad loc.)

In attempting to decipher this poem, Ellis places it in a time sequence
that demands a final alienation to follow ("a temporary reconciliation").
Lenchantin de Gubernatis, on the other hand, looks to the prehistory of
the poem and, guided by the light imagery common to 107.6 and 8.3
("fulsere quondam candidi tibi soles"), attempts to fix a textual *terminus
post quem:* "after c.8." Quinn is more specific in searching for c.107's exact
place in the putative narrative of the relationship: perhaps the two lovers
have been reconciled after one of Lesbia's affairs with a rival; perhaps after
Catullus traveled to Bithynia in Asia Minor as a member of the governor's
(C. Memmius') entourage.

The poem invites such speculation because it refers to a story line outside the boundary of the poem. If Lesbia has been "restored" to Catullus, then she must have been lost to him. But when? where? how? for how long? Such details are suppressed, part of the "before" and "after" left to the imagination. Insofar as restoration of the beloved implies prior loss, interpretation links this poem to other poems in the corpus that refer to loss, whether in terms of a physical journey away from the beloved (10: Bithynia), absence in pursuit of rivals (68.136: Lesbia's other love affairs), or a more general "estrangement" (c.8). Poem 107 suggests a narrative sequence on the basis of what is the same (absence) and what is different (restoration) between itself and the other poems of the corpus.

Sameness and difference are two poetic modalities whose interaction, according to Tzvetan Todorov, produces narrative plot (*le récit*) and its movement through "narrative transformations."[9] Narrative transformations are changes in a term (a motif, for example—like the light imagery of cc.8 and 107) common to different parts of the text.[10] The resemblance, and the difference, between repeated elements in a text links them together in a chain of meaning, but as well suggest temporal sequence:

> The simple relation of successive facts does not constitute a plot: it is necessary that the facts be organized, which is to say, in fine, that they must have some elements in common. But if all the elements are common, there is no more plot because there is nothing more to tell. Now, transformation represents exactly a synthesis of difference and resemblance; it ties together two facts without making them exactly the same. More than a "unity with two faces," it is an operation with a double meaning: it affirms at once resemblance and difference; it sets time in motion, and suspends it; it permits discourse to acquire sense without it becoming pure information; in a word: it makes possible plot and gives us its definition at the same time.[11]

The search for significance is implicit in *erōs*. Diotima herself characterizes Eros as "a lover of wisdom throughout his life" ("philosophôn dia pantos tou biou," *Symp.* 203d7). Indeed, her sketch of the lover's ascent toward the Beautiful Itself is largely a matter of coming to see resemblance in the midst of difference—how the beauty in one body is like the beauty in another, how beauty in souls is related to beauty in institutions, and how all instantiations of beauty are finally related to the Form of the Beautiful. And in the *Phaedrus,* the erotic *mania* that visits the lover will, under the best of circumstances, make her a philosopher capable of discovering truth revealed in resemblance shining through apparent difference (in "collections and divisions"—*sunagōgai* and *diaireseis*—of which Socrates declares himself a "lover" ["erastēs"], *Phaedrus* 266b3–4).[12]

Plato brings to Todorov's picture an awareness of desire's role in creating legible wholes from apparently disparate elements—the operation that underpins *metaphor* (as Peter Brooks has pointed out).[13] But metaphor is static without Todorov's principle of transformation—which he assimilates to *metonymy*,[14] and which (as Brooks notes) is a trope equally powered by desire, the desire to get *to* the meaningful whole promised by metaphor. Lacan aligned metaphor and metonymy with the two basic operations Freud distinguished in the Unconscious—condensation and displacement, respectively.[15] Condensation is "a sole idea represent[ing] several associative chains at whose point of intersection it is located"[16] and displacement is "an idea's emphasis, interest or intensity . . . detached from it and . . . pass[ed] on to other ideas."[17] That is, in part, what Lacan means when he says that "the Unconscious is structured like a language": that *erōs* passing through us creates a signifying chain, a *récit* from which we, as subjects, hang suspended.

Thus the tropological changes rung on our desire as readers are not fundamentally different from those we experience as lovers or as philosophers. We seek meaning—we interpret—in noticing the points of resemblance and difference between different parts of the Catullan corpus. We are invited to do so, by repetition and difference in subject matter and imagery (as we saw in cc.107, 10, 68, and 8), but as well in meter, vocabulary, and the like. We are simultaneously frustrated, because the Lesbia cycle falls far short of the totality of a novel, a play, or an epic poem. Resemblance and transformation in key terms assures us that these poems are not simply "an assemblage of facts." Yet the gaps in what we are given obscure the meaning of this particular discourse—rather like a painting or a statue of which only parts remain.

Given their fragmentary nature and the elements repeated between various poems, the Lesbia cycle lends itself to recombinatory reading—as exampled in the commentators quoted above, each of whom achieves a provisional stasis by supplying a subject to his reading. Where Lenchantin de Gubernatis sees a purling innocent, Ellis perceives a man schooled by previous betrayal to know the reconciliation only temporary. Quinn treads a middle path by adding, "Catullus' extravagant reaction seems devoid of irony"—cautiously laying claim to Lenchantin's *ingenu* while reminding us that Catullus is quite capable of dissimulation.

I do not review these readings as "bad," "false" conclusions, which an enlightened methodology could replace with a "good," "true" conclusion. Rather, the model of narrative I have sketched in the previous pages *requires* unifying icons such as Lenchantin, Ellis, and Quinn have supplied. But if

43

we forget the provisional nature of such icons, we will miss the text's self-multiplication and prematurely close down our inquiry. C.107 could be the sequel to 8—or to 68—or to 10—or to a variety of other plot sequences. That introduces the possibility of narrative *exhaustion* as an alternative to narrative *completeness*. A great many combinations of these poems can be constructed based on transformation in terms repeated between poems. If the gaps between poems cannot be filled in, they can at least be shuffled and reshuffled in different orderings to yield different putative sequences of events. The poems can, in fact, encompass a wide variety of possible "plots" of desire. Thus their very limitation—the absence of surrounding detail that would allow us to *fix* them in a logically determined sequence—lends itself to an expansion of narrative possibilities (as we will see in more detail in our discussion of poems 11 and 51).[18] As in the *fort/da* game, or Aristophanes' half-people trying to reunite into wholes, frustration leads to (conceivably infinite) repetition.

The Subject Dissembled

In the necessity of narrativization to elicit meaning from the text, the Lesbia cycle resembles nothing so much as the rich but perplexing details of a dream, a symptom, a parapraxis,[19] presented by the analysand for interpretation with the analyst. Reading the cycle requires sorting out, into meaningful opposition and sequence, otherwise meaningless elements. Yet overdetermination—the concept that multiple strings of causality may be forged between these disparate elements, each string autonomously capable of "explaining" the dream, the symptom, the parapraxis—makes it clear that this task can never be considered determined and completed. And if, further, we keep in view the fact that these narrative strings are all implicitly anchored to (creating) a subject, the *mise en abîme* of determinate sequence becomes all the more dizzying. The Catullan text constantly suggests, but spirits away, a subject through the subterfuges of the signifying chain and its infinite possible connections.

Take, for example, the ironies we touched upon in c.1, where Catullus' diction dissimulates his aesthetic attitudes toward his own work and Nepos'. Is Catullus' *libellus* to be esteemed as *expolitus* or contemned as a collection of mere *nugae*? Did the effort expended on Nepos' *Chronica* create a work "laborious" for its author, or its reader? We cannot just say "Callimachean irony" and pass on; we must note what the figure of irony does to the subject fitfully visible in the poetry. Irony hopelessly obscures the subject's "true meaning"; irony thereby spirits away the subject's "true self"; an ironized text is a text enacted without definable reference to the subject's agency or consciousness. To the question, What did Catullus *really* mean? no answer can be given. C.16 offers a more extended example of irony's effect:

> Pedicabo ego vos et irrumabo,
> Aureli pathice et cinaede Furi,
> qui me ex versiculis meis putastis,
> quod sunt molliculi, parum pudicum.
> nam castum esse decet pium poetam
> ipsum, versiculos nihil necesse est;
> qui tum denique habent salem ac leporem,
> si sunt molliculi ac parum pudici,
> et quod pruriat incitare possunt,
> non dico pueris, sed his pilosis
> qui duros nequeunt movere lumbos.
> vos, quod milia multa basiorum
> legistis, male me marem putatis?
> pedicabo ego vos et irrumabo.

Fuck you, boys, up the butt and in the mouth, you queer Aurelius, and you fag Furius! You size me up, on the basis of my poems, because they're a little sexy, as not really decent. A poet has to live clean—but not his poems. *They* only have spice and charm, if somewhat sexy and really not for children—if, in fact, they could cause body talk (I'm not saying in teenagers, but in hairy old men who can barely move their stiff bums). But you, because you happen to read about "many thousands of kisses," you think *I'm* not a man? Fuck you, boys, up the butt and in the mouth!

The self-contradiction of this poem needs no elaborate rehearsal.[20] The central conceit rests upon the irremediable indeterminacy of a vocabulary that ricochets between general abuse and specific sexual slang: *irrumare* and *paedicare* refer to homosexual sex acts—but they can also mean as little as "go to hell." Does that confirm, or deny, Furius' and Aurelius' charge that Catullus is "not a man"? Catullus ostentatiously forbids us to ask the question by placing an unbridgeable gap between his poetry and his life— and then, with his suggestive poetic conceits, proceeds to tease us into speculation all over again. What I suggest here is that irony makes the subject ultimately unlocatable within the text and yet, by that very indeterminacy, magnetically lures the reader into trying to locate the subject (as Furius and Aurelius have attempted).

I raise irony as an issue because I wish to suggest that the mechanics

45

of irony that obviate closure of either subject or text operate throughout the Catullan corpus, in single poems and in groups of poems, and in different registers, even in the absence of manuscript difficulties. The Catullan subject is less forged, than torn, between different signifying systems and their institutional loyalties. Turning now to c.2, I shall focus on sexuality and gender as institutional constructs supporting subjectivity, but in a decidedly shifty fashion—a shiftiness that affects the text itself.

We have already seen, in chapter 1, that the subject's accession to gender and sexuality means her accession to Law, insofar as gender and sexuality are institutionally determined and supported by the surrounding cultural order. Accordingly, the general problem of constructing the subject in the Catullan corpus, arising from a collection of data with no fixed bounds of "beginning" and "end," no automatic narrativization, infects the specific categories gender and sexuality.[21] C.2 is a salient example of this—and reciprocally, the gender/sexuality problems trouble the narrative and textual boundaries of the poem. C.2 has a long history of interpretation as sexual allegory,[22] combined with an equally vexed history of text-critical problems. I wish to show that the two problems are not unrelated but commonly rooted in the problematized subject.

C.2 assumes the form of a hymn, addressing the *passer*[23] as though it were a god.[24] The specific office Catullus desires from the *passer* is that he himself be able to play with the bird as his mistress does, and to relieve his sorrows. Yet the description of her "play" resonates in the sexual register because of its vocabulary.

Sexual allegorical interpretation of c.2 dates from the work of Politian[25] in the fifteenth century: interpretations differ in details, but they all hinge on the equation *passer* = "penis," so that what Catullus alludes to in cc.2 and 3 would be either a form of masturbation or (in the minority view) some specific manipulation of the penis he desires, obliquely, from Lesbia. The textual and contextual evidence for the equation is woefully slim, resting chiefly on the facts that:

1. Some of the words in the poem can function as sexual slang (but do not require such interpretation).
2. Contemporary Italian usage equates *passero* with penis (which does not tell us anything certain about Late Republican Latin usage).
3. Greek slang of the third century C.E. included a term for penis (*strutheus*) that appears to be based on the Greek word for *passer* (*struthos*) (but again, the gap in time and between languages argues against this as conclusive evidence).

Why, then, if the evidence is so exiguous, have intelligent commentators subscribed persistently to this tradition? I believe that although the sexual allegorists may not have accurately aligned all the elements, they are responding to a slipperiness in the text that cries out for explanation. "Puzzling" is the adjective most often used to describe this poem; and commentators most often finger as the puzzling part the strophe on Atalanta, in which Catullus compares some unspecified relief to Atalanta's sexual initiation.[26] What readers stumble over is Catullus' sexual masquerade.

The feminine masquerade, as discussed in chapter 1, rests upon constructing Woman's sexuality around a term that posits her solely as exclusion—the phallus Imaginarily seen as the male organ's Platonic Ideal. What the sexual allegorists point toward is not simply a penis but a phallus— both in the Freudian sense of the penis seen as detachable, therefore an object of exchange, and in the Lacanian sense of an empty set, a pure, arbitrary signifier—therefore a ruse. The poem views Lesbia's pet as an equally efficacious means to assuage erotically resonant *dolor, ardor,* and *curae*[27] for both a man (Catullus) and a woman (Lesbia). The *passer* anchors a system in which its very lack of specificity makes it *the* object of exchange, *the* sexual signifier—a fetishized object charged with Catullus' displaced desire for Lesbia.

Moreover, a simple equation with penis would leave oddly unexplained the *passer*'s metaphorical transformation into a little *girl* in c.3, the companion poem to 2 ("nam mellitus erat suamque norat / ipsam tam bene quam *puella* matrem"—"for it was her honey, and it knew its own mistress as well as a little girl knows her mother", 3.6–7). Yet if we regard the *passer* as the phallus, much becomes clear. C.3 mourns the death of the *passer*—a moment the sexual allegorists generally gloss as impotence— a suggestion that, if allowed to render *passer* strictly as "penis," makes of 3.6–7 a jarringly puerile joke. By retaining the concept of "loss" from impotence, while discarding literal detumescence, we can see the larger concept of "castration" adduced here—castration in the Lacanian sense, an irremediable lack in the subject. This lack permits the phallus' operation as that which underpins exchange and substitution, thereby allowing desire to glide through the signifying chain.

Even in Freud's more anatomically literal version of such substitutions, the penis, as the detachable phallus, is subject to metaphoric substitution and to circulation in exchange. Freud outlines a series of metaphorical transformations that lead to the equation "penis" = "baby";[28] Otto Fenichel zeroes in on the fantasmatic refusal of difference underpinning this whole metaphorical chain in order to narrow the equation down to a *girl* child.[29] Finally, Lacan incorporates Fenichel's insight into the slippery and insubstantial nature of the central gender token into his own work on feminine sexuality.[30] If the *passer* supports a sexual allegory, then its appearance in feminine garb marks it both as the phallus and as signifying the refusal of difference that grounds the Symbolic's construction of gender when anchored to the anatomical signifier of one sex. Weaving as it does between male and female positions, while unable to be pinned down to either, the *passer* both undermines the "naturalness" of these gender positions apparently marked by anatomical difference and mocks the empty majesty of the penis Imaginarily promoted to the status of the phallus. Catullus twits the central self-deception of patriarchy: that a miserable fleshly signifier could be assimilated to the pure signifier of desire.

But what else is this locus of transvestism doing here in cc.2 and 3— what is its relevance to two charmingly humorous poems? The answer lies in the concept "refusal of difference." The reader will recall chapter 1's discussion of gender relations, where I pointed out that Lacan formulates sexuality as a concerted attempt to deny the division *between* subjects as perfectly homologous to the Imaginary denial of the division *within* the subject. The denial of difference in both cases is an effect of the Unary Signifier—a denial equally operative in the humor of these two ironic poems and in the controls they erect around *dolor* (including poetry itself as control), the pain of (intra- and intersubjective) division. Joking, like sexuality, both denies and reinforces such division. C.2 explicitly links joking (*iocari*) to the pain peculiar to love (*dolor*):

> cui primum digitum dare appetenti
> et acris solet incitare morsus,
> cum desiderio meo nitenti
> carum nescio quid lubet *iocari*,
> ut solaciolum sui *doloris*
>
> (2.3–7)

to whom she is accustomed to give her little finger when he is in a pecking mood, and to incite him to sharp bites, when the shining object of my desire wants to play some dear little game, as a bit of solace to her pangs of love

Jesting, as an activity, suggests wit; the ability not to take one's own (or anyone else's) dignity too seriously; a delight in nugatory poetry, seen as playful and childlike. All of these find support as aesthetic values in Callimachus' remarks on his own poetry.[31] "Like a child," he says, "I roll

48

forth a short tale"[32]—and also like a child, he delights in upsetting decorum, however subtly.[33] Catullus accepted such a poetic precedent with relish and alacrity. Jokes enter the context of judging or writing poetry, not only in c.2 but throughout the Catullan corpus, featured as subtle *hommage* to the Callimachean aesthetic credo[34] but also as the controlled irruption of an entirely different order into the polite forms of social observance. Freud saw jests as a means of control over tendentious material—a control over *dolor*, material too painful to be allowed undisguised over the borderline separating Conscious from Unconscious.[35] Like clever smugglers, jokes dissimulate the division between two alien territories, as if the split in the subject necessitated by her submission to language and social norms promised to disappear when it revealed itself as bridgeable. But jokes cut both ways: while they are the salvos aimed at civilization from its discontents, their discreet disguises for painful material also capitulate to that social order, including its orchestration of sexuality. Its failures are bled off in the relatively innocuous form of jokes.

Dolor and *iocari* are two sides of the same coin—a signifying pair exactly analogous to *fort/da*, in that (like *fort/da*) they posit, and fracture, a fantasized original unity, prior to the subject's induction into the Symbolic. The whole *passer* joke (whether or not *passer* = penis) turns on the Unconscious mechanism of condensation, or metaphor. The mock hymn to the *passer* rests upon the equation *passer* = god in that each is posited as able to fulfill wishes (as the *passer* does for Lesbia, so Catullus hopes it will do for him). Condensation in joke-work imaginatively grants one's wish for a fantasized lost whole: *da* of the *fort/da* game, as presence and plenitude.

But just as *da* became visible only as lost in *fort/da*—so that unity only emerges as what is conceptually prior to disunity, the *dolor* of the divided subject relegated to the Unconscious—so *dolor* is inextricable from *iocari;* we can see this in c.50, to whose juxtaposition of the same elements c.2 ineluctably refers. *Dolor* names the sorrow of lovers: Lesbia seeks some control over desire and its inevitable, concomitant pain. So does Catullus— and the wish to control the experience of desire and loss, to replace passivity with mastery, is a motivating force in poetry for both author and reader. We metaphorize for the same reason Catullus does, according to his own portrayal of his authorship in c.50: to deny the experience of division, loss, substitution—in short, to palliate metonymy. Jesting exercises parallel control, fictively "healing" the split. In c.2, jesting (*iocari*) is functionally analogous to poetry insofar as it circumscribes pain for Lesbia.

The limits that I suggest operate in cc.2 and 50 exercise erotic "damage containment." The *passer* controls love's pain by offering an eye-catching, playful diversion from the divided, dolorous self—and as such the bird resembles a poem. Does either diversion, game or poetry, "work" in the sense of freeing the subject permanently from *dolor*? C.50, which arranges the same three elements (*iocari, dolor,* and poetry) in a slightly different configuration, suggests not. Therein lies a further resemblance of the *passer* (as well as poetry) to the phallus—it promises unity and fulfillment without supplying the substance.

Bons Mots

In c.50, joking qualifies the atmosphere in which poets *conceive* their poems. Catullus and his friend Licinius compose poetry "for a lark"— affecting *sprezzatura* such as we saw in c.1, a careless attitude toward creations executed in play.

> Hesterno, Licini, die otiosi
> multum lusimus in meis tabellis,
> ut convenerat esse delicatos:
> scribens versiculos uterque nostrum
> ludebat numero modo hoc modo illoc,
> reddens mutua per iocum atque vinum.
> atque illinc abii tuo lepore
> incensus, Licini, facetiisque,
> ut nec me miserum cibus iuvaret
> nec somnus[36] tegeret quiete ocellos,
> sed toto indomitus furore lecto
> versarer, cupiens videre lucem,
> ut tecum loquerer simulque ut essem.
> at defessa labore membra postquam
> semimortua lectulo iacebant,
> hoc, iucunde, tibi poema feci,
> ex quo perspiceres meum dolorem.
> nunc audax cave sis, precesque nostras,
> oramus, cave despuas, ocelle,
> ne poenas Nemesis reposcat a te.
> est vemens dea; laedere hanc caveto.

Yesterday, Licinius, being at leisure, we played around a lot with my writing tablets, as we had agreed to be poet(ry)-lovers:[37] each of us writing little verses, playing now in this meter, now in that, replying back and forth in our laughter and our cups. And I came away from it inflamed with your charm, Licinius, and with your witty ways, so that, wretched as I was, neither

50

could food please me, nor sleep quietly steal over my eyes, but I tossed all over the bed, unable to be quieted in my excitement, wanting to see the dawn, so that I could talk with you and be with you. But, afterward, worn out with my struggle, my half-dead limbs sprawled on the bed, I wrote this poem for you, charmer, from which you can clearly see my distress. Now, take care, I pray you, lest you be foolhardy and reject my prayers, my love; beware lest Nemesis demand proper requital from you. She's a savage goddess: watch out, don't annoy her.

C.50 reverses the cycle—or catches it at a different point in its revolution: game precedes pain, rather than the other way around, as in c.2. Note that Catullus and Licinius *agree in advance* upon the boundaries that will give shape to the disruptive force of pleasure (and pain). Like experienced poker players, they assume roles dictated by the rules of the game: "it had been *agreed* between us to be *delicati*"—so that their attitudes of indulgent *déshabillé* are as conventionalized as the most stringent Ciceronian interpretation of *Romanitas*.[38] Callimachus would have approved the subtle irony that keeps us, as readers, continually on our toes, unable to pin the image of poets-at-play securely to absolute frivolity, absolute seriousness, or anywhere in between. In the aftermath, Catullus produces c.50 because he too (like Lesbia) wants a *solaciolum sui doloris:* he wants to spend more time with Licinius as he spent the previous night. But *dolor* in c.50 (17) results *from* witty games, and *in* poetry (4–6—an amoebean exchange of verses?). *Dolor*'s erotic implications are reinforced by the use of amatory vocabulary—"incensus" (8); "miserum" (9); "furore" (11)—and amatory topoi—he cannot eat (9); he cannot sleep (10–12); he wants to see Licinius again (13).[39] Wit, as Licinius' squibs, so delights Catullus as to strike him with pain—the symptoms of love-sickness. He must in turn write c.50 in order to find some relief.[40]

The limits posited in c.2—pain contained by jesting, whether pure game or an allusion to Callimachean poetry—rupture as we probe a little deeper into the relationship between pain, wit, and love in c.50. Wit promises to contain *erōs* (c.2)—but wit, paradoxically, inflames it (c.50). Witty poetry fed the flame, and yet Catullus resorts to more of the same to relieve his pain. We are endlessly caught on the horns of a dilemma: every attempt at containment itself undermines that containment; every attempt at constructing a healing narrative, with a safe terminus, fails. These failures reveal, in different registers, the internal contradictions and partial truths of the Symbolic about gender, desire, decorum, and language—ultimately, about Law, which founds all. The promise of any one

51

of these to make us "whole," in a smooth alignment of our being, our desires, and our knowledge, always turns out to be empty.

Jouissance and *Otium*

Cc.2 and 50 align along the conceptual boundary line splitting the subject: between the fantasized original whole and the present divided and lacking self. Insofar as jokes, poetry, and amorous pains depend for their function upon the positing of unity—through, respectively, condensation, metaphor, and the mirage of amorous unity with the Other—they are functionally linked as effects of the Unary Signifier. They celebrate its partial failure and its partial success.

The concept of *jouissance* fastens upon these failures, as a "beyond" to the Symbolic, insofar as the concepts of limit and restraint ground the latter. To get to *jouissance*, I must detour through the term that supports the possibility of imagining this beyond—*otium* ("leisure"). Jokes, *dolor*, and writing poetry are all underpinned by *otium*, a concept prominent in c.50 and crucial to the corpus as a whole. Charles Segal has argued for the poetic and erotic significance of *otiosi* in 50.1, basing his argument, in part, on the intricate interweaving of erotic and literary terminology throughout the poem.[41] Part of his argument depends upon the double valuation of key terms in the poem, which signify both within a literary and an erotic context. The recurrent verb *ludere* can mean "to write poetry" (as at 50.2 and 50.5) or can refer to sexual play.[42] *Lepos* (50.7) applies both to people who are erotically attractive[43] and to pleasing poetry;[44] *delicatus* (50.3) alludes to *deliciae*,[45] sexual and intellectual pleasures—and in Catullus' case, to poetic pleasures as well.[46]

The logic behind this double valence of *otium* rests on its status as the unencumbered time necessary both to creativity and to love. Play evolves from *otium*—whether erotic play or Licinius' and Catullus' creative play exploring the possibilities of different meters.[47] Juxtaposing c.3 (c.2's companion) with c.50 shows that the line between play and poetry grows very unclear at times. Similar phrases—at 3.9 and 50.5—describe the poets' switching between different meters as a form of amusement and the *passer*'s movement in Lesbia's own game with her bird in c.3.

nec sese a gremio illius movebat,
sed circumsiliens *modo huc modo illuc*
ad solam dominam usque pipiabat

(3.8–10)

nor would he move himself from her lap, but hopping around now to this side, now to that side, he used to chirp constantly to his mistress alone.

> scribens versiculos uterque nostrum
> ludebat numero *modo hoc modo illoc,*
> reddens mutua per iocum atque vinum.
>
> (50.4–6)

each of us writing little verses, playing now in this meter, now in that, replying back and forth in our laughter and our cups.

This pendulum swing—"now to this side, now to that side"; "now in this meter, now in that meter"—captures the circularity of desire's movement between the poles of binary opposition—*fort/da;* I/you; *iocari/dolor;* and so on. It is the curvilinear path described by desire, which always "comes back to the same place" as a function of the Real, the impossibility of its own fulfillment. But how sedate it is! The predictable regularity of the rhythms controlling Lesbia and Catullus' play suggests a curious positioning of their activities on the borderline between Law and outside-the-Law. Segal, in teasing apart the multiple connotations of *otium,* notes that it slides between a scurrilous association with idleness and mischief, especially erotic mischief (its regular connotation in Roman comedy) and a decorous companionship with peace and civic harmony (Cicero's *cum dignitate otium*). It is a term always reformable, never quite reformed—and in its double valence, it defines the borderline between two economies of desire. One is well confined within the limits of the Law that would restrain desire by channeling sex into marriage and procreation and harnessing creative energies to the demands of the *res publica;*[48] one looks beyond these limits. Where would we situate Catullus' *otium* on this continuum? Certainly not on the end occupied by Cicero:[49] Catullus stands at the edge of what is legible as *dulce et decorum* to the conventional Roman order. His poetry regularly favors the staging of a private moment over the public arena (Segal shrewdly notes that in c.10, Catullus *otiosus* is led "e foro" [10.2], away from Rome's civic center of gravity); he celebrates the pleasures of love over the rewards of *negotium,* "business"; his aesthetic allegiances are predominantly Hellenic and Hellenistic, rather than Roman. This provocatively unconventional *otium* sets the stage for an irruption of another order—like that of jokes—into the Ciceronian order.

But like the jokes and poetry it accommodates, this is a *controlled* irruption, as c.50's momentary concentration on the protocol of naughtiness reminds us ("ut convenerat esse delicatos," 50.3)—Catullus' *otium* and its consequences are not entirely exempt from the constraints of Law (indeed, as we saw in the last chapter, a shared guardrail is precisely what announces the functional kinship between jokes and poetry). *Otium* plays with the idea of a bath in bliss but carefully hugs the shoreline nonetheless.

What is the advantage of invoking a term so determinedly ambiguous—has Catullus no more vivid colors to run up the mast? Certainly, but it would hardly be in his interest to do so. Since the creation of poetry depends on desire—on describing its flight out into the glittering possibility of fulfillment and the inevitable fall back into want—the satisfaction of desire would mean the end of Catullus as a poet. No one writes poetry at the top of Diotima's ladder: they sit and stare at the Beautiful and bring forth "virtue" (*aretē*), not poems.

What I wish to probe here are the first timorous glimpses of a "beyond" to the Symbolic—the system that installs and maintains the guardrails— and a gradually deepening terror of exactly what that "beyond" represents. *Jouissance* is the beyond without limit, whose necessary (but not entirely sufficient) condition within these poems is *otium*. Being without limit, *jouissance* dissolves every familiar landmark of the Symbolic—gender, sexuality, desire, subjectivity, signification, Law, pleasure (the pale, groomed, and restrained version of *jouissance*). Though lightly invoked, *jouissance* shimmers on the horizon of c.50 as the wasteland of bliss.

In c.51, the other prominent locus of *otium* in the Catullan corpus, Catullus stares straight at the wasteland by acknowledging *otium*'s double-edged quality: "*otium* is harmful to you Catullus—but you revel in it."

> otium, Catulle, tibi molestum est;
> otio exsultas nimiumque gestis;
> otium et reges prius et beatas
> perdidit urbes.
>
> (51.13–16)

leisure, Catullus, is troublesome to you; in leisure you rejoice and you desire it excessively; leisure has before destroyed both kings and blessed cities.

The appropriate gloss on these lines is 68.103–4, which describes the Trojan War as a movement ranged against Paris' erotic enjoyment of *otium* with his stolen beloved:

> ad quam tum properans fertur <lecta> undique pubes
> Graeca penetralis deseruisse focos,
> ne Paris abducta gavisus libera moecha
> *otia* pacato degeret in thalamo.
>
> (68.101–4)

[Troy] the city for which at that time Greek youths are said to have deserted their hearth fires, hurrying from everywhere lest Paris, rejoicing in his stolen adultress, should spend his unencumbered leisure in a peaceful marriage chamber.

In mythology, that is *indeed* a case in which *otium* "destroyed kings and happy cities"—destroyed the very institutions set in place and supported by the Symbolic and Law. Hence, the need for the guardrail: pleasure uncontained can easily tip over into its opposite. The Trojan War is recuperable only by being fed back into the restraining signifying chain that supports both the Symbolic and Law; Troy is an erotic debacle, motivated by the same kind of "stolen" union[50] Catullus himself enjoys with Lesbia and yet redeemed (like the affair with Lesbia) by its poetic heritage.

Cross-Dress

Our leisurely divagation through gender, jokes, poetry writing, the pain and gamesmanship of love, and *otium* has followed an ideational chain of association in which each link represents a different stratagem for coming to grips with the subject's division imposed by the Symbolic. We have looked at accommodations that are more and less graceful, more and less candid about their own conditions of restraint. Finally, with our last term *otium,* and its connection to *jouissance,* we have pressed up to the very edge of the Symbolic's careful ordering of human experience and seen something that looks as much like terror as freedom. Armed with this referential frame, we can now return to c.2, to its final strophe,[51] and render intelligible its puzzling mobility of gender categories.

> tam gratum est mihi quam ferunt puellae
> pernici aureolum fuisse malum,
> quod zonam solvit diu ligatam.
>
> (2.11–13)

this is as grateful to me as they say the lovely golden apple was to the swift maiden, which loosened her sash, long tied.

I have earlier argued the case for the *passer* to be seen as the phallus, i.e., a detachable signifier that in its mobility subverts gender categories. The glimpse thus afforded of the provisional and fragile nature of gender construction causes to emerge, on the imaginative horizon, the beyond-gender that is *jouissance.* But is *that* the moment crystallized in 2.11–13? No, it is not: rather, like our familiar paradigms of jokes and poetry, 2.11–

13 is that moment partially resubmitted to the constraints of the Symbolic as it erects and enforces gender. True enough that Catullus blurs sexual boundaries here. But he ends by assigning this image of sexual consummation to an invisible, masculine third term. The apple is "grateful" because it recuperates Atalanta for a heterosexual economy firmly anchored in gender fictions: behind the apple stands Hippomenes. Catullus simultaneously points to *jouissance féminine* as a site for interrogating gender, and falls back from it, erecting the more limited concept of *jouissance phallique*— with its suspicion of feminine sexuality unreferenced to Man—against that measureless unknown.

I do not argue, therefore, that Catullus creates here the, or even a, "feminine" experience. Rather, I point to a species of male ventriloquism[52]—or better, male transvestism, putting on and taking off the penis-as-phallus like a costume. Catullus posits that which exceeds the Symbolic, but ultimately retreats into terms weighed down by that system. I shall, however, make the more modest claim that this poem is an interrogative lever: simply by producing a moment, however brief, in which the Symbolic's apparently firm conceptual props slide and sway dizzyingly casts doubt on how legitimate that order is—even if this poem does not fully press the issue yet.

Within the whole Atalanta simile expressed in 2.11–13, Catullus himself figuratively crosses the boundary separating male from female sexuality, and in doing so, acquires a semblance of sexual and creative autonomy by mimicking both sexes in one body. On the one hand, he expresses masculine desire for Lesbia ("cum *desiderio meo* nitenti / carum nescio quid lubet iocari"—2.5–6). He covets the *passer*'s ability to relieve Lesbia's *feminine* desire (2.8). But at the moment of experiencing his desire's fulfillment, he himself assumes the feminine role of Atalanta. The sexual consummation depicted in 2.11–13[53] finds Catullus temporizing the apparent limitations imposed by anatomy on gender. In so doing, the poem points toward a model of creative autonomy: Catullus-as-figurative-hermaphrodite. The image arises from metonymic substitution—*passer* for Lesbia, as object of desire—and moves, very tentatively, toward reducing Lesbia's importance as the other half of the creative equation. In c.2, Catullus stages, not *jouissance*, so much as a dream of autonomous male reproduction—here channeled into a model for autonomously produced (love) poetry. We will see this movement explored more fully in the *carmina maiora* and some of the elegiac poems that follow them.

In c.3, the *passer*, facilitator of *erōs*, dies—yet the poetry generated

around its own erotic significance lives on. Its epithet becomes its epitaph—
it is "*passer,* my sweetheart's darling" in 3.4 as well as in 2.1:

> Lugete, o Veneres Cupidinesque
> et quantum est hominum venustiorum:
> passer mortuus est meae puellae
> *passer, deliciae meae puellae,*
> quem plus illa oculis suis amabat.
>
> (3.1–5)

Mourn, o Venuses and Cupids and however many there are of charming
men, Venus' own! The *passer* of my sweetheart has died, the *passer* who was
her darling, whom she loved more than her own eyes.

That poetry can cross over the borderline its cherished subject cannot
itself negotiate is one of the darkly humorous ironies derived from the
confrontation of the signifier with the body. The specific subjects upon
which poetry is based (like the *passer*) are finite in time and space. Poetry,
on the other hand, is potentially infinite (like the signifying chain), insofar
as it historically precedes and succeeds any speaking subject, and can express
fantasy—like acquiring another gender—unbounded by the confines of
reality.

Poetry, therefore, holds out the promise of immortality—but at what
cost? Death in small doses—as alienation, loss, absence. There is some
inkling of this in Diotima's *scala amoris,* predicated as it is not only on the
fear of mortality but also upon the cost of ever-increasing losses throughout
its progress. Beautiful bodies are discarded for a beautiful soul, one beauti-
ful soul for all beautiful souls, all beautiful souls for the beauty of Law
and institutions, and so on—a long list of bereavements tied in a chain of
metonymic substitution ending in the ultimate signifier, the Beautiful Itself.
Freud's conceptualization of desire's motor, the drive, as a signifier of the
lost object, further refines Diotima's relation between desire, the signifier,
and death: the always-already "lost" object is as good as dead to the
one who desires it. But when Lacan seizes upon Freud's model and its
indifference to the object's specificity, he reformulates desire as a unified
field, partitioned off into separate drives only as a matter of rhetorical
convenience. Insofar as all drives ultimately signify the irredeemable ab-
sence of the object—of that impossible object that would heal the split in
the subject conferred by the signifier—*all* drives are the death drive. Death

is therefore immanent in the signifying chain: any attempted escape in poetry carries its own contradiction with it.

Upon rereading, this makes the dead *passer*'s anticipation of the amoebean poetry exchange—"modo huc modo illuc" (3.9); "modo hoc modo illoc" (50.5)—a sinister foreclosure of any possible escape from mortality in the excesses of poetry. The *passer* is barely visible as a susurration of rhythm and movement before it is dead. The evening with Licinius is hardly less fragile, when Licinius' very facility with words and meter leaves Catullus "wretched" ("miserum," 50.9), afflicted with "half-dead limbs" ("membra . . . / . . . semimortua," 50.14–15) and "love pangs" ("dolorem," 50.17).

Granted, the issue is not broached with tragic gravity here—we are, after all, speaking about the death of a pet bird, and Catullus' description of his post-Licinius symptoms is decidedly hyperbolic. But the burden of such losses grows heavier in some of the *carmina maiora*. In c.65, for example, the price paid for unending subject matter is the death of Catullus' own brother ("semper maesta tua carmina morte canam," 65.12). Every expression of love (such as "passer deliciae meae puellae") inevitably becomes an epithet, a mourning for the loss of that love.

Perhaps the reason this formula is so lightly invoked in cc.2, 3 and 50 is that for Catullus qua poet, this is a fortunate fall: lack enables the continual renewal of the signifying chain in poetry, in a happily doomed attempt to overcome a poem's own conditions of possibility. Insofar as poetry hinges upon desire, and desire necessarily and logically implies lack, separation, and limit, Poverty is not only the mother of Eros (she who seduces Resource, in Diotima's mythic-allegorical account of Love's origin)[54] but grandmother to poetry. Lack is Catullus' ultimate Muse—if completely satisfied, it would not power the signifying chain of poetry; both Catullus, qua poet, and his art would cease to be. Lack makes things move; therefore, paradoxically, desire cannot be satisfied within the Catullan text, or the poetry itself would stop.

The Numbers Racket

The equal impossibility of death and (satisfied) desire—their shared "Realness," that inspires the poet's repeated attempts to capture them in signification—clarifies their juxtaposition in the next two Lesbia poems, cc.5 and 7. These two poems form a diptych that sketches a moment on the repetitive path of desire—an arc from the finite to the infinite and back again.[55] Death itself prompts Catullus' exuberant desire for Lesbia in c.5.

Poems One Through Eleven

Vivamus, mea Lesbia, atque amemus
rumoresque senum severiorum
omnes unius aestimemus assis!
soles occidere et redire possunt;
nobis, cum semel occidit brevis lux,
nox est perpetua una dormienda.

(5.1–6)

Let us live, my Lesbia, and let us love, and let us rate all the rumors of fuddy-duddy old men at the worth of a plugged nickel! Suns are able to set and to rise again: but for us, when once the brief light sets, we must sleep through one perpetual night.

Recognizing the boundary death sets on life and on desire inspires wild battology, with nearly the same phrases repeated again and again, to hedge about this unsignifiable with a huge number of kisses and a nearly equal number of requests for them:

da mi basia mille, deinde centum,
dein mille altera, dein secunda centum,
deinde usque altera mille, deinde centum

(5.7–9)

give me a thousand kisses, then a hundred, then another thousand, then a second hundred, then—keep going!—another thousand, then a hundred.

But even so, a huge number is still a number: once someone counts it up and confines it within the limits of a precise accounting and an exact figure, the edge becomes visible again—that unaccountable emptiness that yawns just after the last inventoried kiss. So in a last push to put off the final reckoning, Catullus urges himself and his lover to "confuse the lot!":

dein, cum milia multa fecerimus,
conturbabimus, illa ne sciamus,
aut ne quis malus invidere possit,
cum tantum sciat esse basiorum.

(5.10–13)

then, when we have made many thousands, we will mix them all up—lest we should know, or someone evil be able to begrudge, how many kisses there are.

C.5 aligns death with number as, paradoxically, the predicates *and* the enemies of Catullus' desire, bound together by the underlying concept of

59

"When the Lamp Is Shattered"

limit and lack. The prominence of one particular signifying chain—the numerical chain—speaks volumes in two poems so concentrated on the operation of desire and of its vehicle, the drive. Number nicely epitomizes the irretrievable division within the subject that is both the source of desire and, as the most complete loss the subject already knows, an earnest of death. C.5 stages the impossibility of *one,* scanning it as either an incalculable enormity, the imponderability of death (*"semel* occidit brevis lux"; "nox est perpetua *una* dormienda"), or an incalculable trivium, in a monetary unit so small its lone existence is but a conceptual placemarker, a synonym for *"no* value" (*"unius* . . . assis"). The subsequent burgeoning spiral of numbers simultaneously conceals and reveals the impossibility of the Unary Signifier. One—the number of the Absolute Subject—is impossible. Wherever we have fallen from, be it Aristophanes' undivided aboriginals, the *Phaedrus'* precarnate souls, or the putative union with the mother Freud assigns to infancy, we as postlapsarian subjects exist by reason of our relation to something else, something lost to us: the Forms, the Unconscious, the way we (think we) used to be. That impossibility transfers onto erotic relations, where we prevaricate its disruptions with the comforting fiction "we two are as one." But one is only possible with the cancellation of all desire—in death.

Accordingly, after the surface exuberance of c.5, c.7 elucidates the complexities of a desire whose roots sink deep into death and loss. Catullus recognizes, with just a touch of bitterness, the limitations necessarily imposed on all mortals—himself among them. As if she has gone over to the enemy camp—those grim ancients with the minds of bookkeepers—Lesbia herself wants him to submit a request for an *exact* number of kisses:[56]

Quaeris quot mihi basiationes
tuae, Lesbia, sint satis superque.
quam magnus numerus Libyssae harenae
lasarpiciferis iacet Cyrenis
oraclum Iovis inter aestuosi
et Batti veteris sacrum sepulcrum,
aut quam sidera multa, cum tacet nox,
furtivos hominum vident amores;
tam te basia multa basiare
vesano satis et super Catullo est,
quae nec pernumerare curiosi
possint nec mala fascinare lingua.

You ask me, Lesbia, how many kissifications of you would be enough and more than enough. As many as the huge number of the Libyan sands that

60

lie on asafetida-bearing Cyrene, between the oracle of hot and lusty Jove and the sacred tomb of old Battus; or as many as the stars, when the night is silent, that watch the stolen loves of mortals. To kiss you with so many kisses would be enough and more than enough for mad Catullus, kisses which the busybodies could neither fully reckon up, nor an evil tongue bewitch.

In answer, Catullus requests infinite kisses—only that will foil the *curiosi*, who would otherwise try to inventory rigorously (*"per*numerare") the total number of kisses. Yet similes that illustrate his answer consistently imply the chief bound on mortality (death) and the vast gap separating the human condition from infinite immortality. The Libyan sands lie between two poles, one mortal, one immortal. The monument to Jove, the divine king, contrasts sharply with that of the mortal king, Battus: Battus' tomb commemorates old age and death ("Batti *veteris* sacrum *sepulcrum*," 7.6), while Jove's temple is dedicated to an immortal uncircumscribed in his life or passion—he is, was, and always will be "hot and lusty Jove" ("Iovis ... aestuosi," 5).[57] So too, the stars whose number the kisses must equal look down from a realm of quiet, plenitude, and immortality on human beings, who must snatch moments of love like petty thieves ("aut quam sidera multa, cum tacet nox, / *furtivos* hominum vident *amores*," 7–8). The repetition of the key word *nox* from 5.6 reinforces the contrast:

> . . . cum tacet *nox*
>
> (7.7)

> . . . nobis, cum semel occidit brevis lux,
> *nox* est perpetua una dormienda.
>
> (5.5–6)

The stars of c.7 will continue their immortal nighttime voyeurism long after death's night has enfolded Catullus, Lesbia, and all the "stolen loves of humankind."[58]

The contrast drawn between the mortal and immortal poles of the Libyan desert in c.7 is also elaborated in terms of poetry and types of discourse. The reference to King Battus and to Cyrene brings to mind the most famous poet born in Cyrene, and said to claim descent from King Battus: Callimachus.[59] Callimachus evokes a standard of severely limited speech, a poetic discourse whose possibilities have been restricted by a poetics of rejection.

The *oraclum* ("oracle") defines the other pole of speech in this poem. There, the gods speak—a place where speech bridges the unbounded vision of the immortals and the comparatively narrow purview of mortals. Or rather, *would* bridge that gap, were oracles not such notorious riddlers. The gods belong to the Real: they define plenitude as an imaginative horizon to mortal existence (as Diotima notes, when she rebukes Socrates for thinking something so indigent as Eros could be a god).[60] The gods cannot, therefore, participate in the economy of lack imposed by the signifier—they are unsignifiable, and thus Real. The difficulty of rendering their will in words is therefore logically apt—as Diotima specifies, when she posits that mortal and immortal are absolutely incommensurable realms, such that only the mixed nature of the "spirits" (*daimones*) can carry messages back and forth.[61] The paradox that oracles embody enforces the contrast between mortal and immortal vision. The *oraclum*, as a juncture between these two realms articulated by speech that nonetheless manages to keep them disjunct, parallels cc.5 and 7 themselves. *Oraclum*—derived from *oro*, "to ask"—designates the place where mortals make requests or ask questions of the infinite realm. C.5 takes shape in recording Catullus' request of Lesbia for infinite kisses; c.7 stems from Lesbia's question that ineluctably pulls the request back from infinity by asking Catullus to number infinity—to pull what cannot be contained in the Symbolic (predicated as it is on limit) out of the Real and back into the Symbolic.

Renunciation

Cc.5 and 7 phrase the antinomies of *erōs* in terms of limit and limitlessness (whether with respect to number, to life, or to love). C.11[62] expands that interplay by bringing the aesthetics of limit into dialogue with the psychology of *erōs*.[63] In 11, the psychological and aesthetic limits interact synergistically: progressive circumscription of the desiring subject leads to greater refinement in the subject (*materia*) of the poem, and thus to aesthetically better poetry. As this movement stretches through several threads from the beginning to the end of the poem, we must have the whole poem before us in order to discuss its various patterns.

> Furi et Aureli, comites Catulli,
> sive in extremos penetrabit Indos,
> litus ut longe resonante Eoa
> tunditur unda,
>
> sive in Hyrcanos Arabasve molles,
> seu Sagas sagittiferosve Parthos,
> sive quae septemgeminus colorat
> aequora Nilus,

sive trans altas gradietur Alpes,
Caesaris visens monimenta magni,
Gallicum Rhenum horribile aequor ulti-
mosque Britannos,

omnia haec, quaecumque feret voluntas
caelitum, temptare simul parati,
pauca nuntiate meae puellae
non bona dicta.

cum suis vivat valeatque moechis,
quos simul complexa tenet trecentos,
nullum amans vere, sed identidem omnium
ilia rumpens;

nec meum respectet, ut ante, amorem,
qui illius culpa cecidit velut prati
ultimi flos, praetereunte postquam
tactus aratro est.

Furius and Aurelius, comrades of Catullus, whether he shall penetrate the
far-off inhabitants of India, where the shore is struck by the far-resounding
dawn-wave; or among the Hyrcani or the effeminate Arabs, or the Sagae, or
the arrow-bearing Parthians, or the seven-mouthed Nile that dyes the sea;
or if he shall cross the lofty Alps, gazing upon the monuments of great Caesar,
and the Gallic Rhine (troubled water!) and those who come last, the Britons;
since all these things, whatever the will of the heaven-dwellers shall bring,
you are prepared to attempt together: take a message to my love—a few brief
words, not very pretty. Tell her to live and prosper with her adulterers, whom
she embraces three hundred at once, loving none truly—but, over and over,
breaking their groins. Let her not look back, as before, for my love—which
her offense has cut down, just like a flower on the very edge of the field,
touched by the passing plow.

At first glance we can see that the poem moves from the vast to the
microscopic: starting from the edges of the known world, Catullus gradu-
ally pares down the vista.[64] Starting from the Far East ("the far-off inhabit-
ants of India," 2) we move to the Near East (land of the various tribes
catalogued in 5–8, and of the Nile). Along the path from East to West
we are traveling, we would next expect to pass on to Rome as a geographic
entity. Rome appears, at the very center of the geographic catalogue—
but not as a metropolis. Rather, the signs of her own citizens' egregious
accomplishments represent her, such as Julius Caesar's expansion of the
empire (9–12) and later, in 17–20, Lesbia's expansion of sexual possibilit-

ies, embracing three hundred lovers at once. Rome is a center both absent and present, suggested by her own transgression of natural geographic boundaries (the Alps), propelled by the desire for conquest; the poem represents the same desire in a Lesbia inhumanly greedy for indiscriminate sexual conquest.

Lines 1–12 catalogue, for the most part, horizontal geographical expanse. We track from Far East to Far West with but one ascent in the vertical direction—over the Alps ("sive trans *altas* gradietur Alpes," 9). In 13–14, the summary of expanse leaps vertically beyond the Alps into the sky, as Catullus summarizes the preceding meditation as a subset of the possibilities of what "those who dwell in the sky" (the gods) could will as part of his fate. Yet at the same time, expanding into another dimension is circumscribed by a movement, set in play in 13–16, to delimit the enormous horizons he has opened up. "You, Furius and Aurelius, are prepared to attempt *all these things* ("omnia haec," 13); but I only want you to say a *few* harsh words to my sweetheart" ("pauca . . . / non bona dicta," 15–16). The process of circumscription continues in the final similes (21–24), as we move from the overwhelming spectacle of Lesbia in Rome, clutching all her lovers at once, to a humble meadow. The meadow then recedes as the poem focuses on the *edge* of the meadow, whereon a tiny flower is further minimized by the passing plow. The subject matter of the poem is progressively delimited, in accordance with Callimachean aesthetics—yet the limits are simultaneously undercut and contravened.

As we might expect, desire shoots through this contradictory landscape, creating another axis of orientation besides that of space. Furius' and Aurelius' speculative hyperboles as to where they would go for Catullus' sake assume a sexual tone: they are willing to "penetrate" into the outermost peoples of India ("in extremos *penetrabit* Indos," 2). Their formidable "friendly" offer uncannily mirrors the voracious appetites behind Caesar's and Lesbia's conquests. Desire sorts out the nations according to secondary sexual stereotyping: the Arabs are "effeminate" ("Arabasve *molles*," 5). By contrast, the Parthians carry arrows ("*sagittiferos*ve Parthos," 6), whose phallic shape evokes masculine desire as well as military readiness. The axis of desire postulates sexual divisions and contrasts—and, again using sexually significant terms, undercuts the geographic basis for such distinctions (little good the Indians' distance will do them against Furius and Aurelius).

The final strophe of c. 11 not only upsets such an overrapid naturalization of gender fictions but ties it to other ideological failures. Catullus' love is itself confined and immobile as the Indians, a flower helpless before

Lesbia's "offense" as the indifferent blade of the plow. The simile figurally castrates him, by transferring the mobile symbol of masculinity to Lesbia,[65] while he himself assumes the equally traditional sign of feminine sexuality.[66] I understand "castration" here in its largest sense, as the lack in the subject that both erotic desire and ideological allegiance promise to heal, under the aegis of the Unary Signifier. Now the grand geographical catalogue that opens the poem, and gradually narrows until it strangles the speaker, begins to make sense: the single sentence of the poem organizes the failures of ideology exemplified by eviscerated *points de capiton*. *Romanitas* casts its shadow as rapacious imperialism ("Caesaris visens monimenta magni," 10) that has spread over the known world, and as equally rapacious sexual conquest and betrayal (Lesbia and her three hundred adulterous lovers, 17–20). Both private and political delusions are linked in one vast signifying chain, hinging on the illusion of the penis-as-phallus, as the guarantor of masculine identity and authority. C.11 looks back upon a culture unmasked by its own excesses: the least Roman of all her citizens are those whose *Romanitas* has made them barbarians.[67]

3

Poems Eleven and Fifty-one: Repetition and *Jouissance*

And like the wind on the high seas, veering,
the god strode, almost as to one dead,
and at once was distant from her husband,
to whom he tossed, implied in the gesture,
one hundred lives of earth.
He rushed, reeling toward the pair,
grasping for them as in dream. Already
they approached the entrance crowded
with red-eyed women. But once
more he saw the virgin's face, that turned
with a smile, bright as a hope,
almost a promise: to return grown,
from the deep death,
to him, the living one—

Then he flung
his hands before his face, just as he knelt there,
in order to see nothing more after that smile.
—Rilke[1]

St. Tiresias in Rome

IN CHAPTER 2, we examined the expansion of the conceptual pair boundary/transgression, initially founded in Callimachean aesthetics, out into the broadly interrelated realms of narrative, subjectivity, gender, and sexuality. In elucidating the ways in which all these hinged upon lack, difference, and desire—thus upon the founding concepts of the Symbolic—we also discovered the merest intimation of *jouissance*, which exceeds all such conceptual categories anchored in difference. But when we traced, in cc.2, 3, and 50, the repetitive, controlled rhythms of pleasure, we found *jouissance* ultimately excluded by a repetition infinitely repeatable because it carefully preserves the conceptual poles that anchor its circuit around difference (*fort/da;* I/you; pleasure/pain; and so on). In this chapter, by reading closely *another* version of repetition in cc.11 and 51, we will see how *jouissance* breaks against that sedate repetition, that pleasure without destruction, and that knowledge without risk.

Like the rhythms of the *fort/da* game, the observances of sexuality also oscillate repetitively to establish two conceptual poles: Man and Woman. As noted in chapter 1, Woman is fantasized as the complement to Man,[2] who will allow him to achieve the mythic wholeness promised by the Unary Signifier.[3] As such, she represents the fantasmatic hope that something could banish the very lack that inaugurates the subject, *and yet not destroy the subject*. The sexual relation's continual failure to achieve its mythic end in perfect unity and completion—in an unconditional "yes" from both sides, as if neither were fundamentally divided and haunted—fuels repeated disavowal of this failure and repeated assault on the utopian goal. If people continue to go to bed together, it is because they strive, vainly, to overcome a structural flaw in the sexual relation: the Unary Signifier rests on a lie.

And they continue, as well, as a defense against the imagined achievement of the goal—against *jouissance*, that terrifying, tantalizing possibility of self-annihilation in the Other. Like the predictable rhythms of the *fort/ da* game, conventionally constructed sexual relations strive to preserve difference as if it were identity—as if "Man" and "Woman," "I" and "thou," were terms founded not upon the signifier but upon the bedrock of pure Being.

Lacan thus views sexual relations much as does Aristophanes: a grudging *faute de mieux* that ironically saves its dupes from destruction. Aristophanes' dramatic anecdote of Hephaistos appearing to two lovers and offering to weld them together for eternity hints at this terror (*Symp.* 192d2–e9). Tellingly, the amorous pair are struck dumb when the god repeatedly asks them if they would like to be so fused: Aristophanes has to step in and answer for them, papering over their embarrassing reluctance to sacrifice their limited subjectivity in order to essay *jouissance*.

Repetition, in the dual service of disavowal and futile striving, also characterizes the "fortunate fall" of poetry I mentioned in chapter 2—with reason, in that both sexuality and poetry hinge on the relation of desire to the signifier. Insofar as poetry (like all signification) is forever inadequate to express (and thus cancel) the subject's desire, it is by the same token commissioned to renew itself in attempts to express that desire. The two repetitive circuits mutually entwine insofar as the difficulties of the sexual relation that ensure its repetition are difficulties founded upon signification—particularly upon the phallus as the Master Signifier of difference and desire, which nonetheless posits Woman *only* as exclusion. The phallus, though it is *the* signifier anchoring gender and sexuality, cannot signify Woman's desire and thus cannot signify her as subject. "*Was will das Weib?*" returns persistently to the account, as a symptom of its failures.

Freud's infamous question posed to Woman's desire opens the question of knowing gender onto the larger question of knowing per se. At the basis of Man's pretension to false unity and consistency in his identity is his knowledge that he is not a woman. And for him, that knowledge suffices, it is whole and complete: he rejoices in what Lacan calls the "*jouissance* of the idiot," playing upon Greek *idios*—"private, self-referential." Woman, by contrast, is a position of interrogation ranged outside and against certainty, as well as against its ideological cohorts, Law and limit. She inhabits a realm *hors-sens,* "outside-sense," where the usual manifestations of Law in language—grammatical rules, clearly denoted subjects and objects, smooth transitions along the signifying chain—give way to gaps and nonsequiturs, the "parapraxes" of language, that track *jouissance.* Here the position of Woman and the bliss of the text join hands to point to a knowledge and an enjoyment that is beyond the *logos.*

Lacan points to *hors-sens* as historically visible in mysticism, a discourse not entirely controlled by phallic rationality. The connection between *hors-sens* and Woman certainly fits the contours of ancient Graeco-Roman conceptualizations of prophecy, the direct connection with the divine. When Socrates prefaces his speech on erotic, philosophical *mania* with instances of divinely inspired *mania* (*Phaedrus* 244a8–b5), he lists women as its mystic religious channels: the Pythia, the priestesses at Dodona, and the Sibyl. Ruth Padel[4] and Giulia Sissa[5] have both laid out the close conceptual connections between the female body as hollow receptacle of the divine *pneuma* and prophetic possession in Greek thought. Sissa, in particular, illuminates Socrates' careful distinction of prophetesses from augurs by pointing out that the distinguishing feature of female mystics is to be inspired instruments for the divine voice, as opposed to augury's sober readers of divine signs.[6]

With some modification, Sissa's and Padel's findings can shed light on the admittedly more restricted loci of female prophecy in Roman culture. Though its sphere was greatly diminished in a landscape of divinatory functions controlled largely by men,[7] inspired female speech[8] was nonetheless reverently preserved in the Sibylline books, closely guarded by the *quindecemviri* and consulted on occasions august enough to require a motion of the Senate.[9] I argue that by the very fact of being anomalous[10] to a system of state-controlled male divinatory functions, the Sibylline texts stood out within the landscape of Roman religious functions, as a place where God spoke through Woman.

In Catullus' own corpus, Woman's alignment with mystic vision emerges forcefully in c.63: divine possession causes Attis to cancel his male gender and position himself as Woman, the *famula* of Cybele. For a poet so imbued in the Greek tradition, taking up the idea of Woman as divine instrument from Greek culture—an idea still visible, if circumscribed, in his contemporary cultural landscape—makes perfect sense. Perhaps more sense, in fact, for c.51, our particular interest in this chapter, than for c.63: c.51 directly translates a Greek poet.[11] Catullus uses Sappho's text as a Sibylline text, prophetic of the phenomenology of his love; he even fashions a name for his beloved that refers ineluctably to Sappho[12]—a poet Socrates himself names as an authority on love (*Phaedrus* 235c3) and whose phenomenology of love Socrates borrows in his description of the soul fretting and seething under the influence of divinely inspired passion (251a6–b1).[13]

With this as background, I return to Lacan's account of Woman, reading it against the ideational palimpsest of Graeco-Roman conceptualization of the feminine and mystic knowledge. Lacan's account will make clear the more delicate connections I wish to trace in c.51 among textual anacolutha, mystic vision, and the indictment of "reason." Lacan organized much of his twentieth seminar's (*Encore's*) discussion of *jouissance* around Bernini's statue of St. Teresa in Santa Maria della Vittoria. Bernini shows her in an ecstasy that points to the collapse of "rational" categories polarized in the Symbolic: soul and body; divine and human; intellection and sensuality; sex and worship—and thus captures the disturbing resistance to these categories that the bliss of Teresa's own text poses. Consider Jacqueline Rose's comment on the "bliss" that manifests itself in Teresa's sacred exegesis.

"When the Lamp Is Shattered"

If we cut across for a moment from Lacan's appeal to her image as executed by the man, to St. Theresa's own writings, to her commentary on "The Song of Songs," we find its sexuality in the form of a disturbance which, crucially, she locates not on the level of the sexual content of the song, but on the level of its enunciation, in the instability of its pronouns—a precariousness in language which reveals that neither the subject nor God can be placed ("speaking with one person, asking for peace from another, and then speaking to the person in whose presence she is") . . . (Commentary on the line from the "Song of Songs" [1:1]—"Let the Lord kiss me with the kiss of his mouth, for thy breasts are sweeter than wine.")[14]

The collapse of rational categories in the sacred text Teresa scrutinizes exceeds any accounting for the divine voice: "I don't understand why this is," Teresa continues as she reflects on the displacement of pronouns, "and that I don't understand gives me great delight. Indeed, daughters, the soul will not have to reflect upon the things it seems we can grasp with our lowly intellects here below as intensely as it will upon those that can in no way be understood; nor will the former make it respect God as much as do His mysteries."[15]

Plato is as interested in such moments *hors-sens* as Teresa. Though he cannot be said to embrace them wholeheartedly,[16] they offer the opportunity to question easy complacence with any position achieved in the dialogues. Consider (as Martha Nussbaum does, to brilliant effect)[17] the sacred illogic of Alcibiades' intervention in the *Symposium* (212d3–222d6). Crowned with the violets of Aphrodite and the ivy of Dionysus, Alcibiades bursts uninvited upon an abstemious group devoted to praising the god of Love. In drunken eloquence, he speaks seductively of his lover Socrates' address to his soul as snakebite (217e6–218a7) and divine madness (215e1–2, 218b3–4). Alcibiades' speech wanders incoherently, fails to follow the symposium's rule to praise Eros, praising Socrates instead—and disturbs the austere tranquillity of Diotima's philosophic summation of love, such that it no longer seems unimpeachable. A later Socrates also finds such irregularity instructive when, in the *Phaedrus,* he undertakes his palinode to rehabilitate erotic *mania*—*mania* of just such a type as Alcibiades describes, and Diotima scorns, in the *Symposium.*[18] Socrates quotes "bad" Homer, apocryphal, unmetrical lines, to support his *volte-face:*

τὸν δ᾽ ἤτοι θνητοὶ μὲν Ἔρωτα καλοῦσι ποτηνόν,
ἀθάνατοι δὲ Πτέρωτα, διὰ πτεροφύτορ᾽ ἀνάγκην.
(*Phaedrus* 252b7–8)

70

Now mortals call him winged Eros but immortals call him Pteros, because of the wing-growing necessity[19]

The unmetrical word—*pterōs*, punning on *pteron*, "wing"—points to sacred intervention in human art and language as a break in decorum.[20] The gods do not scruple at metrics where *jouissance* is in question.

Man does, however. Against the knowledge of this *jouissance*, which would radically disturb the certainty of his phallic "knowledge," Man erects a number of conjectures around Woman. One such guess is misogyny— resentment at the impossibility of the sexual relation relegated to Woman's side of the equation, as fantasized whore, castrating bitch, and the like. Another is courtly love—the rendering of the impossibility as Woman's inaccessibility, her elevation into the position of distant, goddesslike being.[21] And one can see the outlines of both cc.11 and 51 emerge as an oscillation between these two available positions—misogyny and courtly love—each disavowing the impossibility of Woman, i.e., denying that she exists solely as a fantasy guaranteeing the identity of Man. Let us, then, address ourselves to the issues of repetition, knowledge, and *jouissance* in cc.11 and 51 and see what they have to say to us.

Eyeless in Gaza

Catullus sets up the problem of repetitive oscillation between two poles in the penultimate strophe of c.11. There he uses the word quintessentially representative of repetition—"identidem," "over and over." Yet this word occurs only twice in his whole corpus, and calls attention to itself in each occurrence.[22] The poems in which it appears are metrically paired; only 11 and 51 are written in Sapphics. "Identidem" propels us out of the narrow confines and nihilistic disillusionment of c.11's end to the intoxication of c.51, where the word recurs. "Over and over," says Catullus, someone listens to Lesbia "sweetly laughing"—a Lesbia now as fascinating, idealized, and inspirational as the adulteress of c.11 is repellent and destructive. But no narrative sequence connects 11 and 51, to tell us which state of mind came first and which later, which is true and which false—as indeed it cannot and still truly reflect the operation of desire implicit in the word "identidem." Over and over, Lesbia is lovely, Lesbia is disgusting, depending on just what position in desire one settles on.

It is no accident that Catullus chooses to articulate his fascination in a translation; in doing so, he sets his love against a poetic paradigm of desire established nearly six hundred years before he was born. The translation implies that desire (like some transhistorical *fort/da* game) repeats

71

itself throughout not only individual but collective history—but with a difference.[23] Nothing in Sappho's poem, as we have it, corresponds to the fourth strophe of c.51 and its chill revulsion against erotic takeover (even taking into account the subtle self-arrest of the last halfline, "alla pan tolmaton epei"—"but all must be endured, since . . ."). The magisterial remonstrance voiced in that strophe can be tied, I think, to terror of an even more wrenching experience of *jouissance* than Sappho experiences, and over which, momentarily, the smooth repetition falters.

Let us compare these poems,[24] especially the strophes of each that outline the physical symptoms of what "Longinus" calls "love-madness."[25]

φαίνεταί μοι κῆνος ἴcoc θέοιcιν
ἔμμεν' ὤνηρ, ὄττιc ἐνάντιόc τοι
ἰcδάνει καὶ πλάcιον ἆδυ φωνεί-
cαc ὑπακούει

καὶ γελαίcαc ἰμέροεν, τό μ' ἦ μὰν
καρδίαν ἐν cτήθεcιν ἐπτόαιcεν·
ὡc γὰρ ἔc c' ἴδω βρόχε', ὥc με φώναι-
c' οὐδ' ἒν ἔτ' εἴκει,

ἀλλ' ἄκαν μὲν γλῶccα †ἔαγε†, λέπτον
δ' αὔτικα χρῶι πῦρ ὑπαδεδρόμηκεν,
ὀππάτεccι δ' οὐδ' ἒν ὄρημμ', ἐπιρρόμ-
βειcι δ' ἄκουαι,

†έκαδε μ' ἴδρωc ψῦχροc κακχέεται†, τρόμοc δὲ
παῖcαν ἄγρει, χλωροτέρα δὲ ποίαc
ἔμμι, τεθνάκην δ' ὀλίγω 'πιδεύηc
φαίνομ' ἔμ' αὔται·

ἀλλὰ πὰν τόλματον ἐπεὶ † καὶ πένητα†

(Sappho)[26]

He seems to me equal to gods that man
who opposite you
sits and listens closely
to your sweet speaking

and lovely laughter—oh it
makes my own heart beat fast,
for when I look at you a moment, then no speaking is left in
me

but the tongue breaks, and a thin fire is racing under the
skin I cannot see with my eyes, the ears ring

and a cold sweat holds me and shaking grips all of me, paler
than grass I am, and I seem to myself almost to die

But all must be endured, since . . .

Ille mi par esse deo videtur,
ille, si fas est, superare divos,
qui sedens adversus identidem te
    spectat et audit

dulce ridentem, misero quod omnis
eripit sensus mihi: nam simul te,
Lesbia, aspexi, nihil est super mi
. . . .

lingua sed torpet, tenuis sub artus
flamma demanat, sonitu suopte
tintinant aures, gemina teguntur
    lumina nocte.

otium, Catulle, tibi molestum est;
otio exsultas nimiumque gestis;
otium et reges prius et beatas
    perdidit urbes.

(51)

That man seems to me equal to a god,
that man—if it be right to say it—seems to surpass the
gods,
he who sits facing you, and over and over gazes upon you
        and
hears you

sweetly laughing—that which snatches away all my senses
from me: for the minute I have looked upon you, Lesbia,
nothing is left to me . . .

but the tongue is thick, a thin flame drips down the limbs,
ears ring with their own sound, eyes are covered with double
night

leisure, Catullus, is troublesome to you;
in leisure you rejoice and you desire it excessively;
leisure has before destroyed both kings and blessed cities.

The first image of either poem is the cool self-possession of the beloved's
auditor. He is "like a god" to Sappho but in addition, "surpasses the gods"

73

in Catullus' eyes. The auditor is not robbed of any of his faculties, like the lover. He "listens" to the beloved in Sappho's poem—but 51.4 adds that he also "gazes upon" the beloved, exposing *two* of his senses to the assault of desire. What happens when Catullus merely looks upon Lesbia? He is deafened, blinded, made dumb, in an erotic takeover that puts his subjectivity at issue—and yet, at the same time, makes the distinction between subject and Other all the more acute.

The similarities and the differences between these two moments must be carefully mapped. The triangulation between lover, Woman, and the divine speaks to mystification as defining the borders of the Symbolic: Woman and god are both boundary markers for Man's identity. Yet insofar as both continually exceed the conceptual categories established within signification, they menace the entire Symbolic order in its dependence on limitation and Law and in its support of the subject. Catullus is far more concerned with this menace than Sappho: Catullus hesitates where Sappho presses forward from her equation of auditor and god. He lingers over the formula he inherits from her, pauses and expands equation into a surprisingly reversed hierarchy—"he . . . surpasses the gods." But paradoxically he checks this hyperbole with a formula that makes Law visible as equally support of language and enforced by language: "si fas est"—"if it is lawful to say it, if it can be said." Whatever menace there may be in envisioning the auditor's excess, and thus invoking an order that surpasses everything human, for Catullus it will reveal itself in a resistance to the human order of symbolization. We should not be surprised, then, that when Catullus assumes the position of the auditor and tries to articulate his own experience, the support the Symbolic order affords the subject evaporates, and we are left with chaos.

Sappho finds the conceptual dividing line between human and divine less interesting and, accordingly, stages it as less menacing to her subjectivity. While inventorying the breakdown of her separate body parts, Sappho nonetheless asserts the persistence of an integral ego by using first-person verbs ("orēmmi," "emmi," "phainom'," etc.), first person pronouns ("*m*'idrōs psuchros kakcheetai," "*em*' autai") and substantives ("tromos de *paisan* agrei") representing Sappho. Catullus, on the other hand, catalogues his own dissolution into malfunctioning body parts using only third-person verbs. He disintegrates completely: no "I" remains within the words of the strophe. Out of this dissolution comes an alienated voice, some split-off piece of Catullus himself, that surveys the wreckage and bitterly admonishes the poet that "otium"—the unencumbered time necessary to desire and its recollection in poetry[27]—is his undoing.

On the other hand, desire, in robbing Catullus of his senses in 51.9–12, emphasizes the persistence of a boundary outside the self—that between Catullus and Lesbia. Sappho says "my ears ring"; Catullus says "my ears ring *with their own sound*"—the aural barrier is self-generated, absolutely specified as not originating externally, cutting him off from the outside world. Sappho says "I cannot see with my eyes," a failure of the senses. Catullus says "eyes are *covered* with double night": a distinct barrier to sight has closed over him. The focus of the poem shifts back and forth between establishing the boundary between observant lover and observed beloved, and dissolving the bounds that define the locus of desire, the lover himself.

What is happening here? A veil is being drawn over the site where Woman and the divine commune in their shared excess. Bernini's statue of St. Teresa, and Lacan's analysis of it, are illuminating here. Lacan construed the relationship among Man, Woman, and God as a triangle, a "ménage à trois." God is the "other man" who comes between Man and Woman, to the degree that Woman is made God's support as the lesser and the greater object of nonknowledge, respectively. They are thus both the excluded supports of Man's phallic knowledge, his stupid certainty. The more Woman is mystified, the further she is pushed toward the position of complete ineffability and inscrutability ascribed to God, the more impossible does her position become and the less legible to its supposed beneficiary, Man. Accordingly, in Santa Maria della Vittoria, Bernini filled the gallery surrounding his statue of St. Teresa with images of cardinals and doges, who are (in Jacqueline Rose's words) "*witnesses* to the staging of an act which, because of the perspective lines, they cannot actually *see*."[28] Similarly, Catullus is transformed, between the two moments crystallized in 51.1–4 and 51.5–12, from a witness who can see to one who cannot. He can see the auditor listening to Lesbia; but once his attention focuses on Lesbia alone and she alone assumes the position of mystified Other (the auditor having vanished from the poem), Catullus is deafened and blinded. He is a witness to the degree that he attests his own inability to read the moment he is recording.

But we must note a crucial difference between the triangle of Santa Maria della Vittoria and that of c.51: Catullus occupies *two* apexes of the triangle, as both the one mystically transported and the one blindly witnessing the transport. This poem pulls vertiginously in two directions: between the experience of *jouissance* (an understanding without an account) and the record of it (an account without understanding). What Catullus is staging, and Bernini is not, is immense pressure applied to the conceptual limits the Symbolic places on "knowing," and to the way in which these limits are made to support masculine subjectivity in patriarchy. We will see the pressure return, and grow much greater, in the *carmina maiora*— but for the moment, the fourth strophe pulls us back to cool survey, warning, and dismissal.

And here arises the question of the fourth strophe's pertinence: does it belong here, or is it the detached fragment of another poem? Arguments have raged back and forth on the grounds of perceived structural and thematic similarities or dissimilarities to the rest of the poem[29]—all of which proceed precisely from a point of view the poem is staging and then radically undermining. The poem poses for us a choice between *des jouissances:* between the certainty of the idiot's *jouissance,* that refuses doubt; and the persistent skepticism of *jouissance féminine.* We were warned, in Catullus' delicate hesitation over framing his hyperbole in language (50.2), of a resistance to signification in the auditor's excess. Now Catullus has momentarily taken the auditor's place—and what the poet experienced there continues to resist signification, refuses to be gathered back into rhetorical rules of pertinence or logical progression, opening up a gap in the text. The moment staged in strophe three and that staged in strophe four are incommensurable, as divine and human are incommensurable— and the jarring break in tone and shift in perspective, by refusing to cover over these moments' inconcinnity, dramatize a *jouissance* effect.

Having seen in this chapter how Catullus rethinks another poet's crystallization of a moment, in the next we shall look at Catullus rethinking his *own* poetic statements, as he works and reworks themes in the epigrams. The theme of repetition will be our entry into that set of poems.

4

The Epigrams: "I Am Lying"

A. borrowed a copper kettle from B. and after he had returned it was sued
by B. because the kettle now had a big hole in it that made it unusable. His
defence was: "First, I never borrowed a kettle from B. at all; secondly, the
kettle had a hole in it already when I got it from him; and thirdly, I gave
him back the kettle undamaged."

—Freud[1]

I loved her; I was sorry not to have had the time and the inspiration to insult
her, to do her some injury, to force her to keep some memory of me. I knew
her to be so beautiful that I should have liked to be able to retrace my steps
so as to shake my fist at her and shout, "I think you are hideous, grotesque;
you are utterly disgusting!"

—Proust[2]

Reading the Other

IN CHAPTER 3, we saw how the question of gender positioning opened
up into questions of epistemology and representation, with Woman posited
as partially escaping signification and therefore exceeding phallic knowl-
edge of her. To the impassable divide between Man and Woman, such as
we saw open up in c.51, Lacan attributes the difficulties of the sexual
relation[3] and the repeated futile attempts to bridge this divide. In this
chapter, we will expand our investigation of Catullus' repeated attempts
to know Lesbia, as a specific example of attempting to expand phallic
knowledge to encompass Woman. Moreover, we will see that, in the
epigrams, the problems of knowing gender as the foundation for knowing

77

expand outward to encompass some of the thematic difficulties we have traced in earlier chapters:

1. The divided subject as agent, and object, of knowledge
2. The difficulty of narrativizing the Catullan corpus, so as to yield knowledge
3. Repetition as a function of that which escapes signification and thus escapes phallic knowledge: the Real

Cc.2–11 and 11 plus 51 present different models for reading the history of the affair, thus different modes of coming-to-know that impose their own peculiar restraints upon conceptualizing the objects of knowledge. In poems 2 through 11, we saw a narrative laid out as a linear progression through stages of desire, from the first glimmers of interest through disappointment to disgust. C.11 caps that sequence—and yet its metrical symmetry and verbal repetition tie it to c.51 as well. Construing 11 in relation to 51 sends the reader in circular repetition between putative beginning[4] and end of the affair, without any sequence of causality or progression to bridge the gap.

Cc.2–11 thus offer containment, order, logical progression from love to hate—but end with 11. C.11, in its reference to 51, refuses to sustain that order's closure. Cc.11 and 51 are suspended moments in time; reading them together links love to hate, but without an end. The metrical and verbal symmetries between the poems send the reader back and forth between the two poles without any unambiguous signal to stop. The key word in each poem presents them as scenes of repetition: "identidem."

The epigrams pose yet another model of reading, thus of knowing— but not *just* another model. Rather, the epigrams pose, more starkly than any other group of poems in the corpus, the question of what can be known by the subject-in-language. In these poems, epistemological certainty fractures, not primarily upon what is missing from the text nor from our information about its historical context but upon what is "missing" from the subject: the lack, or division, that proceeds from being subject to the signifier (being an "I" only insofar as one can represent oneself as "I" in language), and that founds desire. This division radically problematizes the reader as agent-of-knowing, and the text as object-to-be-known— a relationship Catullus explicitly stages in the epigrams. Catullus sets himself up as "reader" of Lesbia-as-text, in his obsessive attention (peculiar to the epigrams) to decoding her speech: he obsessively investigates her "true" meaning and her true desire. He also dramatizes his repeated failure in his quest, balked by the nature of language and his own desire. Language ensures that the subject of the speech will never be the same as the speaking subject; Catullus' own desire works assiduously to deny this. The epigrams thus hew to a Lacanian model of reading as a transaction between an irremediably flawed subject and an equally flawed object; they destroy the classic paradigm of reader as a transparent, focusable lens and text as a difficult, ambiguous, but ultimately knowable object. Both falter upon the failures and the shortcomings of signification.

These failures hinge upon the division of the speaking subject, as evidenced in the paradox of "I am lying"—but so does the intrigue of attempts to overcome this structural impediment to communication. This announced dissimulation effectively encapsulates the problems of ad-dressee/speaker, reader/text, and subject/object as positions in interpreta-tion and in the quest for knowledge—pursuits ultimately pinned to the positions of two desiring (and correspondingly mysterious) subjects. The speaking subject's mythical[5] intention is not manifest in her statement but *ipso facto* poses an intriguing riddle that seduces the listener to "solve" it. The listener is solicited to interrogate the desire of the subject as hinted, but never revealed, in her speech. The listener's question is (as Lacan puts it), *"Che vuoi?"*—"you are telling me this, but what do you *really* want?" *Che vuoi?* ultimately translates into our familiar Hegelian terms, as posing to the Other the question of the subject's desire to be the pure desire of the Other—the impossible desire that would render the subject as Absolute Subject. Thus, *che vuoi?* ultimately translates "what do you want?" into "what am I for you? who am I in your eyes?"

The impossible enigma at which *che vuoi?* is directed surfaces in the epigrams as lies, elegant variations on "I am lying." Catullus organizes the epigrams as his repetitive interrogations of "lies" told by Lesbia, i.e., interrogations of the subject's desire occluded by her statement. Catullus addresses a *"che vuoi?"* to Lesbia's statements and comes up with a plethora of mutually incompatible, and therefore competing, answers. The principle of noncontradiction that governs phallic knowledge, based as it is on the principle of difference the phallus signifies, simply will not accommodate all of them.

All of this is suspiciously familiar: Catullus again faces a desire that (as we saw in chapter 3) exceeds signification in the Symbolic—the enigma of Woman's desire, which lacks a signifier beyond the phallus, again mapped onto Lesbia. Faced with this irremediable lack in the Symbolic—the "hole in the Other"—Catullus papers it over with wildly multiple conjectures as to what Lesbia might want, and what might account for the "failure" of her desire for him. When his conjectures fall short of accounting for the phenomena, he ascribes the blame to her: "she lied, she is a whore, she is faithless." These are the failures of the sexual relation, as rehearsed in chapter 3, transposed into the register of reading and interpreting the Other's message. What cannot be known about Lesbia as Woman returns to Catullus as a cluster of persecuting "messages" read in the actions of his beloved: she becomes his symptom.

Similarly, in the act of reading and interpreting any text, the imagined—and ardently desired—horizon is a significant, legible whole, bounded and complete, that would make even the gaps and omissions in the text signify and thus render up knowledge. We approach the sentence (poem, lyric collection) with the *point de capiton* in mind that allows us to supply closure and thus meaning to any discourse, at least in the form of provisional punctuation. However, something must always escape the quilting (*capitonnage*): the Real. Thus the desire to know Lesbia is mapped onto the desire to know Woman, fix her essence, symbolize her desire (*"Das Weib will . . . ; Das Weib ist . . ."*)—and onto the repeated frustration of that desire.

In the epigrams, in response to this frustrating repetition, Catullus reaches for *points de capiton* in a vocabulary that offers (illusory and ironic) escape from these repeated defeats because its own myth about itself promises secure anchorage by the chief ideologemes of *Romanitas: fides, veritas, pietas,*[6] and the like. I speak of the language of politics, treated as a set of signifiers (such as *foedus* and *amicitia*)[7] whose relation to their signifieds never changes. Unfortunately, these terms come to Catullus no more, and no less, impossibly ironized by the noncoincidence of the signifier with its signified, than any amorous vocabulary. Catullus' attempts to articulate a different kind of desire in a different kind of vocabulary come to nothing—*not* because of Lesbia's failing to live up to this new vocabulary's meanings, but because it never intrinsically meant anything at all.

As closely as the epigrams' workings parallel *capitonnage,* they can also be seen as a disillusioned version of Platonic love in action. In chapter 1, I touched upon the parallels between the *Phaedrus'* harnessing of desire to the pursuit of truth through language and *capitonnage.* But I did not there elucidate the degree to which the *Phaedrus* rests its program upon just such an obsession with rereading as exampled in the epigrams. Socrates' correct philosopher-lover pursues a triangular circuit of diligently "reading" her own soul and her beloved's continuously against human knowledge of the divine, to match the image of the god in one soul to that in the other, and both ever more closely to knowledge from any source about the god (*Phaedrus* 252d1–253b1). Catullus' own essays in psychic herme-

80

neutics repeat the *Phaedrus'* prescribed exercises—but as if the god's image had been replaced by an obscured palimpsest, that grew dimmer, rather than clearer, upon scrutiny. Yet not irretrievably so: we will see this concern to resurrect an internalized image for the lover's *sole* edification resurface as a glimmer of hope and independence at the end of examining the epigrams.

Advancing in Circles

The frustrations of the epigrams sketched above lead, as I have said, to repetition rather than cessation—but not precisely the kind of repetition encapsulated in cc.11 plus 51. The epigrams spin out narratives bridging the two poles of misogyny and courtly love that anchor the affair with Lesbia under the guise of *odi* and *amo*. But in doing so, they combine the dynamics of cc.2–11 and of 11 plus 51. Like the former, they articulate moments in the passage from one pole to the other in a rationalized temporal progression. But like the latter pair, they repeat—verbally, metrically, topically. The epigrams go over and over the same moments in time, the same words, the same emotions—and often in ways that work counterpoint to a straightforward, linear reading. The epigrams pose the questions, How does Catullus read Lesbia? and How do *we* read Lesbia? as functions of the question, How do we read this particular poetic text?— and that more starkly than anywhere else in the cycle. Elegy's tendency to articulate thought in end-stopped couplets—coming to completion, or at least a distinct pause in its elaboration, at the end of each distich—encourages concision. Catullus' use of the form in the epigrams correspondingly strives to wring maximum possible significance from this already pithily laconic form, through suggestive analytical antithesis and repetition.[8] Consider 75.3–4 as a simple example:

> Huc est mens deducta tua, mea Lesbia, culpa
> atque ita se officio perdidit ipsa suo,
> *ut iam nec bene velle queat tibi, si optima fias,*
> *nec desistere amare, omnia si facias.*

To this degree is my mind distracted, my Lesbia, by your fault, and does so destroy itself by doing what it must, that it could not now cherish you, if you became the noblest of women, nor could it stop loving you, no matter what you did.

Catullus exploits the metrical resemblance always possible (though not necessary) between beginnings of hexameter and pentameter to reinforce the contrast between the ideas contained in each.[9] Metrical similarity of both lines' openings (a spondee, a dactyl, and a long half-foot before the line break) plays "ut iam nec bene vel[le]" off against "nec desistere ama[re]"[10] in a way that cuts across the structural distinction between hexameter and pentameter and urges a nonlinear construction of the couplet.

Or, as a more detailed example of nonlinear, repetitive reading, take c.107. C.107 not only contains internal verbal symmetries but echoes and repeats other poems in the cycle, as it talks *about* repetition in desire:

> Si quicquam cupido optantique obtigit umquam
> insperanti, hoc est gratum animo proprie.
> quare hoc est gratum nobisque hoc carius auro
> quod te restituis, Lesbia, mi cupido.
> restituis cupido atque insperanti, ipsa refers te
> nobis. o lucem candidiore nota!
> quis me uno vivit felicior, aut magis hac quid
> optandum vita dicere quis poterit?
>
> (107)

If anything ever befell someone who wanted it and wished for it, but did not expect it, this is especially pleasing to his heart. Wherefore this is pleasing to me, and to me this is dearer than gold, that you restore yourself, Lesbia, to me who desire you. You restore yourself to one who desires but does not hope, when you yourself bring yourself back to me. O day with a whiter mark! Who lives who is happier than I alone, or who shall have been able to say that anything ought more to be wished for in this life?

Note the verbal repetitions of "cupido," both before and after the line breaks (the hexameter's principle caesura, and the pentameter's diaeresis). "Cupido" occupies the same metrical position in the hexameters of 107.1 and 5, *before* the logical (though, in 5, elided) caesura, balanced by "cupido" repeated in 4's pentameter *after* the diaeresis. "Optanti" and "insperanti" occupy the same metrical positions in 1 and 5, with the same balancing of "insperanti" repeated both before (2), and after (5), the pauses—as was the case with "cupido."

But this is also repetition in the history of the affair: Lesbia has come back ("te *re*stituis, Lesbia, mi cupido," 107.4). In one sense, Catullus presents the moment as abstracted out of time: the poem says nothing about past or future, why she left, why she came back, or what either lover envisions for the future. Yet verbal echoes undermine the construction of this moment as static and tie it to a narrative of instability and repeated *peripeteia*. "*Cupido* optant?" (107.1) and "*cupido* . . . insperant?" (107.5) echo *"cupido . . . amanti"* in 70.3. The impassioned lover of 70.3 listens to *words* that mean nothing, and are unstable: "though she says she prefers no one to me, what a woman says to her *impassioned lover* I write in wind and water." This echo and others in the poem suggest that Lesbia's actions mean little more than her words in c.70. Neither lover can step out of the repetitive oscillation between pain and joy, betrayal and return. For example "lucem candidiore nota" (107.6) echoes 68.148—Catullus' construction of Lesbia's sexual behavior as habitual infidelity:

> quae tamen etsi uno non est contenta Catullo,
> rara verecundae furta feremus erae,
> . . . illud satis est, si nobis is datur unis
> quem *lapide illa diem candidiore notat.*
> (68.135–36, 147–48)

> even if she is not content with Catullus alone, hers are the occasional thefts of a modest mistress—we shall bear them . . . it is enough, if the day that is given to me alone, she marks with a whiter stone.

In these lines, Catullus does not expect Lesbia to put an end to seeing other men: he only wishes that her trysts with *him* be special. In that light, 107 is merely a moment abstracted from the turn of the wheel between absence and presence, *odi* and *amo.*

On the other hand, the epigrams' reworkings progress, rather than just repeat, in that they articulate the affair in finer and finer detail. Catullus carefully, obsessively refines his interpretation of the dynamics at work between himself and Lesbia, by construing (and reconstruing) the erotic history between them. In the process, he applies different interpretive *points de capiton* to the events. Each of these *points de capiton* articulates a provisionally meaningful relation between the extremes of desire pinpointed in 11 and in 51. This progressive refinement results, however, in interpretive *aporia*, precisely because the connection between one extreme and the other is overdetermined. Too many signifying chains in the epigrams compete to read the affair—chains that are each consistent within themselves but incompatible taken together. The epigrams multiply and undermine antitheses on many different levels—structural, linguistic, psychic—resulting in a conflict of interpretations. The narrative collapses in its own plethora of attempts to articulate closure.

Reading the Verso

Catullus focuses upon Lesbia's speech as a problem of interpretation in cc.83 and 92—of correct reading, analogous to the puzzle of how, and in what order, one is to read 11 in conjunction with 51. He explains the relation between Lesbia the whore and Lesbia the goddess as an erotically founded metaphorical relation between signifier and repressed signified (= her mythical intent). Though Lesbia verbally mistreats him, that signifies the opposite intent—she meditates passionately on their connection:

> Lesbia mi praesente viro mala plurima dicit;
>   haec illi fatuo maxima laetitia est.
> mule, nihil sentis? si nostri oblita taceret,
>   sana esset; nunc quod gannit et obloquitur,
> non solum meminit, sed, quae multo acrior est res,
>   irata est. hoc est, uritur et loquitur.
>
> (83)

> In the presence of her man, Lesbia spouts a torrent of abuse about me; it's the source of the greatest happiness to that oaf. You jerk, don't you know anything? If she had forgotten about what's between us and were silent, she'd be heart-whole; now, given that she snarls and rudely breaks into the conversation, she not only remembers, but, what is by far the more bitter fact, she is angered. There you have it: she burns and she talks.

Catullus reads himself into what Lesbia says, into the desire of the Other: if he were gone from her mind, she would be silent ("si *nostri oblita taceret*," 3). Her obloquies indicate that he is mentally present to her ("non solum *meminit*. . . . / hoc est, *uritur et loquitur*," 5–6)—thus they reassure him of her love rather than threaten him. "*Che vuoi?*" is answered, in his interpretation, with "you."

How is it that Catullus knows how to interpret her speech? C.92, looking again at this topos, shows that he reads her talk as corresponding to the split between himself as speaking subject and as subject of the speech when discussing her; his insults elaborately translate "I am lying":

> Lesbia mi dicit semper male nec tacet umquam
>   de me: Lesbia me dispeream nisi amat.
> quo signo? quia sunt totidem mea: deprecor illam
>   assidue, verum dispeream nisi amo.
>
> (92)

> Lesbia spouts abuse of me all the time, and she never shuts up about me: I'll be damned if she doesn't love me. How do I figure? Because it's all the same thing with me: I curse her constantly, and I'll be damned if I don't love her!

The Epigrams

Catullus' reading of Lesbia's speech supplies to it an Imaginary *point de capiton* ("she's just like me, my mirror image") that finds the repressed significance of "black" is "white."

That *point de capiton* signals as well a bond between the two lovers: as Catullus sets up the correspondence, he can interpret Lesbia's speech, but his rival, the dull-witted *vir*, is effectively shut out of the communicative circuit. Reading their talk as conditioned by opposition makes it a *recherché* communicative system similar to that established by Callimachean poetics. The lovers' speech, like Callimachus' erudite poetry, is understandable only to an elite interpretive community—to themselves and to the *cognoscenti* who read Catullus' poetry and are thus let in on the secret.

Cc.83 and 92 also say "the Whore's abuses really signify the Divine Lady's love, provided that you read them correctly." These poems effectively interpret the relation between 11 and 51 as between fact and its fictionalization, where fiction protects lovers' secrets. And if Lesbia's abuses *prove* that she desires Catullus, then 83 and 92 radically revise the disappearance of the subject envisioned in c.11. In 11, Lesbia's lack of erotic discrimination—"embracing all at once, but loving none truly"—makes Catullus, qua Lesbia's lover, indistinguishable from any one of her three hundred adulterers. She takes as much notice of him as a plow does of a flower, so that he fades in the desire of the Other. In 83 and 92, she privileges him as her paramour (in contrast to the *vir*), because he alone can truly understand her. He thus constructs himself as the Master, the subject-supposed-to-know. He himself, and his own behavior, become the code by which she may be properly read. Not only *what* he reads from her talk, but that he *can* correctly read her talk, proves their exclusive erotic bond, based on psychic mirroring. Callimachean exclusiveness defines him as a lover, as well as a poet—and Lesbia becomes, in the classic relation of Woman to Man, the guarantor of Catullus' identity and self-knowledge.

Other epigrams, however, do not allow that guarantee to stand unchallenged. The extreme example is c.104. The slippage between signifier and signified that grounds interpretation in 83 and 92 undermines any basis for construction in c.104.

> Credis me potuisse meae maledicere vitae,
> ambobus mihi quae carior est oculis?
> non potui, nec, si possem, tam perdite amarem;
> sed tu cum Tappone omnia monstra facis.
>
> (104)

85

> Do you believe that I would have been able to badmouth my life, she who is dearer to me than both my eyes? I couldn't have—nor, if I were able, would I love so desperately; but you and Tappo make every little thing into a portent!

C.104 runs headlong against 83 and 92: the premise of interpretation in the latter two epigrams turned on curses that signified passion. In 104, Catullus not only denies that he could curse and love with such abandon but denies any basis of interpretation to the poems that denigrate Lesbia. This casts uncertainty upon the whole fragmented narrative of the Lesbia cycle: if you can deny that a spade is a spade, or that saying "spade" means "spade," then you destroy the whole basis for interpreting signifers.

Or so it seems, from the perspective that views language as "code", with a fixed relation between signifier and signified; the matter is in fact more complex. C.104 destroys the simple Saussurean assumption that the relation between signifier and signified resembles that between two sides of a piece of paper—synchronically rigid and stable, though it may gradually change diachronically.[11] Lacan demonstrates[12] that the signifying chain works against any such simplistic welding of meaning to individual signifiers, treated as independent and self-contained units. Rather, meaning is numinous and immanent in the chain as a whole: substitute one word for another—any word, it does not matter which—and *some* meaning effect will accrue. He quotes as illustration a line from Victor Hugo's "*Booz endormi*": "His sheaf was neither miserly nor spiteful" ("Sa gerbe n'était pas avare ni haineuse"). The word "sheaf" is a metaphor for "Boaz," yet bears no logical relation to "Boaz," no Aristotelian relation of similarity[13] that legitimates the substitution. Only the signifying chain as a whole allows the substitution to work, making "sheaf" (as grammatical subject) produce "Boaz" (as conceptual subject).

The hermeneutic reach of the signifying chain is vast, as c.70[14] shows by drawing in a substantial chunk of the literary tradition as interpretive key to Lesbia's speech. C.70 sets up the problem of interpreting Lesbia's speech, and Catullus' self-reflection in that speech, from a perspective opposite to that of 83 and 92. Now Lesbia's speech flatters rather than abuses: she says "I would prefer you to Jove."

> Nulli se dicit mulier mea nubere malle
> quam mihi, non si se Iuppiter ipse petat.
>
> (70.1–2)

My woman says that she would marry no one in preference to me, not even if Jove himself asks her.

86

That defines Catullus as unique in the desire of the Other, insofar as she prefers him to the highest of the gods, the pinnacle of the cosmos. Her speech—read as a straightforward expression of her intent—would define the bond between them *and* his worth to her, shoring up her estimate's reflection of his identity. But Catullus reverses that reading in the second half of the poem; he "rereads" her speech in the light of another signifying chain: that of the literary tradition's articulation of erotic insincerity as a poetic topos.

> dicit; sed mulier cupido quod dicit amanti,
> in vento et rapida scribere oportet aqua.
>
> (70.3–4)

So she says; but the words a woman says to her impassioned lover, one must write in wind and in the flowing water.

The reversals of c.70 have clear precedents in erotic poetry;[15] the most obvious model is an epigram by Callimachus:[16]

Kallignotos swore to Ionis that he would never hold any woman or man dearer than her. So he swore; but they say truly that oaths spoken in love are unable to reach the immortals' ears. And now he burns for a man, while of the poor young maiden there is, as the Megarians say, "neither count nor reckoning."[17]

Catullus assimilates Lesbia's betrayal to a cliché of the erotic tradition—"*così fan tutti*."[18] He contravenes the uniqueness he read into their relationship in 83 and 92: now they occupy the well-worn positions of betrayer and betrayed. C.70 flips the relation between the images of the beloved set out in 11 and 51 in a fashion incompatible with 82 and 93: now the Goddess, though she says she sets him above the king of the gods, must be disbelieved and read as the Whore.

But why should Callimachus, or any other poet for that matter, be privileged to provide special insight into Lesbia's motives? The same meta-phorical urge that allowed Hugo's Boaz to be usurped by his sheaf, and yielded us, the readers, the pleasure of a legible whole, is at work in c.70. The *point de capiton* operating here is "Woman is a whore," as specifically articulated in the poetic tradition. Catullus has switched the gender of the perjurer from Callimachus' epigram and borrowed the image of wind and water from a plethora of sources, notably from a misogynistic Sophoclean line: "I write the oaths of a woman in water."[19] As a result, he raises an

individual woman (Lesbia) to the dimension of Woman (the overarching
fictive construct that guarantees Man's identity) and then interprets her
in the light of misogyny, as a *point de capiton* that papers over the lack of
any signifier for her desire in the Symbolic. As Woman's desire cannot be
signified, it is assumed to be limitless, voracious—whence the crude sexist
wisdom that when women say, "no!" they really mean an emphatic, "yes!"
Their "no!" invites a doubly aggressive assault. C.66.15–20 examples this
analysis:

> estne novis nuptis odio Venus? anne parentum
> frustrantur falsis gaudia lacrimulis,
> ubertim thalami quas intra limina fundunt?
> non, ita me divi, vera gemunt, iuerint.
> id mea me multis docuit regina querellis
> invisente novo proelia torva viro.

Is sex an object of hatred to new brides? Or are the joys of their parents
frustrated by false (though becoming) tears, which they pour forth abundantly
within the threshhold of the marriage chamber? May the gods help me, they
don't complain sincerely! This my queen taught me, with her many objections,
when her new husband looked enviously on savage battle.[20]

"Woman is a whore" is the return of "*Was will das Weib?*" as an insistent,
unanswerable question.[21]

I'm Missing Something

In c.70, the paradox of 83 and 92—that the speech of the two lovers
signifies the opposite of what it says—expands into a principle impossible
to stabilize. C.70 does not emphasize that Lesbia's speech, as a sign of her
desire, always means the opposite of what it says: that would lend itself to
stable, though convoluted, interpretation. Rather, her speech (as Catullus
constructs it) defies stabilization altogether. The images and the elisions
of 70.4 (there are no elisions in 70.1–3) match the fluid media in which
Catullus proposes to inscribe her words. Edges dissolve in flowing wind
and water and in elisions between words describing that flow; the ratifica-
tion of the lover's (Catullus') desire, and the signifier of the lover's unique
identity, dissolve along with them.

In c.72,[22] destabilization as a problem of reading recurs, though it
operates at a different level and on a slightly different basis. The interpreta-
tion of 72 is destabilized, not because of edges erased, but because of what
is missing from the text. C.72, like 70, looks at disbelief, but this time

88

arranges Lesbia's declarations as a series viewed from a point in time that succeeds them. Catullus' formulation in 72 is at once more and less clear: 72 transforms the worldly wise, easy cynicism of 70 into a finer and more meticulous articulation of precise moments in the process of disenchantment, and of the emotional shift that accrues to that knowledge. In looking back upon his own experience, Catullus signals us in the very first line of the poem that repetition is intrinsic to his reading (and ours): *re*reading forms part of the attempt to construe sensibly this erotic history.

> Dicebas quondam solum te nosse Catullum,
>   Lesbia, nec prae me velle tenere Iovem.
> dilexi tum te non tantum ut vulgus amicam,
>   sed pater ut gnatos diligit et generos.
> nunc te cognovi; quare, etsi impensius uror,
>   multo mi tamen es vilior et levior.
> qui potis est, inquis? quod amantem iniuria talis
>   cogit amare magis, sed bene velle minus.

(72)

At one time, Lesbia, you used to say *solum te nosse Catullum nec prae me velle tenere Iovem*. I loved you then not only as the common herd loves a girlfriend, but as a father loves his sons and his sons-in-law. Now I've come to know you; for which reason, even if I burn more passionately, you are to me much cheaper and of less account. How is this possible, you ask? Because your sort of offense forces a lover to desire more, but to cherish less.

The first line poses a question of reading: what precisely did Lesbia say to Catullus—"I know Catullus alone"? "Catullus alone knows me"? "I wish to know Catullus alone"? "I wish Catullus alone to know me"? The construction of the indirect statement makes her reported enunciation ambiguous, but we do not perceive the ambiguity until the second line of the distich.[23] One must carefully reread the sentence in order to arrive at a *decision*—not a certainty—as to what it says. That decision rests upon *assumptions* about the distich's grammatical working—what is to be read with what and in what order, and what needs to be supplied. Poet *and* audience engage in reinterpreting Lesbia's speech and its precise articulation of the lovers' relationship.

Moreover, what is missing from this poem, as much as what is there, forces us to reread Lesbia's remembered declarations. The poem's gaps function as do the gaps in the Lesbia cycle's narrative of the affair, which also invite the reader to construe and reconstrue the poems in different

89

orders to realize different narrative sequences. And we as readers repeatedly attempt to "master" the text and its gaps, just as Catullus repeatedly attempts to master his erotic loss by transforming it into "knowledge," knowledge of Lesbia.

My point is that repetition, as a strategy to deal with lack—for us as readers, what the text lacks—inheres in the act of interpreting the cycle. And that obtains not only for the fragmentary whole but within discrete and clearly unified poems. C.72 indicates that our perplexity as readers, which urges us to repeat and to reconstrue, cannot all be ascribed to a faulty manuscript tradition or to the mystery surrounding Catullus' ordering of his poems.

Rereading[24] functionally matches the poet's interrogation of his own erotic history in order to define a self; rereading also seeks definition—definition of the text to be interpreted. In c.72, that search is ultimately frustrated—as, in the Lesbia epigrams as a whole, no stable sense of the subject emerges, because no stable sense of the Other('s desire) does.

Interpretation fails in c.72, and yet the fruit of interpretation—knowledge-as-mastery—is at stake in this poem for the lovers as well as the readers. Knowledge promises to ratify an erotic bond, and to define those who share that bond, so that desire defines self through knowledge. In the first distich of the poem, Lesbia's blandishment couples an erotic expression of desire ("nec prae me velle *tenere* Iovem," 72.2) to a desire to know the Other: she wishes to have known Catullus alone (or for Catullus alone to have known her). Whichever way we read the sentence, she declares that desire will discover *who* the Other is—erotic knowledge defines the Other, and thus also secures the basis of self.

But c.72 also pins an elusive knowledge, and a divided self, to shifting gender positions. The contrast between 72.3–4 and 72.5–6 represents Catullus as an innocent at the time Lesbia made her declarations. The second of these distichs isolates two divergent elements within his love, tied to feminine and masculine positions, respectively: the love the common herd feels attaches to Woman, while his more exclusive bond accrues to Man, matching the love of a father for his sons and sons-in-law. Catullus' paternal love for Lesbia rests on the presumption that her speech represents herself and her desire transparently, faithfully, completely—exactly the false assumptions about the Symbolic's adequacy upon which phallic certainty rests. Little wonder, then, that he makes her gender masculine in a comparison that measures his remembered love for her as "known quantity." His fantasy of Lesbia's transparency was convenient: it dissimulated each lover's division, presenting them to each other's view as the impossible "one"—

meaning both "whole; not troubled by unrepresented desires, unconditionally consenting," and "my exclusive complement—the only one for me." Lesbia defined Catullus as a party of one ("solum . . . Catullum," 72.1), preferring him even to the king of the gods; he defines her as exclusive, precious and ingenuous as male heirs. "*Che vuoi?*" clearly operates here, in the naïve fantasy that the desire of the Other is known and known to be the subject, exclusively. Fantasy thus momentarily prevaricates the tension between the divergent elements Catullus has already acknowledged within himself: the love of the *vulgus* and that of the *pater,* two different ways of imagining the Other.

But when erotic knowledge discovers a slippage between signifier and signified—when phallic certainty stumbles over language's own incapacity to represent the subject completely—then the poem returns Lesbia to feminine unaccountability: no more talk of sons and sons-in-law after the apocalypse. Lesbia said she would not prefer Jove to Catullus—yet she "wronged" him ("iniuria talis," 72.7): her actions, in his eyes, contradict her words. How, then, to save the appearances and rescue masculine knowledge gracefully? Construe the sequelae under a different *point de capiton* and call that "knowledge."

Yet the difficulties of this task mock the threadbare logic of the very misogyny the poem stages. "Now I know you" Catullus says—and the connotations of *cognovi* (72.5) combine in one epistemological function what Lesbia's declaration linked but articulated separately: sexual and intellectual knowledge. His rude awakening sorts out himself and Lesbia as erotic subject and object, between too-familiar glosses on the positions Man and Woman: she is a necessary, but despised, complement, like Hegel's Slave to his Master. She becomes more an object of desire (72.5, 8), yet "cheaper and a thing of greater contempt" (72.6). He correspondingly admits to more passion, but less regard, for her (72.8).

C.72 articulates the relation between *amo* and *odi*—corresponding to the first and second halves of the poem—as resting on the fulcrum of enlightenment. But this revised knowledge reveals itself as mere *capitonnage,* where interpretation has spun abruptly in its allegiance from one *point de capiton* to the other, from "Woman is a goddess" to "Woman is a whore." Lesbia has a *vir* in much of the Lesbia cycle, to whose claims Catullus himself cedes precedence;[25] Lesbia's trysts with *Catullus* constitute *iniuria* to that other man. Catullus' gloss on the changed *capitonnage*—"I was a fool then; now I know the truth about you"—in its own desperate logic, dramatizes an insufficiency in masculine knowledge of Woman. Catullus begins to look a lot more like the asinine *vir* of c.83, who never

91

really grasps that Lesbia's words do not match her wants—and neither Catullus *nor* the *vir* can fathom Lesbia's desire.

Unrealpolitik

Reflecting upon precisely what went wrong between "then" and "now," Catullus adduces yet another system of signifiers by which to interpret Lesbia's speech and behavior versus his own—that of political alliance. The significance of the switch lies in the fact that this system is supposed to operate in a manner directly opposed to the interpretive keys Catullus has applied in 83, 92, and 70 to Lesbia's speech and his own. Those elegies assumed contradiction between speech and intent—in 83 and 92, as the sign of their mutual bond; in 70, as the sign of Lesbia's lack of credibility. Yet D. O. Ross' 1969 analysis of the epigrams emphasizes the solemnity that invests the epigrams' underlying political vocabulary.[26] These terms ratify social and political bonds with religious and legal rigor. Failure to honor such bonds in deed as well as in word is considered an offense against both piety and law.

> Catullus, then, has portrayed his affair with Lesbia in the terminology of a political alliance: it is to be an *amicitia*, a *foedus*, based on *fides*, the concrete expressions of which are the mutual *benevolentia* and *benefacta* of the two parties, resulting in *gratia* arising from the performance of *officia;*[27] the relationship is to be protected by divinity, as it must be religiously observed with *pietas* by both parties; and Catullus can imagine the alliance, too, as one resulting from a marriage between families, a bond of *pietas* linking the father-in-law and sons-in-law.[28]

Ross defines *foedus* as "used to mark the formal necessity of the obligations inherent in a political *amicitia*," and though "a metaphorical extension of its basic meaning, treaty," it rests upon no light comparative term.[29] Ross quotes P. A. Brunt to illustrate the implications of the metaphor: "Treaties were ratified by solemn oaths and to break them was perjury."[30]

On this reading, Catullus sets up an implied antithesis between the language of politics, assumed to enjoy a straightforward correspondence between word and meaning under the aegis of religious and contractual rigor, as opposed to an amorous register, which assumes a contradictory relationship between word and meaning. C.109 illustrates the contrast between the two: as an explicit act of rereading, it tries to retranslate Lesbia's words into political terminology and to pinpoint the difference between the operation of the amorous and the political vocabularies.

The Epigrams

Iucundum, mea vita, mihi proponis amorem
  hunc nostrum inter nos perpetuumque fore.
di magni, facite ut vere promittere possit,
  atque id sincere dicat et ex animo,
ut liceat nobis tota perducere vita
  aeternum hoc sanctae foedus amicitiae.

(109)

You propose to me, my life, a pleasant love—that this love, between us, will be pleasant and forever. Great gods, grant that she can promise truly and speak this sincerely and from her heart, so that we may live out to the very end of our lives an eternal bond of sacred alliance!

The difference between Lesbia's proposal and Catullus' is not articulated in terms of time: she, too, says that she wants this love to be "forever" (*perpetuum*, 109.2). Rather, the sign of their bond will be exact correspondence between word and meaning, word and deed, instead of the recondite amorous cryptography that in 83 and 92 signaled love between Lesbia and Catullus. C.109 asks that she speak *vere, sincere,* and *ex animo*—that contradiction between word and intent be abolished—so that the two lovers may enter into a relationship that will have the force of a bond (*foedus*) protected by law and by divinity (*sanctae . . . amicitiae*).

Yet it is instructive, in this context, to compare Ross' 1969 estimation of political vocabulary with his quite different stress six years later: "In a political alliance, a Roman statesman would have admitted, expediency is the most powerful element, that and cold obligation: sincerity has no place."[31] The shift of emphasis between Ross' 1969 and 1975 views on alliance, from sacred obligation to mundane instrument of self-interest, concurs with P. A. Brunt's conclusion to the very same study quoted above of the key terms in political vocabulary. Brunt sees the central term, *amicitia,* as ranged on a denotative continuum from pure political expediency and self-interest to selfless devotion.[32]

Amicitia's hospitable embrace of contradictory concepts illustrates that Catullus grapples with a problem ultimately no less insistent in the political vocabulary than in amorous speech: that of the floating signifier. Given that the signifier is not nailed to the signified in a fixed relation (as we saw in discussing "*Booz endormi*"), no word means *anything* in isolation. It "floats above" the signified, suspending and deferring meaning until the last word of the utterance is in place. And if one replies, "yes, but its meaning is fixed contextually," then the pressing question arises: where and how is context delimited? Let me turn back to consideration of c.109 to illustrate this problem.

93

David Konstan has analyzed c.109 to elucidate from it a pattern of unfolding meaning that depends upon a series of the reader's radical revisions, depending on how the boundaries defining context are drawn.[33] He considers first the opening line in isolation ("Iucundum, mea vita, mihi proponis amorem"), which he translates "you offer me, my life, pleasant *amor*." But he points out, when the second line is supplied to the first, yielding "Iucundum, mea vita, mihi proponis amorem / hunc nostrum inter nos perpetuumque fore"

> The meaning and syntax of the hexameter are quite altered. *Proponis* no longer means, "you offer," but rather means, "you promise," and it introduces the construction of indirect discourse, the emphasis shifting from the act to the word. The lines read: "you promise, my life, that *this* love, ours, between us—*this* love will be pleasant and forever." If we recall, now, the traditional [Roman] attitude toward *amor* as a kind of temporary insanity, then the idea of *perpetuus amor, amor* that lasts forever, seems almost an oxymoron, just as in English there is an odd or self-contradictory note in the expression "eternal infatuation."[34]

As Konstan demonstrates, the addition of the second line to the first in c.109 propels all the key terms from the sublime to the ridiculous ("perpetual infatuation"). The same may be said of the terms that fall under the influence of the political field: more than one commentator has noted that c.109's legalistic piling up of synonyms ("vere"/"sincere"/"ex animo"; "tota . . . vita"/"aeternum") progressively weakens the force of each one.[35] If the promise has meaning, multiplying parameters is needless; if not, multiplying them is useless. Thus, no individual word in the line means anything at *all* in isolation.

Further, every word, every signifying unit we read or utter, is in isolation to some degree, since context can be expanded indefinitely: word added to word, sentence to sentence, paragraph to paragraph *ad infinitum*. As *points de capiton* offer only temporary respite (however ideologically charged), they palliate, but do not solve, this problem. We can see this if we turn back to c.72, and follow up its gravitational pull on other poems, which, when added to its sphere of influence as *point de capiton*, are rendered opaque.

In c.72, the political code that assumes one-to-one correspondence between word and deed redefines and reexplicates lover and beloved but destabilizes the interpretations of other poems. It articulates the nature of Catullus' love more finely—love that was both *bene velle* and *amare*. The split between word and deed that 83 and 70 perceive as originating in the object (Lesbia) corresponds to a split in the subject's own emotion in 72, between "cherishing" and "desiring." Catullus anatomizes two emotions that work according to diametrically opposed principles. In order to cherish, he must believe in the worth of his object—which, the first quatrain implies, amounts to her granting him an exclusive image of himself as Jove. By contrast, her failing (a faltering in her attention?) increases the force of *amare*. That in turn suggests a reinterpretation of 83, 92, and 70, as poems resulting from Catullus reading his own subjective schism onto Lesbia. He takes her obloquies to be a sign of love, and then, applying the same principle to opposite effect, reads her blandishments as the clichéd insincerity of lovers.

Further, 72 construes the relation between joy and sorrow not as end and beginning of the affair but as the eclipse of a particular element of Catullus' love and the waxing of another, precipitated by his construction of Lesbia's behavior. That forces us to reconstrue 11 and 51 yet again, not as oscillation between awe and disillusionment, but as a change in the nature of the bond or feeling perceived between subject and object. It denies an end to the relationship: he does not say in 72, as he does in 11, "I'm through." Rather, he says "I'm through feeling about you in this way, though my other feeling is in fact augmented."

Assessing the Fault Line

In 75, the destabilizing of the tools of reading spreads from words (as in 70) and syntax (as in 72 and 109) to narrative itself, and perceived closure in that narrative. C.75 expands both on the antitheses of feeling discovered in c.72 and the denial of an end as announced in c.11. Here is the same word—*culpa*, "offense"—that destroyed Catullus' love in 11.22:[36]

> Huc est mens deducta tua, mea Lesbia, *culpa*
> atque ita se officio perdidit ipsa suo,
> ut iam nec bene velle queat tibi, si optima fias,
> nec desistere amare, omnia si facias.
>
> (75)

To this degree has my mind been distracted, my Lesbia, by your fault, and has itself so destroyed itself by doing what it must, that it could not now cherish you, if you became the noblest of women, nor could it stop loving you, no matter what you did.

"When the Lamp Is Shattered"

nec meum respectet, ut ante, amorem,
qui illius *culpa* cecidit velut prati
ultimi flos, praetereunte postquam
tactus aratro est.

(11.21–24)

and do not let her look back, as before, for my love, which her fault cut
down just like a flower on the edge of the field, touched by the passing plow.

Yet in 75, Lesbia's *culpa,* far from ending the affair, binds Catullus more
firmly to her. The poem elucidates the antitheses and splits in Catullus as
desiring subject. Note, for example, the way in which the poem formulates
Catullus' irrationality. He represents himself as engaged in an internal civil
strife in which his mind sacrifices his own best interests in pursuit of his
desire: "my mind . . . / . . . itself has destroyed itself by doing what it
must" (75.1–2). The structure of the poem emphasizes this: the elision
between "se" and "officio" in 2 makes it *sound* as though "self" is being
sacrificed to "what it must do" in that the articulation of the latter nearly
swallows the former. Moreover, "se" before the diaeresis balances "suo"
after the diaeresis. Balancing the two cognates emphasizes how counterin-
tuitive is the opposition that allows "*suo* [officio]" to win out over "*se*" in
this conflict of interests.

C.75 makes nonsense of the antitheses encapsulated in the object in 11
and 51 that provoke readings of the two poems as "end" and "beginning,"
respectively. The same indiscrimination that embraces three hundred lovers
and destroys Catullus' love in 11 is no obstacle to his desire in 75. On
the other hand, the supernaturally desirable vision of 51 cannot restore
his regard for her ("ut iam nec bene velle queat tibi, si *optima* fias," 75.3).

C.75 suggests that the polarity of Whore versus Goddess perceived
in Lesbia as desired object resides rather in Catullus as desiring subject.
The subject reading himself in the Other is the locus of both poles in
desire. Desire and disgust we have construed in cc.2–11 as respectively
beginning and end of the affair. We can read the mutual reference of 11
and 51 as beginning and end also, if we assume that love and hate are
incompatible, and that the poems' metrical and verbal symmetries can only
be read in one direction, from love to hate. C.75 sees these emotional poles
as not only simultaneous (therefore not, in this perspective, describing a
temporal or narrative sequence) but juxtaposed in one person rather than
transacted between two people. C.75 suggests that the destabilizing split
desire manifests in the subject has little or nothing to do with an "unwor-

96

thy" object but proceeds from the nature of the desiring (thus, by definition, divided) subject.

The subjective division at which c.75 points we know founds desire and the futile repetition of its circuit *ad infinitum*. The lack Plato felt as keenly as Lacan or Freud compels the divided subject organized around it progressively to annul his objects, since none can answer this lack— save, for Plato, the Forms. The rampant hermeneutic mischief we have documented in the epigrams reflects this futility. The signifying chain's idiotic circulation around the verge of non-sense is only pinned and made provisionally meaningful by desire's momentary attachment to a signifier, making of the signifier a *point de capiton*. But *capitonnage* cannot provide an ultimately satisfactory answer to *"che vuoi?"*—"who am I for you?" The epigrams contemplate the adequacy of such answers as *amans* (lover) and *amicus* (friend/partisan) and eventually discard both, not by open repudiation, but by radically problematizing the terms' bases of intelligibility. The etiolation of these terms is as inevitable as, and homologous to, the inadequacy of any object (not just Lesbia qua object) proffered to desire: none can heal the split in the subject.

Thus, it should come as no surprise that the object—Lesbia-as-object, simulacrum to Catullus' desire, occupying the fantasized position of Woman—completely disappears in c.85. C.85 fully realizes the division between love and hate as residing in the subject exclusively, in the complete absence of an object:

> Odi et amo. quare id faciam, fortasse requiris.
> nescio, sed fieri sentio et excrucior.
>
> (85)

> I hate and I love. Why do I do this, perhaps you inquire? I do not know—
> but I feel it happening, and I am laid on the cross.

Of the eight verbs in this epigram, six are first-person singular.[37] No sign of Lesbia remains: she is not named nor referred to as *vita, puella,* or anything else. These two lines do not even have any grammatical object, much less an object of desire. The split in Catullus exists independent of his object. He plays the verbs off one another for their antithetical connotations and denotations:[38] hate and love ("odi" and "amo"); active and passive ("faciam" and "fieri"); ignorant mind, perceiving senses; ("nescio" and "sentio"). The last word of the poem—also a verb—envisions the subject pulled in opposite directions: "I am laid on the cross."

97

In quella parte del libro de la mia memoria
dinanzi a la quale
poco si potrebbe leggere, si trova una rubrica la quale dice:
"Incipit vita nova"

The first third of c.76 also contains the relationship between Catullus and Lesbia within the subject alone, as a memory couched in political vocabulary:[39]

> Si qua recordanti benefacta priora voluptas
>   est homini, cum se cogitat esse pium,
> nec sanctam violasse fidem, nec foedere nullo
>   divum ad fallendos numine abusum homines,
> multa parata manent in longa aetate, Catulle,
>   ex hoc ingrato gaudia amore tibi.
> nam quaecumque homines bene cuiquam aut dicere possunt
>   aut facere, haec a te dictaque factaque sunt.
> omnia quae ingratae perierunt credita menti.
>
> (76.1–9)

> If there is any pleasure for a person who remembers previous acts of kindness, when he considers himself to be loyal and mindful of his obligations; not to have broken any trust, nor to have abused, by any false oath, the power of the gods, to deceive people—many joys await you, Catullus, in the long time to come, from this senseless waste of love. For whatever people can do or say in kindness and truth, this has been done and said by you. But everything goes to waste when sunk in the debt of a selfish heart.

In these lines, Catullus carefully articulates his self-definition as a man who has honored his commitments to gods and to human beings as a fact independent of what the object of his love is supposed to have done. He defines his worth and his identity independently of Lesbia, based on the memory of his good deeds. That should end the problem of interpreting his lover's behavior and trying to ascertain his worth in relation to her. And the frail utopian exception Plato makes to the psychoanalytic concept of lack—that Ideals exist to fulfill it, however removed in their empyrean serenity—comes to Catullus' rescue here. Catullus speaks of internalizing an Other comparable to the Platonic Ideals that will define him as virtuous, and he leans upon Plato's conceptualization to do so. As Robinson Ellis notes, "Catullus in speaking of the benefits performed by lovers to the beloved uses Platonic language,"[40] and points to the *Phaedrus,* "where however the opposite view is stated, that lovers *regret* the kindness they

98

have done, after the passion is over."[41] Catullus, like Socrates, repudiates this view and borrows from the same dialogue Socrates' vision of the benefits conferred by love. Love activates an image of virtue within the lover, that has to be called back by memory ("têi mnēmēi" *Phaedrus* 253a3); contemplating this internalized image causes the lover to perfect herself (*Phaedrus* 250a–253c). The vision of the divine goodness and beauty external to the lover in the *Symposium,* guiding her steps up Diotima's ladder, resides within and returns from memory in the *Phaedrus* and in c.76.

Yet the second half of 76 radically undermines this idyllic vision of a transcendent Other who will heal the lover, seeing the desiring subject again as split, conflicted, unstable. The poem gathers together the imagery and vocabulary of erotic split outlined in cc.85 and 51:[42]

> quare cur tete iam amplius *excrucies?*
> quin tu animo offirmas atque istinc te ipse reducis
>   et dis invitis desinis esse miser?
> difficile est longum subito deponere amorem,
>   difficile est, verum hoc qua lubet efficias;
> una salus haec est, hoc est tibi pervincendum,
>   hoc facias, sive id non pote sive pote.
> o di, si vestrum est misereri, aut si quibus umquam
>   extremam iam ipsa in morte tulistis opem,
> me *miserum aspicite* et, si vitam puriter egi,
>   *eripite* hanc pestem perniciemque mihi,
> quae mihi *subrepens* imos ut *torpor in artus*
>   expulit ex omni pectore laetitias.
> non iam illud quaero, contra me ut diligat illa,
>   aut, quod non potis est, esse pudica velit:
> ipse valere opto et taetrum hunc deponere morbum.
>   o di, reddite mi hoc pro pietate mea.
>
> (76.10–26)

But why do you not strengthen your resolve and withdraw from that vile situation and cease to be wretched, when the gods are unwilling that you be so? It is hard to let go suddenly of a longstanding love; hard, but in truth, this is what you must do, insofar as you can. You have but one chance of salvation, that you conquer this thing; and you must do this, whether impossible or possible. Oh gods, if you have any pity, or if you have ever brought help to anyone at the final moment, even in the grip of death itself, look at me! Wretch that I am, if I have lived my life clean of stain, rip out this disease and this torture from me—which, creeping like a deadly languor into the marrow of my bones, has driven out all happiness from my heart. I do not now ask this, that she love me in return, or, what is not possible, that she should want to be good: I just want to heal and get rid of this foul disease. Oh gods, grant me this in return for my devotion to you!

As in 85, Catullus finds himself again on the cross (76.10). But 76 mirrors c.51 even more—as the words and phrases underlined in 76.19–21 show. Catullus describes his desire as an invasive force, and asks the gods to return him to a putative state of wholeness and autonomy he believes love has wrested from him.[43] The terms of his petition echo c.51—the poem in which Catullus experiences erotic invasion and splits into disorganized body parts:

> . . . *misero* quod omnis
> *eripit* sensus mihi: nam simul te,
> Lesbia, *aspexi*, nihil est super mi
> . . . .
> lingua sed *torpet*, tenuis *sub artus*
> flamma demanat . . .
>
> (51.5–10)

. . . which snatches the senses from me, wretch that I am: for as soon as I have looked upon you, Lesbia, nothing remains to me . . . . but the tongue is slow, a thin flame drips down beneath the limbs . . . .

Even further, *subrepens*—"creeping in from underneath"—recalls Sappho's crystallization of the classical view of desire as violent and invasive:

> Once again, love the limb-loosening shakes me,
> bittersweet, not-to-be-fought-against *creeping thing*
> [*orpeton*]
>
> (LP 130)

In 76, Catullus, like Sappho, feels the tremor even with eyes averted from the object. As he says, "I do not ask that she love me in return—I only ask that this sickness be removed from me." Yet the split cleaves the subject, even when he ceases reaching after the object.

Memory returns as a *topos* in c.68, which forms the focus of the next chapter. That *carmen maius* finds a way of resolving, without erasing, the amatory split in both subject and object.

5

The *Carmina Maiora:* Hercules and the Engineering of Desire

> There has fallen a splendid tear
> From the passion-flower at the gate.
> She is coming, my dove, my dear;
> She is coming, my life, my fate;
> The red rose cries, 'She is near, she is near;'
> And the white rose weeps, 'She is late;'
> The larkspur listens, 'I hear, I hear;'
> And the lily whispers, 'I wait.'
>
> She is coming, my own, my sweet;
> Were it ever so airy a tread,
> My heart would hear her and beat,
> Were it earth in an earthy bed;
> My dust would hear her and beat,
> Had I lain for a century dead;
> Would start and tremble under her feet,
> And blossom in purple and red.
> —Tennyson[1]

IN THIS CHAPTER, I propose to look at some of the *carmina maiora*—specifically, those longer poems that deal, directly or allegorically, with the Lesbia-Catullus affair. I shall discuss cc.63 (Attis), 64 (Peleus and Thetis), and 68 (the [M]Allius poem). I see the explication of c.68 as the goal toward which [M] are progressing in this chapter, and cc.63 and 64 primarily as steppingstones toward that goal. Cc.63 and 64 represent reprises of some of the topics we have broached in analyzing the *carmina minora*—topics such as troubling the defining borders of the subject, particularly those marking gender position and the closed certainty of phallic (self-) knowledge; and the text as inviting, while frustrating, unilateral construction. Cc.63 and 64 offer grounds for comparing the ways in which the longer Catullan narrative poems treat these topics. Up to this point in our discussion, we have explicated the topics broached not only within single poems, but using separate poems linked by verbal, metrical, and topical similarities. The *carmina maiora* are an important testing ground for our treatment of these issues. Do our working hypotheses still hold when the linkage between portions of the interpretive field is not a matter of the reader's choice? Cc. 63 and 64 will also set up issues that are peculiar to the *carmina maiora*—thus forming a bridge to c.68. C.68 is my "cap" for several reasons. It combines two representational approaches to the Lesbia affair—explicit, relatively realistic references, with allegorical-mythological representations. Its elaborate, nonlinear structure (the famous "Chinese boxes")[2] represents a narrative complexity greater than that of any other poem of the corpus. Finally, it is a text that insists upon its own problematic nature as a key to interpretation, as I will show. Günther Jachmann offered no hyperbole when he called c.68 the "Schibboleth des Catullinterpreten."[3]

Let us begin by looking at c.63 in comparison with c.51—a *carmen maius* and a *carmen minus*, respectively, that both focus on dissolution of the subject. We will then compare c.63 with c.11, a *carmen minus* that shares with 63 an interest in disturbing gender positions. To do so, we will need to bring the term *identity* back into sharp focus, alongside the looser concept of subjectivity, as a subset of the latter. By *identity* I understand (as discussed in chapter 1) the seeming cohesion of different facets of the subject—such as gender and knowledge—into a smooth alignment, a consistent "self." Illusory as it may be, identity and its synonyms provide a necessary vantage from which to trace the transformations and odd meldings of different agents in the *carmina maiora*. Attis' reflections on the effects of his castration, for example, proceed from someone who is certainly a subject: when he reviews his actions the morning after, he is anguished, but not psychotic. Yet he sees his experience as having fundamentally transformed *who he is*. To be rigorously faithful to the terms in which these poems are set out, we must make visible that sense of transformation under the term *identity*, as a function of Imaginary fixity, while also setting against it the more fluid assumptions of *subjectivity* that proceed from Symbolic heterogeneity and movement.

L'etranger(e)

In chapter 3 of this book, we looked at c.51 as exemplifying the transgression of psychic, physical, and poetic boundaries necessary to define the lover and the poem. C.51 contrasts the lover's disintegration with a godlike wholeness, impervious to desire, in Lesbia's auditor, who can listen to her "sweetly laughing again and again" and not, like Catullus, fracture under the force of desire pushed toward *jouissance* and the divine. Two radically different planes of being clash in this poem: the auditor's godlike impassivity parallels Diotima's analysis of divinity in the *Symposium* (202c). Desire does not affect the divine because the gods lack nothing, therefore can desire nothing; the phallus means nothing to Plato's gods. Human beings, on the other hand, define themselves—and desire, create, and strive after knowledge—all on the basis of their own limitations and their disruptive hunger for a token of the divine: vicarious immortality. Diotima sees confronting the divine as rapt tranquillity, but the *Phaedrus,* and Lacan's conceptually parallel account of *jouissance,* portray divine and human conjoined as a profoundly unsettling experience, a *mise en abîme* of all previous rules and procedures—even the very structure of one's life— verging on madness. C.51 posits Diotima's model of divine-human confrontation as a curious and inexplicable, distant phenomenon—how can the auditor maintain his stony tranquillity in the face of bliss? Yet all that is available to Catullus in 51 and in the *carmina minora* is to risk *mania* in facing divinity. Accordingly, the fourth strophe yields to fear over interest and retreats into cool contempt for any disturbance to phallic knowledge and self-definition.

I have recapped the discussion of c.51 in order to show, in brief, the confines within which the *carmina minora* of the Lesbia cycle operate and why the complacent sanctuary that rescues Catullus at the end of c.51 is systematically refused in the *carmina maiora*. Allusions to, and symbols of, gods and the divine state of being appear in the *carmina minora,* but subordinated to the premise that the Lesbia cycle records moments in a human love affair. While Jove's oracle appears in c.7, for example, Jove himself does not—and his oracle is an imaginative background to the focus of the poem, the infinite kisses of the lovers. By contrast, in the *carmina maiora* mythology lends Catullus greater latitude in which to explore con-

103

ceptual borderlines articulated in the contrast and rapprochement between the divine and human planes of being. Mythology transports us into the unfettered realm of fantasy, where encounters between the bounded and the boundless—the Symbolic and that which exceeds the Symbolic—and the traffic of desire with each, can be dramatized.

We can see the differences this entails by examining c.63 in order to trace the changes mythology allows in the treatment of problematized identity and disturbance of gender positions. From there we will branch out into other topics adduced in c.63, versions of which we have seen in the *carmina minora*—as, for example, geography as cultural iconography (comparable to geography's significance in c.11).[4]

C.63 combines the interests of cc.11 and 51 by emphasizing gender as a crucial parameter of the self; once disturbed, identity is put into question. Attis' emasculation tosses him between gender positions: the pronouns referring to him switch between masculine and feminine throughout the poem. Yet he has not clearly reenlisted with either gender. Rather, he is "notha mulier"—"a spurious woman" (63.27), neither truly male nor truly female but an indefinite *tertium quid*. He bewails his physical metamorphosis in terms that emphasize the confusion it entails:

> "*eg*one a mea remota haec ferar in nemora domo?
> patria, bonis, amicis, genitoribus abero?
> abero foro, palaestra, stadio et gyminasiis?
> *miser a miser, querendum est etiam atque etiam, anime.*
> quod enim genus figurae est, *ego* non quod obierim?
> *ego* mulier, *ego* adolescens, *ego* ephebus, *ego* puer,
> *ego* gymnasi fui flos, *ego* eram decus olei:
> *mihi* ianuae frequentes, *mihi* limina tepida,
> *mihi* floridis corollis redimita domus erat,
> linquendum ubi esset orto mihi sole cubiculum.
> *ego* nunc deum ministra et Cybeles famula ferar?
> *ego* Maenas, *ego* mei pars, *ego* vir sterilis ero?
> *ego* viridis algida Idae nive amicta loca colam?
> *ego* vitam agam sub altis Phrygiae columinibus,
> ubi cerva silvicultrix, ubi aper nemorivagus?
> iam iam dolet quod egi, iam iamque paenitet."
>
> (63.58–73)

"Shall I be borne into these woodlands, far removed from my home? Shall I be absent from my fatherland, my goods, my friends, my parents? absent from the marketplace, the wrestling ground, the racetrack and the sport-school? Oh my wretched, wretched soul/self—you/I must mourn again and again! What kind of shape is there, that I have not undergone? I, a woman, I have been a young man; I, a stripling; I, a boy; I was the flower of the athletes' hall, the ornament of the wrestling ground. My door was often visited, my doorstep body-warmed, my house was encircled with flowery wreaths, when, with the risen sun, I was obliged to quit my chambers. Shall I now be called the handmaiden and the houseslave of Cybele? Shall I be a Maenad—I who am a part of myself, I, a sterile man? Shall I dwell in the chilly places, wrapped in snow, of green Ida? Shall I live beneath the cliffs of Phrygia, where the doe dwells in the forest, where the wild boar wanders the glades? Now, yes, *now* I regret what I have done—now, *now*, it haunts me!"

Even grammar and syntax fail Attis, as they assert and disavow the coherence of the speaker. He repeats various forms of the first-person pronoun: "ego" and "mihi" dot almost every line, hysterically asserting the existence of an "I" at the very moment they deny it exists any longer. Attis can now only call himself "a part of myself" (69). His syntax mirrors his confusion by sliding ambiguously around subject positions. Who, for example, is "miser" in 63.61—Attis, or his *animus*? And in the absence of a "mihi" or "tibi" to this line, where the passage otherwise so generously distributes personal pronouns, which of the two must lament for the other?[5] The inadequacy of Attis' language to capture his situation highlights a conceptual insufficiency in the Symbolic, marked by *jouissance* and the feminine, that has reached out and claimed him.

Attis' complaint focuses upon the way in which his castration dislocates him from the positions that have defined his self in the past as opposed to the present. Geographical alienation matches alienation from his former identity. He will be absent from the civic spaces (60) that defined him as a youth ("I was the flower of the athletes' hall," 64), because he will dwell in the woodlands (58) and "the chilly places on green Ida" (70). He will no longer be a part of civic social relationships (63–64)—that which defines him as "what he is for the Other."[6] In particular he will no longer be defined by the desire of others as a *paidika*, a role he dwells on at length (65–67). His protean physical changes ("what kind of shape have I *not* undergone?" 62) tie identity to structure and social milieu rather than to abiding essence—but more importantly, see that social milieu as a fragile boundary against an outer darkness and unreasoning indistinction, where human beings live like beasts (71–72).[7]

Attis suffers this *jouissance*-like disintegration of self in approaching what is divine. His journey brings him from Greece to the forests of Ida, the realm of the goddess—a Dark Continent[8] indeed, that enfolds a mystery alien to everything he knows about human desire. Ida displaces his familiar home, encircled ("redimita," 66) by his lovers' wreaths, with "the dark places of the goddess, *encircled* by forest," ("opaca silvis *redimita* loca deae," 3). He proposed the journey to please the goddess:

> "agite ite ad alta, Gallae, Cybeles nemora simul,
> simul ite, Dindymenae dominae vaga pecora,
> aliena quae petentes velut exules loca
> sectam meam exsecutae duce me mihi comites
> rapidum salum tulistis truculentaque pelagi,
> et corpus evirastis Veneris nimio odio;
> *hilarate erae citatis erroribus animum.*"
>
> (63.12–18)

"Come, let's go together, Gallae, to the deep glades of Cybele, let's go at once, wandering cattle of the Dindymian mistress, you who, seeking strange places, just like exiles, have followed my path, I as leader, you my comrades; you who have endured the swift salt sea and the fierce deep, and who have emasculated your bodies out of excessive hatred of Venus' work; rejoice your mistress' heart with your hurried wanderings!"

The consequences make him the goddess' "handmaiden" for life (90).

But c.63 is more than a theoretical examination of self-disintegration. Attis' situation coincides with Catullus' own, as he constructs it in the Lesbia cycle. The figure of Attis extravagantly expands upon the icons of Catullus' suffering that dot the Lesbia cycle, but particularly upon his tortures in c.11. The last strophe of c.11 also translates the effect of mental alienation into physical distance: estranged from Lesbia, Catullus' love languishes on the outer limits of a field beyond Rome. Michael Putnam has pointed to other similarities between Attis and Catullus' self-portraits.[9] Attis suffers under the rule of a mistress portrayed as harsh and domineering; both he and Catullus are driven to madness under her influence.[10] Attis, too, was a "flower" ("gymnasi fui *flos*," 63.64) of young manhood before madness inspired by Cybele led him to castrate himself. Putnam sees the image of the flower cut down by the plow in 11.22–24 as referring to Catullus himself as well as his *amor;* the cutting plow correspondingly symbolizes Lesbia herself, in addition to her perceived indifference to Catullus. As Attis is physically castrated, so Catullus is psychically castrated. "Masculine Cybele deflowers and gelds. . . . Similar energies are imputed to Lesbia who causes loins to burst and 'touches' flowers. It is Lesbia to whom all force is imputed at the poem's conclusion."[11]

106

When we align the erotic dynamics of cc.51 and 11 with c.63, we can see that the *carmen maius* imaginatively bridges the gap between the contradictory images of Lesbia presented in the two *carmina minora*. We addressed attempts to suture that gap in the last chapter, where we spoke of the epigrams as poems that articulate relationships between these images. However, the epigrams perceive Lesbia as in truth either the Whore of 11 or the supernaturally desirable Woman of 51. Looking back on any one moment, Catullus may believe he was deceived about her, but not that *she* really was both Goddess and Castrating Monster at once. C.63, because it operates in the realm of mythology, can combine the Lesbia of 11 with the Lesbia of 51 in one figure at one time—in Cybele. Cybele is all the terrifying things Putnam points to as characteristic of c.11's Lesbia; she is also a goddess whose maddening attraction sweeps away every familiar landmark of a young man's identity. Cybele is *jouissance féminine* personified.

Back to the Future

Peleus, as Thetis' betrothed in c.64, also aligns with Catullus the lover, though at first glance he appears to contradict c.63's pessimistic view of divine and human encounters.[12] Paul Harkins[13] notes that Catullus loves a woman he regards as a *diva* (68.70), as Peleus loves the goddess Thetis. Thetis does not reject marriage with a mortal ("tum Thetis humanos non despexit hymenaeos," 64.20), though we know from Pindar[14] that she was sought by both Zeus and Poseidon. Likewise, Lesbia often tells Catullus that she prefers him to Jove and would wed him in preference to Jove (70.1–2; 72.1–2). But more important for our discussion is Peleus' role in a *carmen maius* that, like 63, meditates extensively on relations between gods and humans. The concept of aboriginal rupture, whose ramifications we have previously traced within the subject, between subjects, and between gender positions, as the common source of anguish and desire, now threads its way between mortal and immortal like a poisonous stain. C.63 focuses primarily on spatially defined and defining scissions between male and female bodies, between the *polis* and the wild places across the sea. C.64, on the other hand, concentrates on time as a boundary separating the mortal and immortal realms. In 64, the passage of time itself brings about a deterioration in the mortal order that irrevocably splits it from the divine order.

Time plays another role in 64: dislocations in temporal sequence complicate the narrative.[15] By contrast with 63, which follows a single story line in linear sequence, c.64 embraces two stories: the "outer," framing narrative of Peleus and Thetis and the "inner," framed narrative of Theseus and Ariadne. Time in the outer narrative, though interrupted by the inner narrative, moves in linear sequence; the inner narrative jumps between past, present, and future. The way in which sections of the poem impose atemporal sequences on events insists, even more sharply than in 63, on alternatives to linear construction of the poem. Sequences connected by position or by subject matter gloss one another, though separated by the text and by strict temporal construction. For example, in his address to the heroes of the first ship, *Argo* (64.22–30), Catullus says:

> o *nimis optato* saeclorum tempore nati
> heroes, salvete!
>
> (64.22–3)

Oh, heroes born in an era of time *nimis optato*, hail!

How is one to take "nimis optato" in this line—as "very much wished-for" or "too much, excessively wished-for" age? The decision demands a choice between an age of heroes that either was truly heroic or was overrated. The dilemma is not trivial in that determining the precise tone in which c.64 presents the age of heroes is a much-discussed issue in criticism of this poem.[16] A first reading need not see the line as at all problematic: Catullus simply praises the age of heroes. However, comparing this passage with other passages recounting the results of heroes' journeys across the seas—such as 64.52–9 (Theseus abandoning Ariadne) or 64.238–45 (Theseus causing his father's death by forgetting to change his sails' color) or 64.343–70 (Achilles at Troy) pessimistically colors the line. Theseus is benighted and faithless, Achilles murderous: as exemplars of the heroic age, they cast doubt on its worth as an ideal.

I do not claim that this kind of intratextual reading of comparative passages is absent from a linear narrative such as c.63. I assume that Catullus' audience are careful readers, and that they supplement first readings with rereadings that construe motif patterns as well as linear sequence. Rather, in c.64 the text more openly draws the reader's attention to its own artful manipulation of narrative sequence—which makes the structuring of data, as well as the data themselves, a more prominent issue in interpretation. The poem insists on its own rereading and reconstruction in various patterns outside temporal sequence in order fully to elucidate its significance. This is the issue of construing "fragmented narrative" realized within

The *Carmina Maiora*

a unified text—a realization we will see taken to extremes in the far more intricate temporal dislocations of c.68.

Temporal dislocation in c.64 makes time a problematic boundary *between* the different sections of the poem, where any moment from past, present, or future may follow any other in the narrative. But time also marks, and shifts, problematic boundaries *within* various sections. The marriage between Peleus and Thetis can be seen as an attempt on Jove's part to maintain time as a border separating mortal from immortal. Moreover, mythological iconography suggests the imposition of other time frames upon the Heroic Age and at the same time undermines the traditional value accorded those time frames. Let us examine in more detail how the poem constructs these complications of time.

Jove's desire for Thetis threatens to set time in motion for the immortals. Jove gives up his love because she is fated to bear a child greater than the father.[17] According to Hesiod, Zeus's father Kronos toppled Zeus's grandfather, Ouranos; Zeus in turn overthrows Kronos.[18] If Thetis were to bear a child superior to Jove, capable of overcoming his father, the succession of generations that Jove's assumption of the throne had stopped would begin again. Time, as measured by the succession of younger generation to the place occupied by the older, would operate again for the immortals.

Yet when Peleus takes Jove's place as the lover of Thetis and prospective father of her fateful child, time begins to move anyway. One can see this happening on the very day Peleus and Thetis marry and formalize Jove's yielding generative power to Peleus. Time begins to flow backward to parody the Golden Age—the age before Jove wrested power from Saturn.[19]

> rura colit nemo, mollescunt colla iuvencis,
> non humilis curvis purgatur vinea rastris,
> non glebam prono convellit vomere taurus,
> non falx attenuat frondatorum arboris umbram;
> squalida desertis robigo infertur aratris.
>
> (64.38–42)

No one cultivates the countryside, the necks of the yoke-team grow soft, the low-lying vinerows are not purged with the curved hoe, the bull does not overturn the clods with the deep-driven plowshare, the scythe of the pruners does not thin the shade of the tree, filthy rust invades the deserted plows.

Works and Days tells us that Jove invented the necessity of work for human beings; before that, when Kronos reigned, no one needed to

109

bother.[20] Because everyone has deserted the countryside to attend Peleus and Thetis' wedding, the fields fall into Golden Age disuse; no one forces them or the animals into service.

However, their state ominously parodies the Golden Age rather than offering a true return to paradise: some things suffer more than they benefit from the hiatus. The vines are not "cleansed" of weeds by the hoes, "filthy rust" invades the plows. Catullus prefaces his description of the dazzling wedding feast with a picture of decay wrought by time—a *memento mori*.

The description of the details surrounding the marriage transfers the projected consequences of a union between Jove and Thetis into the context of the union between Peleus and Thetis. Within Peleus' house, the coverlet enfolding his marriage bed tells the story of a son who destroys his father: forgetful of Aegeus' instructions, Theseus causes the old man to leap to his death. Moreover, the Parcae sing the wedding song (rather than the Muses, as older versions of the legend have it)[21]—goddesses who measure out the extent of mortal life. Their refrain ("currite ducentes subtegmina, currite, fusi"—"run, you spindles, and draw out the threads of life") and the content of their song emphasize time's motion: they sketch the prospective history of the marriage, from the morning after the wedding night to its offspring's (Achilles') maturity.

The movement of time will bring about a moral deterioration in the mortal realm matching the physical deterioration surrounding Peleus' house. Achilles' maturity will be a career of bloodshed and destruction: he even claims the life of an innocent woman (Polyxena) after he dies. The bloody description of his heroic career foreshadows the carnage characteristic of humanity's postlapsarian state, so that the distinction between the age of heroes and the reprobate present becomes less than clear.[22] C.64's vision of the Trojan War's focal figure precedes a view of the deterioration of mortal life, and its increasing distance from the immortal realms.

> sed postquam tellus scelere est imbuta nefando
> iustitiamque omnes cupida de mente fugarunt,
> perfudere manus fraterno sanguine fratres,
> destitit extinctos natus lugere parentes,
> optavit genitor primaevi funera nati,
> liber ut innuptae poteretur flore novercae,
> ignaro mater substernens se impia nato
> impia non verita est divos scelerare penates.
> omnia fanda nefanda malo permixta furore
> iustificam nobis mentem avertere deorum.

110

quare nec talis dignantur visere coetus,
nec se contingi patiuntur lumine claro.

(64.397–408)

but after the earth was deep-dyed in wicked crime and everyone chased justice
out of their greedy minds, brothers stained their hands with the blood of
brothers; the son refused to mourn for his dead parents; the father longed
for the death of his firstborn son, so that he might freely enjoy the favors of
a virgin stepmother;[23] the impious mother lies with her own unwitting son—
she is so gone in wickedness, she does not fear to offend the holy household
gods. All these things—wicked hopelessly mixed up with good by this evil
passion—turned away the mind of the gods, who establish justice for us.
Wherefore they did not deign to gaze upon such human trafficking, nor for
themselves to be touched by the bright light of day.

C.64 looks much like the Platonic aetiological history of an individual
soul and its desires mapped onto human history: each narrative begins in
communion with the gods—a happiness of which we have always been
robbed before we knew we had it, and to which we long to return. But
if we scrutinize that history of lost utopia through a psychoanalytic lens,
the vertiginously shifting boundaries of time and ethos in c.64 become
more intelligible. C.64 is a narrative constructed along the principles of
the *fort/da* game, as a series of retrospective adjustments in reading our
being and our desires. Ernst's game with his wooden reel "rereads" his
past to construct a narrative of a fall from grace and thereby to supplant
logical priority with temporal priority: out of the division and lack repre-
sented by *fort* emerges the unity and plenitude of the (lost) *da*. Insofar as
the *fort/da* game models the system of causality that governs all subjects,
its retroactive mode makes nonsense of temporal boundaries. Like Ernst,
we all construct a past congenial, if melancholy, to recall: thus our *present*
creates our *past* as a retrospective narrative to account for who we are
and what we want. In c.64, the Platonic hope of lost paradise, and the
psychoanalytic suspicion of that illusion, jostle one another constantly.
While the reader is invited to align the time of Peleus' wedding with
the Golden Age, the inconsistencies between the two force a rethinking,
readjustment, and reinterpretation of that alignment. The environmental
deterioration attendant on Peleus' wedding parallels the moral deteriora-
tion leading up to the present, inviting assimilation between the two images
rather than contrast. What is offered as a clear distinction between heroic
past and fallen present blurs and nearly disappears under the force of that
rereading.

111

And what relevance has this to the affair with Lesbia? Clearly c.64, like c.63, allegorically predicts horrific consequences from union between a mere man and a divinized woman—and more, questions the temporal logic behind the narrative the *made* her divine, and the past paradisal. But a ruse unraveled can always be woven again, if it supports a necessary fiction; no subject can exist without a history, however specious. So when we turn to c.68, that also plays with time, with conceptual, narrative, and temporal divisions, and with misalignments that force rereading, we will first examine how these features trouble the interpretation of Catullus' history. But we will move toward a disenchanted synthesis—a synthesis that weaves a past Catullus can live with, and *create* with, in open-eyed acceptance of its fiction.

Enigma Variations

C.68 pulls together the disparate threads traced thus far in the book: the parameters of "personhood" disrupted (gender, identity, psychic integration); narrative sequence problematized; meaning hopelessly gliding beyond the reader's secure grasp. The poem advertises itself as an intricate enigma—not the least of whose problems is the name (or names) of its subject and addressee. But even if we consider the confusion between "Allius" and "Mallius" to be the fruit of a precarious manuscript tradition, the poem still presents problems—the solution to which, as I shall show, requires reference to the whole of the Lesbia cycle.

Like c.64, c.68's many-layered structure realizes a version of fragmented narrative within a unified text. And like 64's disturbingly deteriorated vision of the Golden Age, inconsistencies in 68's mythological iconography insist upon the rereading and realigning of the text to arrive at an exhaustive (if not unambiguous) explication. That insistence upon rereading we have seen before, in the epigrams, though motivated by grammar rather than iconography (as in the irreducibly ambiguous initial lines of cc.72 and 109). Both iconographic and structural misalignment in c.68 point to another level of meaning that works against the poem's own overt declarations.

In particular, the rhetorical figures structuring the poem become an issue—and one that puts into question as well the bounds defining its dramatis personae. Because of the problematic alignments to which I have alluded, lines of identity, gender, and time as distinguishing mortal from immortal, waver and shift.

But whereas such fluidity has proven an irremediable *mise en abîme*

112

of the person and of the human order in cc.63 and 64, c.68 develops the bare suggestion of c.2: that troubling gender divisions leads to a new Adam, who leans upon the conceptual fluidity of the subject—to a new equilibrium (however fictive) in being. In c.2, we spoke of Catullus' figurative fusion with Atalanta as miming the attributes of both gender positions, to render Catullus a metaphorical hermaphrodite. C.68 expands on that vision of creative autonomy, figured as the generous embrace of both sexes in one body, in the image of Hercules that anchors the poem's last section— the hero "super-male and feminine," in Nicole Loraux's richly suggestive phrase.[24] In c.68, Catullus imagines male appropriation of female sexuality more ambitiously than anywhere else in his corpus, fashioning an icon (Hercules) of male procreative autonomy. As such, the poem parallels Plato's construction of Diotima as (David Halperin argues)[25] an ambiguous "feminine" mouthpiece for a concept of sexuality apparently incorporating the feminine but implicitly modeled on the male.

Let us look at the problems c.68 sets up, and the way in which it addresses these, in detail. To do this we must address a textual problem— are we dealing with two poems here or one? I believe that 68a and 68b are a unified poem.[26] Let us consider what kind of reading that would entail.

I have referred to this poem as an enigma, and a self-conscious one at that. If we assume that 68a and 68b somehow belong together—taking as evidence the train of themes repeated and echoed between one and the other section—then we face an immediately glaring problem of reconciliation: who is the subject, and who the addressee, of this poem? Are they the same, or different men? The manuscripts present us with several variant names: Ma(l)lius for 68a; Allius in 68b (with a desperate correction to "Manllius" in the margins of O). Metrical evidence argues for two distinct gentile names, one beginning with a consonant and one with a vowel. Moreover, the situations of Mallius and Allius are entirely different. Allius receives 68b in return for past favors ("pro multis . . . officiis," 150), whereas Catullus explicitly apologizes that 68a does not sufficiently discharge his grateful obligation as guest-friend to Mallius ("hospitis officium," 12). Allius is happy in love (155) whereas Mallius is tormented by love—whether due to a temporary or permanent separation (5–6).

As we are supposing, just for the moment, that these two sections somehow belong together, what kinds of problems in reading do they present? The reader must find a way to align 68a with 68b—and the ingenuity of many has been expended on just that. Perhaps Mallius, despite all evidence to the contrary, is really Allius—as some have tried to assert, speculating that behind the names lay an address to Allius as "mi Alli."[27] Perhaps the poem *about* Allius is an old poem dredged up to fulfill the request to comfort a bereaved lover; it does, after all, speak about several bereavements. Perhaps the poem is composed for the occasion, to show Mallius that his problems are small by comparison.

In any case, the two names present us with problems of aligning personae in the poem. We must also construe the thread of artistic logic guiding this poem: How does the thought of 68b fit the thought of 68a, so that we may articulate a meaningful narrative relationship between the one and the other?

Of course, we could simply cut the Gordian knot and assume that these are two entirely unrelated poems, joined as the accident of a problematic manuscript tradition. But we shall see that this does not, in fact, solve the problems of reading inherent to each section of the poem, and that the same puzzles of identity and alignment present themselves in separatist as well as unitarian readings. I have therefore called the poem a self-conscious enigma: no matter how, or whether, one divides it up, the problems of how precisely to construe this narrative remain. For that reason (among others) I incline to belief that 68a belongs with 68b, and that the refractory elements of each are a principled textual strategy rather than the lamentable evidence of a careless manuscript tradition. Still, my argument claims authority, not on the basis of any putative intention on Catullus' part, but rather on the strength of the reading such an assumed unity can produce— on the reading's cogency, coherence, and tactful preservation of the text's phenomena.

We must first ask ourselves, what is the effect of the name and theme complications, given that neither separatist nor unitarian readings can evade them? The complexity forces us, as readers, to read, reread, and reconstrue the text repeatedly—just as c.64 does. Reconstruction, forced by the text's failure to align smoothly when read the way it tells us to read it, yields another text, another layer superimposed upon the explicit frame of reference. The insistence upon a counterorder in the text is much more systematic and structurally intricate than mere ambiguity. And this doubleness refuses to be reduced to simplicity. As in our reading of the elegiacs, we reach a point of *aporia*, where one signifying chain refuses to enfold another smoothly. In that paradox lies the true richness of the text.[28]

Let me take 68a as a starting point for discussing the focal concerns of this poem (or poems). In my discussion, I will view the poem both from the unitarian and separatist perspectives, so that no argument depends solely on evidence that assumes a unified text.

Chain Mail

Catullus frames 68a as a response to a letter from someone I shall continue to call Mallius, as a reasonable compromise among textual variants.[29] Mallius has recently lost his love ("desertum in lecto caelibe," 6); he cannot sleep and he takes no delight in the poetry of older writers (7–8). He requests poems (and possibly more, though precisely what is uncertain)[30] of Catullus—"muneraque et Musarum hinc petis et Veneris" (10). He also chides Catullus about the poet's own love life, which in Mallius' estimation is suffering (whether one takes him to refer to the provincial puritanism of Verona or to Lesbia's other love affairs in Rome).[31] Catullus replies that he cannot comply with the request for poetry, and that he cares little for his love life at the moment. His brother has died recently; his death spells the end of Catullus' family line. Grief over this misfortune has dispelled Catullus' joys, not only in love, but in poetry.

> multa satis lusi: non est dea nescia nostri,
> quae dulcem curis miscet amaritiem.
> *sed totum hoc studium luctu fraterna mihi mors*
> *abstulit.* o misero frater adempte mihi,
> tu mea tu moriens fregisti commoda, frater,
> tecum una tota est nostra sepulta domus;
> omnia tecum una perierunt gaudia nostra,
> quae tuus in vita dulcis alebat amor.
> cuius ego interitu tota de mente fugavi
> *haec studia atque omnes delicias animi.*
> quare, quod scribis Veronae turpe Catullo
> esse, quod hic quisquis de meliore nota
> frigida deserto tepefactet membra cubili,
> id, Malli,[32] *non est turpe, magis miserum est.*
> ignosces igitur si, quae mihi luctus ademit,
> *haec tibi non tribuo munera, cum nequeo.*
> nam, quod scriptorum non magna est copia apud me,
> hoc fit, quod Romae vivimus: illa domus,
> illa mihi sedes, illic mea carpitur aetas
>
> (17–35)

I have played around quite a bit; the goddess is not unknown to me who mixes sweet bitterness with cares. But all this pursuit my brother's death has taken from me in my grief. Oh, brother stolen from wretched me—you, you, brother, wrecked all my comforts when you died, and with you our whole house is buried at once; all my joys, which your love nurtured in life, in a single blow perished along with you! Since his burial I have chased all these

115

pursuits out of my mind, and all intellectual allurements. Wherefore, regarding the fact that you write "it is shameful for Catullus to be at Verona, because in that/this place every distinguished person warms his cold limbs in a deserted bed;" that, Mallius, is not shameful, more a matter of passing regret. You will forgive me if I do not give you the gifts that mourning has taken from me, because I cannot. For there is no great abundance of writings where I am, due to this: I live at Rome. That is my home, that is my territory, there I live my life.

From the immediate context of "haec studia atque omnes delicias animi," the phrase evidently refers to poetry as well as to lovemaking.[33] Catullus mentions two points from Mallius' letter—the request for poems and a glance at the poet's love life. He addresses the effect of his brother's death on each of these points separately. Venus is not unknown to him, but his brother's death has taken away his interest in this pursuit ("hoc studium," 19). But in 68.26 he specifically expands the summary of effects to include "omnes delicias animi" destroyed. *Deliciae* means, essentially, "allurement." That could cover the sense of "amours"—but would leave *animi* oddly unexplained. Why "amours of the mind"? And if we take *animus* as meaning, more generally, "intellectual seat of the emotions," that makes Catullus redundantly explain (after 19–20) why he no longer cares about his own love life, yet still leaves him without a reason for not sending Mallius the requested poems. C.68.33–36 cannot be the sole reason for his inability: Catullus can write a poem without a library, and nothing in Mallius' reported request specifies a learned Hellenistic exercise (though if this poem is his requital, he got one anyway, books or no books). Catullus says, rather, that Mallius must not ask such gifts "a misero" (14), and then launches into an account of his brother's death to explain why he is wretched. To plunge then into the bathos of saying that he cannot send a poem solely because he forgot his books at home would be ludicrous. Rather, he specifies that he has no abundance of previously written material with him (whether his own or from other writers), so he cannot even send Mallius an *old* poem.

Furthermore, c.65 specifies that one of the effects his brother's death had on Catullus was to make him temporarily incapable of writing poetry:

> Etsi me assiduo confectum cura dolore
> sevocat a doctis, Hortale, virginibus,
> nec potis est dulcis Musarum expromere fetus
> mens animi, tantis fluctuat ipsa malis—

116

namque mei nuper Lethaeo gurgite fratris
pallidulum manans alluit unda pedem,
Troia Rhoeteo quem subter litore tellus
ereptum nostris obterit ex oculis.

(65.1–8)

Yet care has called me away from the learned maidens, Hortalus (me, afflicted
with unceasing pain) and the thought of my mind is not able to bring forth
the sweet fruits of the Muses, because it tosses upon such great troubles—
for just now the wave issuing from the Lethean pool washes the pale, dear
foot of my brother, whom the Trojan earth beneath the Rhoetean shore
grinds down, snatched from my sight.

For these reasons, *deliciae animi* must refer to poetry as one of the
"intellectual delights" his brother's death took from him. Loss, in 68a,
threatens the power to create; given Diotima's pronouncement that cre-
ation (*poiēsis*) through "pregnancy" is our only hope of immortality, loss
threatens that hope. Accordingly, Catullus represents his brother's death
not just as the end of an individual life at a particular moment in time but
as an end to collective future expectations of survival. His brother's death
spells the end of his family line, which has now lost the potential to survive
into future time by creating heirs: "with you our whole house is buried
at once" (22).

Catullus experiences exactly the kind of profound *aporia* against which
Diotima ranges her *scala amoris*—incapacity following the loss of an object
perceived as unique, irreplaceable—a problem Aristophanes' aboriginal
"other halves" pose but cannot solve. (The *Phaedrus* prevaricates the issue
of loss by assuming that ideal philosophical couples live, die, love and stop
loving as one.[34]) Incapacity from bereavement can be viewed, from the
psychoanalytic perspective, as a block to metonymy, to the endless substitu-
tion of objects for one another—a substitutability based (as Diotima would
concur) not on the objects' adequacy but on their *in*adequacy. No object
can grant the subject Absolute Subjectivity; none can replace the Forms.
Therefore, any object will do—though Diotima's agenda designedly de-
scribes a sequence of substitutions that leads eventually to perception of
the Beautiful Itself, while no such *telos* animates the psychoanalytic project.

Fortunately, as Diotima is the only one offering a solution to this
dilemma, her *scala amoris* can be translated without violence into psychoan-
alytic terms: her emphasis on signification over physical gratification in
assessing the mechanics of desire is uncannily Lacanian. Diotima's picture
of *poiēsis* represents creation punctuating a signifying chain: the philoso-

pher-lover brings forth "beautiful discourse" appropriate to the level of the ascent she has attained (with a beautiful body, 210a7–8; a beautiful soul, 210c1–3; in contemplation of the "wide sea of beauty," 210c7–d4). But she does *not* make love: a truer understanding of her desire reconfigures its goal from what a long Greek erotic tradition regarded as *the* goal of love—sex.[35] And but for the culmination face to face with the Beautiful Itself, she never clings to an instance of beauty—her necessary medium of discourse—so as to be end-stopped. She patiently consents to lose and replace her objects repeatedly. In fact, Martha Nussbaum has argued,[36] the various stages of consolidation in the ascent—in which an instance of beauty represents a class of beauty, thus loses its power to detain the philosopher in further admiration—are an *askēsis* specifically directed against excessive attachment to any particular beautiful object. Excessive attachment would end the metonymy that, by allowing one object of desire to substitute for another freely, makes Diotima's ladder work.

After the loss of his brother, Catullus experiences attachment to an object, and loss of that object, so radical that it temporarily abolishes the very possibility of metonymy; his delight in words, in writing poetry, cannot work to assuage the loss by substituting for the brother-as-object. As we shall see, c.68 responds to this problem with a solution that draws in equal measure upon the *Symposium* and the *Phaedrus*, seen through the lens of psychoanalysis: upon Diotima's emphasis on discourse as *the* appropriate emphasis and result of desire; on her appropriation of female reproduction for an autonomous male model; and, finally, upon the *Phaedrus'* reliance on anamnesis to redeem love from mundane stasis in possessing the object.

The death of Catullus' brother also threatens to rob the poet of his immortality, as it robbed his house of its heirs. Because he cannot write poems while grief-stricken, loss threatens to take from him the only *poiēsis* that will perpetuate *his* name after his death. In poems alone resides his hope, as his complete despair for the *domus* upon his brother's death indicates. Presumably Catullus was capable of marrying and having children, had he so wished to direct his creative energies—but he does not. His *domus* now is Rome, where *multae capsulae scriptorum* locate the center of his life. As poems are his sole creative focus and claim to a *Nachleben*, the problem of c.68 is to overcome all obstacles to the signifying chain's continual self-renewal, because poetry carries all the burden of immortality.

nam, quod scriptorum non magna est copia apud me,
hoc fit, quod Romae vivimus: illa *domus*,

illa mihi sedes, illic mea carpitur aetas;
    huc una ex multis capsula me sequitur.

(33–36)

For, there is no great abundance of writings where I am, due to this: I live
at Rome. That is my home, that is my territory, there I live my life. Only
one book-box of many attends me here.

If we take 68a as the introduction to 68b, then the former pinpoints
a problem central to the latter. C.68a broods on the problem of loss,
especially as it threatens creation, and on how to overcome that threat.
But even if we insist that no relation exists between the one section and
the other, immortality, loss in love, and the effect of loss on creative power
open 68b as well.

The Postman Always Rings Twice

C.68b expresses thanks for the help of another man, Allius, who put
at Catullus and Lesbia's disposal a house in which to hold their trysts. The
poem opens with a prayer for poetic immortality. Catullus prays that his
poem may make widely known Allius' "helpful deeds" ("officiis," 42), so
that even when dead, Allius' fame will grow, and his (Allius') name will
not be forgotten. Since Catullus' *carta* shall effect this, Catullus' own name
must necessarily be immortalized as well (especially since he takes the
trouble to name himself in the poem). As yet, though, the vision of
immortality here offered is imperfect: it juxtaposes negative images of
forgetfulness and desuetude against positive ones of growing fame:

Non possum reticere, deae, qua me Allius in re
    iuverit aut quantis iuverit officiis,
ne fugiens saeclis obliviscentibus aetas
    illius hoc caeca nocte tegat studium;
sed dicam vobis, vos porro dicite multis
    milibus et facite haec carta loquatur anus.
. . . .
notescatque magis mortuus atque magis,
nec tenuem texens sublimis aranea telam
    in deserto Alli nomine opus faciat.

(41–50)

I cannot be silent, goddesses, about the way in which Allius helped me in
this affair, and how many were the kindnesses with which he helped me, lest
time fleeing along the corridors of the forgetful ages should cover up his

119

eager assistance in blind night; but I shall tell it to you, and you disseminate it to many thousands and make sure that this page speaks when it is old . . . . and may he, when dead, grow more and more well known—lest a spider, spinning its slender web under the rafters, should weave its work over the neglected name of Allius.

However, a simile immediately follows this prayer mixed of despair and hope, hinting at new hope and new life evolving from destructive passions and attachment to mortal objects in the ensuing poem. Catullus juxtaposes two images in drawing a portrait of his early frenzied and frustrated passion for Lesbia. First his burning passion is like a scalding-hot spring, obviously sterile and painfully hot:

> cum tantum arderem quantum Trinacria rupes
> lymphaque in Oetaeis Malia Thermopylis,
> maesta neque assiduo tabescere lumina fletu
> cessarent tristique imbre madere genae
>
> (53–56)

at that time, I burned just as much as the Trinacrian cliff and the Malian water in Oetaean Thermopylae, nor did my mourning eyes cease to languish with constant weeping, nor to run with sad moisture on my cheeks

But then his tears are like a cool stream surrounded by green life and offering refreshment *from* excessive heat to a weary traveller:

> qualis in aerii perlucens vertice montis
>   rivus muscoso prosilit e lapide,
> qui cum de prona praeceps est valle volutus,
>   per medium densi transit iter populi,
> dulce viatori lasso in sudore levamen,
>   cum gravis exustos aestus hiulcat agros
>
> (57–62)[37]

just as a clear stream on the top of a lofty mountain leaps from the mossy stone, a stream that rolls headlong down its sloping bed, its path crossing through the middle of a densely populated land, a sweet refreshment for the traveler in his exhausted sweat, when the heavy heat splits the blasted fields.

The development from sterile stream to life-giving stream of water parallels 68a's movement from a concentration on loss and separation in love, and consequent creative impasse, to creativity protected from such vicissitudes (figured by the *multae capsulae scriptorum*).[38]

Are these things problems in 68b, if we do *not* read it in the light of 68a? Yes—and that is apparent from the moment Catullus launches into his complex train of similes describing Lesbia arriving at the tryst house.

> quo mea se molli candida diva pede
> intulit et trito fulgentem in limine plantam
> innixa arguta constituit solea,
> coniugis ut quondam flagrans advenit amore
> Protesilaeam Laodamia domum
> inceptam frustra, nondum cum sanguine sacro
> hostia caelestis pacificasset eros.
>
> (70–76)

> where my shining-white goddess betook herself on her delicate foot and, resting her shiny-pale sole in its creaking sandal on the worn threshhold, she stood for a moment—just as Laodamia, burning with love, once came to the house of Protesilaus, begun in vain, because a victim had not yet appeased heaven's lords with consecrated blood.

Catullus compares Lesbia to Laodamia arriving at the house of Protesilaus as his bride. But Laodamia brings with her a story peculiarly burdened with separation, death, and an end to (sexual and artistic) creative power.[39] The Trojan War takes Protesilaus from her: he is killed (says Homer) as he leaps on the beach of Troy, far in advance of all his men.[40] *Domus incepta frustra*, like "domos hēmitelēs" in the Iliadic passage, carries a double sense: that the couple is childless, and their dwelling place unfinished.[41]

The separation of Laodamia and Protesilaus, and his subsequent death, result in a double creative failure. The couple does not produce an heir— thus not renewing the life of the *domus* nor continuing their own lives by passing life on to their flesh and blood. Nor, because of the separation, can Protesilaus complete an artistic creation he had begun: the architectural *domus*. Separation and loss resulting in the *domus incepta frustra* thus connects again (or anew) 68a's links among loss of a loved one, of sexual and artistic creative power, and of a chance to immortalize oneself.

C.68b (91–96) emphasizes the connection between Laodamia's and Protesilaus' history with Catullus' own personal concerns by mirroring, nearly unchanged, the lament for his brother's death from 68a. The 68b lines echo the Greek myth's motif of the *domus* brought to an end by death; once again his brother's death results in "our house buried" ("nostra sepulta domus," 94 [= 22]). But here Catullus expands his account of the brother's death so that it parallels more closely Laodamia's loss of Protesi-

121

laus. Like Protesilaus, the brother died in Troy, far from one who loved him:

> quem nunc tam longe non inter nota sepulcra
> nec prope cognatos compositum cineres,
> sed Troia obscena, Troia infelice sepultum
> detinet extremo terra aliena solo.
>
> (97–100)

he whom a strange land holds fast now, so far away, at the end of the world, not laid away among familiar tombs nor close to the ashes of his kin, but buried in unhappy Troy, barren Troy.

The juxtaposition of myth and personal history, so that each begins to resemble the other, intertwines the concerns of both not only here but throughout the poem. On the one hand, we have loss, separation, and loss of creative power connected to *sexual* love between Laodamia and Protesilaus; and on the other, all these same things connected to *fraternal* love. By joining the two with a thread of repeated motives, Catullus creates a unified problematic focused on loss in love and its consequences, whatever the nature of that love may be.[42]

The further development of the Laodamia simile will make this clearer. For now, we must rehearse in brief some of the parallel details that make the link between separation, loss, and creation sketched in the Laodamia-Protesilaus myth as applicable to the affair with Lesbia as to the loss of Catullus' brother. The paradoxical terms in which the poem represents Lesbia indicate some of the reasons that poems, not children, offer Catullus a chance at immortality. C.68 surrounds Lesbia with a train of metaphors and similes that portray her as a marriage partner and thus as one who promises offspring, who could revive the *sepulta domus*. She is, as we noted, compared to Laodamia coming as a bride to the house of her new husband. Moreover, Catullus envisions Lesbia arriving at the tryst house accompanied by Cupid, dressed in bridal yellow, swinging a torch—the customary gesture at Roman wedding ceremonies (133–34).[43] Lesbia, whose desire Catullus represents as encompassing multiple lovers, plays Jove to Catullus' Juno: like the goddess with her husband, he endures the "rare thefts" of his beloved (136).

And therein lies the frustration of Lesbia's promise: Catullus contravenes his own construction of her with disingenuous excuses. Her father did not lead her to me on his right hand, he reminds himself; whatever she gives to me she steals from the bosom of her *vir* (143–46). Furthermore, she has other lovers (135–36). A third point always intervenes in 68's depictions of relationships, some representation of a barrier between those who love. For Laodamia and Protesilaus—as for Catullus and his brother—it is Troy; for Catullus and Lesbia, it is the rivals.

Thus the schism we have repeatedly mapped between Catullus and Lesbia, insofar as they assume the positions of Man and Woman, now divides Catullus and his brother as well. The poem's diction and imagery (as I shall show) relegate the brother to the position of Woman. Memory elevates him to the courtly-love position of unavailable perfection occupied by Lesbia in c.51, and much of c.68. The brother's exalted distancing makes it clear that c.68 depicts less the failings of this or that particular object than a structural failure in love, to which even the adored brother is subject.

Changing the Subject

Given the relationship sketched in our discussion of the brother's death on the one hand, and Laodamia and Protesilaus on the other, between loss of love and of creative power, 68 at this point looks as bleak as 63 and 64. Those *carmina maiora* respectively end in sterility and the unleashing of a destructive force (Achilles); if now even his brother can fail him, what hope remains for Catullus?. Yet toward the end of 68, a simile expanding on the poem's central organizing topos—Laodamia's love—turns around the destruction of the *domus:* an old man gazes lovingly on his only grandson and only heir (68.119–24). How do we arrive at that vision, and realize the program of movement from sterility to the nurturing of life indicated in 68b's opening water imagery?

I have emphasized the problem's articulation in terms of loss and death, predicated on human limits in space and time. Much of the poem's imagery focuses upon spatial separation as loss and frustration and upon crossing a separating boundary as gain and fulfillment. Laodamia loses Protesilaus when he travels to Troy (84–86); Catullus grieves that Troy entombs his brother "so far away, at the end of the world" ("tam longe," 97; "extremo . . . solo," 100); Greece sends her youth far away to Troy, where they end up as "bitter ash" (90, 101–2). On the other hand, Catullus describes Allius' help to himself and Lesbia as opening up a "closed field with a broad path" ("clausum lato patefecit limite campum," 67);[44] his description of Lesbia's meeting with him focuses on her crossing the threshold (70–72);[45] and Hercules becomes a god "in order that the doorway of heaven might by worn down by more gods / and Hebe not be overlong a virgin" (115–16).

"When the Lamp Is Shattered"

I propose to look at the subtler ways in which the poem defines and breaches boundaries, in order to show that it answers the problem of loss by finding how limit and its corollary, difference, may (figuratively) be transcended without inviting chaos. Yet transcending difference necessarily entails putting identity into question. Identity prevaricates internal division, representing the subject as the cohesive "individual"; but it correspondingly shifts emphasis to *inter*subjective division ("I am me, unique, because I am not *you*"). We have looked at blurred difference between subject and object endangering the self before: in cc.51 and 63 a wavering borderline between divine and human destroys familiar landmarks of the self; in the epigrams, uncertainty about Lesbia as desiring Other undermines Catullus' self-definition.

C.68b reverses the connection between defining divisions and self traced in cc.51 and 63: in 68b, identity blurred calls such divisions into question. And like the epigrams, 68b examines these "selves" as the product of a subject/object pairing—subject facing the (beloved) Other. The divisions thus blurred affect interpretive as well as personal alignments, because the subject/object pairings connect in an elaborate chain of similes. They constitute the text's rhetoric, which must be construed in order to arrive at its meaning. As I shall show in scrutinizing the complex of linked similes that constitute the central portion of 68b, the confines of structure defined within these linked similes—the structure that aligns a with b, then a' with b', then a'' with b'', in order to expand a comparison—are violated. The elaborated characteristics and imagery of the compared elements work against the simile's overt alignment. These suggest alternative alignments— that a is really more like b' and b'' than a' or a'', for example. While the simile explicitly tells the reader to align person a with person a', characteristics and imagery force a match between person a and person b'. The resulting multiple superimpositions confuse identities in 68b. The reader is left wondering, who is *anybody* in this poem?

C.68b thus unites the problems we examined in the polymetrics and epigrams, with greater attention paid to identity as a specific subset of subjectivity. The problem of boundaries branches out to embrace first, the wavering and blurry self; second, troubled reading and interpretation—and rereading and reinterpretation, motivated by the gaps and inconsistencies in the text. The linked central similes of the poem set up this complex of issues and as well point toward a figurative solution to the problems of loss, separation, and creative impasse.

The central similes all expand upon the nature of Laodamia's love, by comparing it to various types and intensities of love. In the process, the suggested alternative alignments blur distinctions between Catullus and Lesbia, Lesbia and the brother, the brother and Catullus. Accordingly, the problem of loss becomes as well a problem of preserving the self, in the sense both of survival and of self-definition. Let us see how this works.

We have already seen that Catullus opens the central complex of similes in 68b by comparing Lesbia entering their borrowed tryst house to Laodamia arriving at Protesilaus' house, "burning with love" ("flagrans . . . amore," 73). But that raises an immediate question: Who shows burning passion in the relationship between Catullus and Lesbia, as represented in the other poems of the Lesbia cycle? Certainly not Lesbia. Catullus depicts the Lesbia of the polymetrics as peculiarly untouched by his type of intense emotion: in c.8, for example, while he experiences volcanic joy, she is only "not *un*willing":

> ibi illa multa cum iocosa fiebant,
> quae tu volebas *nec puella nolebat,*
> *fulsere vere candidi tibi soles.*
>
> (8.6–8)

that was when those many amusing diversions were yours, which you wanted— and the girl was not unwilling; then truly bright suns shone for you.

In c.7, she is cool as can be, asking him just exactly how many kisses does he want, anyway?

Moreover, Laodamia briefly enjoys a love that is "dearer than life and the breath of life" to her—

> quo tibi tum casu, pulcerrima Laodamia,
>   ereptum est *vita dulcius atque anima*
> coniugium
>
> (68.105–7)

by that mischance, oh most beautiful Laodamia, your marriage, sweeter than life and soul, was snatched away

—as Catullus thinks of Lesbia as his light and life, dearer than himself:

> . . . mihi quae me *carior ipso est,*
> *lux mea, qua viva vivere dulce mihi est.*
>
> (159–60)

. . . my light, who is dearer to me than myself; while she lives, living is sweet to me.

125

Laodamia suffers both separation from, and the death of, her beloved. Her experiences fuse into one the motives of grief felt for the brother's death and for the shift of Lesbia's attention elsewhere (implicit in 135–36: "quae tamen etsi *uno non est contenta Catullo,* / rara verecundae furta feremus erae"—"even if she is not content with Catullus alone, we shall bear the rare thefts of our modest mistress").[46] While the simile aligns Catullus with Protesilaus, his passion and his situation as a lover correspond more closely to Laodamia's.[47]

On the other hand, Protesilaus matches Lesbia in that he not only leaves Laodamia but does so apparently without a backward glance, in stark contrast to her *avidus amor.* In fact, Protesilaus is little more than a colorless backdrop to *Laodamia's* emotional intensity: it is she who is "forced to let go of her new husband's neck" (81), she whose "great passion", once she is given in marriage, draws the poet's admiration (129–30). Laodamia passively suffers hurt, and Protesilaus actively (if unwillingly?) inflicts it—just as Lesbia's *culpa* wounds Catullus' *amor* in 11.21–24.

Following this description of Laodamia's married passion, the simile drifts into Troy. C.68.87–90 and 101–4 briefly describe the convergence of the Greek army on Troy, and its subsequent destruction; these lines surround a lamentation over the brother's death. Structurally the whole passage represents a break in the linked similes all designed to illustrate the depth of Laodamia's love. (By contrast, the equally elaborated excursus on Hercules nonetheless connects to Laodamia by comparing her passion to the depth of the drainage channel the hero dug.) That apparent "flaw" in the text's construction forces the reader to construe another order for herself—an order beyond what is explicitly laid down in the text—in order to make the text relevent and logically coherent. Recurring words and images forge the connection to other passages of the poem. These connections conflate Catullus' two major losses portrayed in his corpus and represent them as threatening his own destruction.

Troy effects the eclipse of difference necessary to this conflation; the city becomes the place where the *fact* of loss collapses distinctions among *what* is lost. National differences disappear in the "common tomb of Asia and Europe" (89), as the distinction between men ("virum") and their excellences ("virtutum") disappear into "bitter ash" ("acerba cinis," 90).

The subject of Troy as the site of Protesilaus' death and the Trojan War leads into an exclamation over the death of Catullus' brother in the same place. True to the pattern of confused identity, Catullus superimposes the image of Lesbia on that of his brother—a brother already feminized in the description of his love. Catullus transforms the brother into Woman—specifically, into a feminine parent figure—when he remarks that his brother's death destroyed all his joys, "which your sweet love *nursed* when you were alive" ("quae tuus in vita dulcis *alebat* amor," 24, 96).[48] But more specifically, the vocabulary of this exclamation echoes terminology elsewhere peculiar to Lesbia. The brother is "light stolen" from Catullus, ("lumen ademptum," 93); Lesbia is "my light" ("lux mea," 132). Catullus repeatedly equates each of the two not only with *joie de vivre*, but with his *raison d'être*. In 23 and 95, he mourns his brother, saying "omnia tecum una perierunt gaudia nostra"—"all our joys have perished with you at once"; in 160, he blesses Lesbia as "lux mea, qua viva vivere dulce mihi est"—"my light, who, while she lives, living is sweet to me." *Lumen* and *lux* both can mean "life" as well as "light."[49] Catullus' own light/dark imagery in 5.5–6 equates light with life, darkness with death: "but for us, when once the brief light sets, we must sleep through one perpetual night."[50]

This terminology of affection, besides equating the brother with Lesbia, implies that loss threatens Catullus' own existence. To say that Lesbia is his "light" and that his brother's death is "light stolen" from Catullus, equates each of them with life, according to the connotations adduced above. And rightly so, according to the connection we have drawn above between loss seen as unassuageable and creative impasse. If the death of Catullus' brother stymies his ability to write poetry, if Lesbia's failure to desire Catullus exclusively makes marriage impossible, and no remedy can be found for these impasses, then Catullus loses his two claims to existence beyond death—poetry and children.

The imagery, as well as the terminology, surrounding 68's portrait of Catullus' loves supports that equation between loss of Other with loss of self, and between fraternal and erotic loss. Images repeated between 68 and other poems of the corpus (65 and 64) align the brother with Lesbia, as mythological beauty, and with Catullus himself, as abandoned lover. For example: the whole Laodamia simile, which has led up to Troy, springs from the moment Lesbia decisively becomes Catullus' lover. She crosses the threshold of the borrowed tryst house with a "shiny-pale" foot, and appears as a "shining-white goddess":

> quo mea se molli *candida diva* pede
> intulit et trito *fulgentem* in limine *plantam*
> innixa arguta constituit solea
>
> (68.70–72)

"When the Lamp Is Shattered"

where my shining-white goddess betook herself on her delicate foot and, resting her shiny-pale sole in its creaking sandal on the worn threshhold, she stood for a moment

This concentration on paleness, feet, and separating borders catches up the two prominent motives surrounding the *brother* in c.65—another poem in which Catullus replies to a request for poetry, saying that sorrow has impaired his ability to write:

> Etsi me assiduo confectum cura dolore
> sevocat a doctis, Hortale, virginibus,
> nec potis est dulcis Musarum expromere fetus
> mens animi, tantis fluctuat ipsa malis—
>
> (65.1–4)

> Yet care has called me away from the learned maidens, Hortalus (me, afflicted with unceasing pain) and the thought of my mind is not able to bring forth the sweet fruits of the Muses, because it is tossed by such great troubles

Catullus follows this explanation with a portrait of his brother standing on the border of Lethe. First the water above (the sea between Italy and Troy) then the water below (Lethe) separated Catullus from his beloved brother, whose "pale, dear foot" the waves in the underworld wash.

> namque mei nuper *Lethaeo gurgite* fratris
> *pallidulum manans* alluit unda *pedem,*
> *Troia Rhoeteo quem subter litore tellus*
> ereptum nostris obterit ex oculis.
>
> (65.5–8)

> for just now the wave issuing from the Lethean pool washes the pale, dear foot of my brother, whom the Trojan earth beneath the Rhoetean shore grinds down, snatched from my sight.

In turn, Catullus models this odd picture upon his abandoned erotic heroines. In c.64, the sea separates Ariadne on an island from her faithless lover Theseus. C.64 focuses equally on *her* feet, juxtaposed to the waters dividing her from love:

> omnia quae toto delapsa e corpore passim
> *ipsius ante pedes fluctus salis alludebant.*
>
> (64.66–7)

128

with all these things, fallen everywhere from all of her body, the salt waves played before her feet.

Thus the image of an abandoned lover—like Catullus himself—superimposes itself upon the lost brother's image, which in turn floats above the picture of Lesbia as the beautiful goddess whose amorous "thefts" Catullus endures (68.136).

These equations are made possible, in part, by Catullus' fetishistic concentration on representative features—paleness, borders, feet—as metonymic substitutions for his beloved others. These features—*objets a,* in Lacan's terminology—recall the fetishization of Woman's body discussed in chapter 1, rendering her a collection of magically desirable parts. Just so does Catullus construct Lesbia, as we have seen in his rapturous concentration on her smile in c.51. But consider also c.43 as extending and transforming this idea and offering additional insight into the operational principles of c.68. C.43 anatomizes Ameana as a fragmented negation of Lesbia's beauty:

> Salve, nec minimo puella naso
> nec bello pede nec nigris ocellis
> nec longis digitis nec ore sicco
> nec sane nimis elegante lingua,
> decoctoris amica Formiani.
> ten provincia narrat esse bellam?
> tecum Lesbia nostra comparatur?
> o saeclum insipiens et inficetum!

Well, hello, my dear—you with a nose not small, foot not beautiful, eyes not black, fingers not long, neither dry lips nor (trust me!) a tongue too elegant— *and* the girlfriend of that deadbeat from Formiae. The countryside calls *you* beautiful? My Lesbia is compared with *you?* Oh, tasteless and idiot age!

The transformation of Lesbia and Ameana into collections of body parts— black eyes, long fingers, and so on, against the absences thereof—sketches, albeit in negation, a phenomenology of desire that sees the beloved's beauties as potentially reproducible. Other bodies could have black eyes and long fingers; Ameana just happens not to. Similarly, c.68 catches up c.51's reduction of Lesbia to *objets a* but develops the implications of c.43 to see these features as not unique; in c.68 they are, after all, interchangeable with the brother's features. More significantly, c.68 inserts these *objets a* into a signifying chain linking Ariadne to Lesbia to the brother to Catullus. By assuming the function of signifiers in an onward-moving discourse,

129

these *objets a* begin to reproduce the central principle of Diotima's *scala amoris:* metonymic substitution. Diotima's lover is a lover always open to persuasion that this or that object is best abandoned in favor of a worthier one; she is the more easily persuaded in that her *aim* is signification (*kaloi logoi, Symp.* 210 *passim*), substituted *ab origine* for impossible fusion with the body of the beloved other (what *Aristophanes* constructs as the goal of love). The *kenosis* of Catullus' beloveds in c.68, their reduction to this or that luminous feature as signifiers in an ongoing discourse of love, points forward to a palliation of their loss *with other signifiers*—with poetry itself. This is one of the surprising benefits of the breakdown of identity, the breakdown of its smooth alignment of the subject's "parts" into a "unique whole." We will see how this works presently in our exposition of the poem.

Siren Troy

Separating borders persist as a motif in 68's portrayal of the brother's death: not only is his burial site remote, it is in "a strange land" ("terra aliena," 68.100). But adulterous, rather than abandoned, lovers allow Catullus to insert himself into the triangular equation of lover, brother, self in this poem. C.68.87–90 and 101–4, which frame the reference to his brother's death, point to Helen's theft ("Helenae raptu," 87) as motivating the Greek army to converge on Troy, the city where they will be destroyed. The history of the site causally links infidelity to death: Helen's adulterous union with Paris converts Troy into the "common tomb of Asia and Europe" ("commune sepulcrum Asiae Europaeque," 89). When Troy becomes the site of Catullus' brother's death, the city reaffirms its mythological significance, proceeding from adultery, as the site that steals men to itself and destroys them: just as Helen was stolen from Menelaus, so Catullus' brother was "stolen" from him by Troy ("adempte," 20, 92; "ademptum," 93).[51]

Troy forms a link between adultery and death that allows Catullus to draw himself into the complex equation of loving self with beloved other. He places an adulterous lover (like himself), surrounded by mortal danger, in Troy. The picture of Helen and Paris ensconced in their bedroom while all about them the Greek army threatens death corresponds to his own liaison with Lesbia.

> ad quam tum properans fertur <lecta> undique pubes
> Graeca penetralis deseruisse focos,

ne Paris abducta gavisus libera moecha
    otia pacato degeret in thalamo.

(101–4)

[Troy] the city for which at that time Greek youths are said to have deserted their hearthfires, hurrying from everywhere lest Paris, rejoicing in his stolen adultress, should spend his unencumbered leisure in a peaceful marriage chamber.

Verbal repetitions link this portrait to the similes that describe Laodamia's love—an indirect illustration of Catullus' passion—while thematic and imagistic repetitions link it to direct descriptions of his liaison with Lesbia. Paris "rejoices" ("gavisus," 103) in his stolen love, just as Laodamia's love compares to that of a dove who "rejoices" ("gavisa," 125) in her mate. Catullus also represents his affair with Lesbia as a theft from *her* man ("sed furtiva dedit media munuscula nocte" / "ipsius ex ipso dempta viri gremio"—"but in the dead of night, she gave dear gifts stolen from the very lap of her man himself," 145–46). The island of erotic peace represented by Paris and Helen's *thalamus* mirrors the haven Catullus and Lesbia find in Allius' house, where they can "indulge a shared love" ("communes exerceremus amores," 69).

Paris's love brings death upon himself and his city. Thus Paris is a point of collocation for love and loss, for a love that corresponds to Catullus' stolen love for Lesbia ineluctably drawing toward itself the brother's fate. Helen and Paris allow a connection to the brother that the first comparative couple, Laodamia and Protesilaus, do not. The picture of the adulterous lovers represents human happiness in love—of whatever nature, remembering the Trojan link to fraternal love—as fragile and threatened.

Emerging from this portrait, we connect again with the Laodamia-related similes—and the poem sets in train a series of images offering to solve the besetting dilemmas of mortality and loss sketched in the first half. These images depend upon the same principles set down in the exposition of the problem. C.68 depicts the problem of human limitation in terms that do not strictly respect difference and division, as the latter define identity. Catullus' alignment of himself, his brother, and Lesbia with the figures of mythology (e.g., Paris and Helen, Laodamia and Protesilaus) and with each other blurs the distinctions among personae.

Of particular interest to us is the way in which his representations regularly disrupt gender lines—Ariadne superimposed upon the brother, Laodamia on Catullus, Protesilaus upon Lesbia. The latter half of the poem focuses upon gender fluidity and on palliating mortality and loss as

131

they threaten creativity. To do so, Catullus borrows the metaphoric logic behind Diotima's equation of sexual procreation with artistic creation, as species of *poiēsis* that both aim at immortality. Sexual creation, and the transcending of gender boundaries to achieve autonomy in that creation, point to *poiēsis* independent of an object, an Other.

Heroic Cross-Dressing

Appropriately, Catullus chooses Hercules as his organizing focal figure—the one mortal whom myth credits with effecting the transition between mortality and the gods, and one whose legend shows him frequently crossing between gender positions.

Catullus moves from Troy to Hercules by addressing Laodamia directly and comparing the emotional "deep pit" ("barathrum," 108) into which the tidal wave of her love for her dead husband sweeps her, to the deep drainage shaft ("barathro," 117) dug by Hercules to drain floodwater from a low-lying plain.[52] The water imagery speaks of emotion out of control, that drags its victim down into a seemingly bottomless abyss ("tanto te absorbens *vertice* amoris" / "*aestus* in abruptum detulerat *barathrum*"—"with so great an eddy had the tide of love sucked you down and plunged you into a sheer abyss", 107–8). Water expresses Laodamia's passion, just as earlier the imagery of 53–62 (hot springs transformed into cooling stream) depicts Catullus' own amorous experience—the tortures softened through Allius' help.

Barathrum also means Hades:[53] like Catullus, Laodamia experiences the loss of a loved one as a threatened end to her *own* life, as if *she* were being swept down to Hades. Equally, since both Laodamia's and Catullus' bereavement involve aborted creation (the *domus incepta frustra* and the abandoned poetry), Laodamia's reaction to her loss conjures up again the fragility of ephemeral beings connected to creative impasse and the structural impossibility of possessing completely the object of one's desire.

It makes sense that next, groping for solutions, Catullus pictures a hero taming a body of water as monstrous as that which metaphorically delineates Laodamia's destructive passion. The simile contrasts water out of control (*vertex, aestus*) with water channeled and directed, water's victim (Laodamia) with its master (Hercules).[54] Catullus paves the way to Hercules' apotheosis by depicting the hero's mastery over 68's opening metaphor for desire. Moreover, Hercules provides an icon of successful artistic and technological creation, supplanting the images of blighted production set forth in Laodamia and Protesilaus. His hydraulic engineering creates

132

a technical control over water analogous to poetry's channeling of desire through the signifying chain: each shepherds a force depicted, in 68, as overwhelming and life-threatening.

Not coincidentally, the successful master artisan in this poem—Hercules—assumes both gender positions. In the rest of the cycle, terrifying visions of emasculation have dogged gender mobility: switching gender position becomes a nightmare fantasy of a castrating mistress at the end of c.11, and again in c.63.

But Nicole Loraux's unfolding of the complex sexual significations threaded through the Hercules legend can help us see why and how c.68 adopts a different perspective on gender crossing through him.[55] She points out that the astonishing contradictions of this hero's myth regularly define gender polarities. The hero is both a lover and hater of women: his rites regularly bar women from participation. Yet his stories declare that he deflowers virgins (as many as fifty in one night), marries almost compulsively, and produces scores of children. His lion skin signifies a great male hunter, but he is also a transvestite (exchanging clothes with Omphale as her slave) and so are his priests (at Kos and at the Roman shrine of Hercules Victor). "The female body as an object of conquest and pleasure is continually new for him, and allegorizing erotic interpretations of his amorous career were current in the banquets of the Hellenistic period." In assessing his heroic path from Omphale's slave to Hebe's husband, Loraux notes the anatomical punning on *omphalos* (Greek "navel") and *hēbē* (Greek slang for female genitals): "the life of Herakles is turned into a journey across the female body."[56]

In his slide between the positions of Man and Woman, Master and Slave, *misogynēs* and *philogynēs,* Hercules describes Catullus' own oscillations between these positions as we have traced them through the Lesbia cycle. But the controlling figure of Hercules' life is metonymy: the names of his women (when they are granted names) derive from parts of their bodies, and all are seen as basically interchangeable. Even he himself regularly takes on womanly attributes. No position, either of identity, gender, or sexuality, is seen as unshakeable in the Hercules' legend, and no object as irreplaceable.

But I further argue that Catullus draws from Hercules' legend a concept of playing the Other, so as to replace the Other—with other objects, and/or with one's own autonomous sexuality. So beside the image of Hercules as transvestite—cleverly engineered simulacrum of female sexuality—I place Hercules as hermaphrodite, the fiction naturalized. The fact that Catullus emphasizes Hercules as a successful *engineer* means that the hermaphrodite image is never unproblematic: contrivance is always visible as a factor. Nonetheless, the logic of successful sexual reproduction as a bid for immortality controls the rest of the poem in spite of flawed objects or desperate circumstances.[57]

Hercules models a dream of creative and sexual autonomy for the poet. Not coincidentally, given the connection Catullus elsewhere makes between poetry and immortality (as, e.g., **43–50**), Hercules trades the fatal Deianeira for a bride who embodies eternal life—Hebe (= Greek "youth"). Hebe is handmaiden to the gods and dispenses the nectar and ambrosia that continually renew their lives. Hercules himself ultimately bridges the gap between gods and mortals.

> pluribus ut caeli tereretur ianua divis,
> Hebe nec longa virginitate foret.
>
> (115–16)

[he killed the monstrous Stymphalian birds] so that the threshhold of heaven might be worn down by more gods, and Hebe should not long be a virgin.

Catullus thus closes his portrait of Hercules with an image of productive marriage and immortality—an image that contrasts dramatically with the earlier disasters wrought in the encounter between human and divine in cc.63 and 64, in the figures of Attis and Peleus respectively.

Surprisingly, Catullus' excursus on Hercules has come in for much criticism as an otiose Hellenistic ornament that does not pull its own weight.[58] However, Hercules' image not only models a fantasy of escape from death and sterility but in doing so matches the next point of comparison for Laodamia's love that begins to clothe the fantasy in earthly garments. The grandparent/grandchild vignette recapitulates (in a believably mundane—if too fortuitous—fashion) Hercules' magical circumvention of all impediments to his continued existence. The vignette also explicitly links sexual generation with writing as a means to preserving a human being's substance after death. Hercules' potential for creative autonomy (insofar as he figurally incorporates male and female elements within himself) here opens out, through the linking of similes, into that potential realized: the grandchild. Laodamia's love had earlier been set against the background of a *domus incepta frustra*. The reason behind that "house begun in vain"—Protesilaus' departure for Troy—leads into the image of *Catullus'* house brought to an end by the loss of his brother—"with you our whole house is buried at once" ("tecum una tota est nostra sepulta domus," 94). But the grandchild simile reverses the earlier images con-

134

nected with Laodamia's love, and compares it to the love felt for "the life of a late-born grandson" ("caput seri . . . nepotis," 120), who *saves* a doomed house.

> nam nec tam carum confecto aetate parenti
> una caput seri nata nepotis alit,
> qui, cum divitiis vix tandem inventus avitis
> nomen testatas intulit in tabulas,
> impia derisi gentilis gaudia tollens
> suscitat a cano volturium capiti
>
> (119–24)

nor so dear is the life of his late-born grandson to a grandfather burdened with age, the child whom his only daughter nurses; the child who, found in the nick of time for the wealth of his grandfather, when his name has been entered upon the witnessed tablets, destroys all the wicked joys of his laughing-stock relative, and shoos away the vulture from the old man's white head

The details of the simile argue for the grandchild as an emblem of Catullus' poetry and its potential to preserve a representation of the poet after his death. The whole point of the child's existence is that he will be translated into a *written testament* ("nomen testatas intulit in tabulas," 122), and *only* thus can he negate the old man's mortality ("suscitat a cano volturium capiti," 124). Just so the poem, a written testament to Allius' helpfulness, promises *him* immortality (43–50)—and *a fortiore,* to its creator, Catullus. Little more than ten lines away from the vignette of grandfather and child, Catullus carefully inserts his name in the poem ("quae tamen etsi uno non est contenta *Catullo,*" 135). He makes sure that if the *opus* that promises Allius immortality survives, it shall necessarily transmit its creator's name as well. Furthermore, "alit" echoes the earlier lament for his brother's "nurture" of Catullus' delight in poetry ("gaudia nostra / . . . alebat," 23–24), lost when the brother died. "Alit" both forces a rereading of the earlier "alebat" by activating its connotations of feminine nurture (thus reinforcing the brother's feminization) and retrieves the image of that nurture and that creativity from hopeless loss. The signifying chain that hesitated when the brother died is reknit and goes on; true to the equation hinted in 33–35, words, in poetry, are the true center of Catullus' life. They take the place of human objects—Lesbia, the brother, Catullus' potential flesh-and-blood children.

Aria for Two Voices

The infant of 120, insofar as he represents accomplished poetic creation, points to escape from mortal ephemerality. Memory plays a role in

135

achieving this—a way into, and out of, the problem to which this image poses a figurative solution. In 70–72 and 131–34, which frame the long excursus into the Laodamia myth, Catullus reaches back in memory to Lesbia, as if to that quasi-divine image of the good he conjured up from his own memory in c.76. The first passage presents her as an idealized object of desire—he even refers to her as a "goddess" ("candida diva," 68.70). Her passion and beauty are remembered at the perfect moment— the very *first time* she came to him, which established the paradigm of their erotic encounter.[59]

We come back, ring-fashion, to the same moment—Lesbia appearing at the tryst house. But disturbing inconsistencies appear in the description of Laodamia's passion just before we get there—details that drive the portraits of Lesbia and Laodamia even farther apart. The portrait Catullus has drawn of Laodamia does not, as we have already seen, fit the portrait of Lesbia available from other poems. The studied awkwardness with which Catullus emerges from the extended comparison underlines this fact by setting at odds details from different parts of 68 itself. That narrowing and intensification of interpretive focus urges the reader to review and adjust the explicit alignments of the Laodamia simile within 68. Catullus' comparative terms begin to unravel the sense of earlier similes when pinned to both women, emphasizing the fundamental gap between the two of them.

The last two similes of the Laodamia complex prepare for the transition to Lesbia. Up to this point, the details of the simile have been appropriate to Laodamia but not to Lesbia; now the comparisons begin to reverse and to fit Lesbia but not Laodamia. Comparing Laodamia's love to that of the aged grandparent, for example, clashes with the explicit focus of Laodamia's situation—the *domus incepta frustra*. She is widowed after a brief period of time and utterly devoted to her dead husband; eventually she commits suicide rather than live without him.[60] Therefore, her *domus* can never produce an heir for whom she would feel such love. But Lesbia *is* potentially the focus of such expectations, ringed about as she is with the imagery of marriage. The second simile (of the dove and her mate) alludes to the reason she can never fulfill such expectations: her refusal to emulate Laodamia's single-minded devotion.[61]

> nec tantum niveo gavisa est ulla columbo
> compar, quae multo dicitur improbius
> oscula mordenti semper decerpere rostro,
> quam quae praecipue multivola est mulier.

(125–28)

136

nor has any dove rejoiced so much in her snowy mate, who is said to snatch kisses with a biting beak more greedily than the most wantonly abandoned woman.

The dove is an example of conjugal passion but draws in the "wantonly abandoned woman" (128) as a comparative term—a glance forward to Lesbia as "not content with Catullus alone" ("uno non est contenta Catullo," 135). The "multivola mulier" is an ostentatiously inappropriate, albeit indirect, comparison to Laodamia's passion focused exclusively on Protesilaus. But as a glance forward to *Lesbia's* other desires, the second simile points to the reason why the promise of self-preservation in the first simile depends on writing rather than on the child alone: Lesbia can provide the subject matter for poetry, but she will not provide children to Catullus.[62]

After these last two similes in the Laodamia complex, Catullus reintroduces Lesbia by circling back to the same moment in time from which we entered the complex—her entrance to Allius' house. The second image of this moment once again measures, subtly, the distance between the Whore of c.11 (only suggested here) and the Goddess of c.51 (an idealism that controls the first image of this moment, in 68.70–72). The studied difficulty Catullus has in logically bridging the gap urges (as we have seen elsewhere in the cycle) a rereading of the whole complex of similes as a measure of his desire and of its illusory constructions of his objects. He ostentatiously discounts time and its power to reveal, since he assigns a pristine Lesbia and a tarnished Lesbia to the very same moment: the hour of her first assignation with Catullus.

Upon reentering the stage of the poem, Lesbia pales before the dazzling idealization of Laodamia. Lesbia's love concedes nothing to Laodamia's—or, on second thought, perhaps a little:

> aut nihil *aut paulo* cui tum concedere digna
> lux mea se nostrum contulit in gremium,
> quam circumcursans hinc illinc saepe Cupido[63]
> fulgebat crocina candidus in tunica.
>
> (131–34)

to whom my light deserved to concede either nothing, or maybe a little, when she brought herself to my bosom; whom Cupid, circling frequently now on this side, now on that, shone upon—he resplendently glowing in his saffron-yellow tunic.

The next few lines indicate the reasons behind Catullus' recantation, which casts suspicion upon the whole train of images proceeding from Lesbia's comparison to Laodamia. He now reveals his awareness that he is not the sole object of his mistress' desire ("furta," 136). His glosses on the multiplicity of her desire in 137–48 convey a studied lack of conviction. Catullus picks Juno as his model of marital tolerance, which is unconvincing not only in the light of the goddess' typical treatment of rivals but even in its phrasing in this passage:

> saepe etiam Iuno, maxima caelicolum,
> coniugis in culpa *flagrantem contudit iram,*
> noscens omnivoli plurima facta Iovis.
>
> (138–40)

often even Juno, greatest of the gods, has beaten down her flaming anger at her husband's offense, forgiving the many wrongs of Jove, who wants everybody.

Line 139 points to the fact that, whatever face Juno may be forced to put on the infidelities of one more powerful than herself, she nonetheless suffers "flaming wrath" at her husband's behavior—she cannot be indifferent.

The comparison to Juno works against its overt counsel of tolerance; a series of painfully awkward rhetorical reworkings follow. The cumbrous adjustments Catullus keeps forcing upon the train of cases adduced to excuse Lesbia's other desires underlines that counterpoint. He cancels his evidence by picking up images from earlier sections of the poem that undermine the message. The reader finds herself faced with two trains of thought: one deriving from the initial comparison of Lesbia to Laodamia, another from Lesbia's repeatedly adduced and excused behavior. These work at cross-purposes and cry out for rereading and readjustment—as was the case with the Laodamia simile by itself.

For example: after mentioning Juno, Catullus says "atqui nec divis homines componier aequum est"—"but one shouldn't compare human beings to gods" (141). This statement works not only against the immediate comparison of Lesbia to Jupiter but against the initial image of her as a resplendent goddess ("candida diva," 70). The progress of the poem carries us further and further away from that vision—and 68.141 locates the widening gap, not as proceeding from her *particular* failures so much as an inherent incommensurability between a woman as a human being, and her burdensome apotheosis as Woman, the support of Man's identity, aligned with the divine (as in c.51).

The *Carmina Maiora*

Following this, he says: "ingratum tremuli tolle parentis onus"—
"Stop playing the part of the elderly father—little thanks it will get you!"
(142). Characterizing the *tremulus parens* as a nag and a scold clashes with
the *confectus aetate parens* of 68.119–24. That "grandfather burdened with
age" was an index of tenderness and concern for his offspring.[64] Catullus
speaks of such nonsexual love for Lesbia in the epigrams, without consider-
ing himself officious. Yet as with the comparison to Juno, 68.142 focuses
not on the appropriate attitude of loving subject to beloved object but on
expediency: it would not do any good to protest, so why bother?

Lastly, Catullus exclaims, "and anyhow, she isn't married to me":

> nec tamen illa mihi dextra deducta paterna
> fragrantem Assyrio venit odore domum
>
> (143–44)

and furthermore, she did not come to me led on her father's right hand, to
a house scented with Assyrian fragrance

Yet he surrounded her entrance into the borrowed tryst house (also "do-
mum," 68) with images borrowed from the marriage ceremony (e.g.,
Cupid swinging a torch, dressed in yellow, 133–34). He compares her
entrance to the house to the entrance of a legitimate bride into her hus-
band's house—Laodamia coming to Protesilaus (73–74). The earlier sym-
bolic presentation of Lesbia and Catullus' union denies that infractions
against it are to be viewed as minor offenses.

Memory Circuit

Having elucidated these jarring details, let us step back for a moment
and look at the whole section that begins and ends with Lesbia as a clue
to the interpretation of c.68. The misgivings I have pointed out above are
not simply subtle variants on the topic of defaming Lesbia, engaged at
various points in the cycle. The poem's circular motion in time—beginning
with the appearance of Lesbia at Allius' house, and ending there—cross-
references these two moments and looks closely at the two Lesbias thus
conjured up. The Lesbia who appears on the threshold of Allius' house
as a "candida diva" is not the same woman who reappears at the end of
the simile, perhaps not *quite* worthy to be compared to Laodamia. Yet by
the very end of the poem, her diminution is somehow tolerable. In wishing
everyone well, Catullus extends his joy and goodwill toward Lesbia, too:

139

et longe ante omnes mihi quae me carior ipso est,
lux mea, qua viva vivere dulce mihi est.

(159–60)

and far before all the rest, she who is dearer to me than myself, my light;
while she lives, living is sweet to me.

How is this possible, after the reservations implied in the last third of 68?
Why is the memory of time past in the affair, as compared with time
present, pristine ideal compared with its tarnished deterioration, not in
68 a source of anguish or cold hatred for Catullus—as in cc.8, 11, 72,
and others? He has indeed looked fully at the gap between the ideal and
deteriorated images (whatever their truth value may be, remembering the
illusory nature of the *fort/da* game's "paradise" and "vale of tears"). His
own similes indicate that neither he nor Juno welcomes the mobility of
their mates' desires.

We are again looking at desire as *amo* and *odi* in the conflicting
portraits of Lesbia. On the one hand, we have perfect passion and devotion
attributed to Lesbia, as "shining-white goddess," through comparison to
Laodamia. On the other, we have passion without devotion in the Lesbia
of the "rare thefts" (136), which is a source of pain. Again we face the
problem of reconciling the two—or do we?

The creative potential of these two Lesbias derives precisely from an
unreconcilable oscillation between the Whore and the Goddess, within a
unified text, and ostentatiously not rationalized by temporalization. In
c.68, the circuit of desire around these two foci articulates the gap between
love and hate as *in itself* that which motivates poetic creativity—just as the
perceived gap between paradise and exile is the basis for language and
(self-) narrative in the *fort/da* game. I spoke earlier (in chapters 2 and 4)
of the fact that desire is the operational basis for poetry: poetry derives
from, and depends for its aesthetic lure upon, desire—the writer and the
readers' mutual address to the mystery of the Other. Though desire reaches
for attainment, if it were to achieve its object, desire *and* the subject would
be obliterated. Keeping desire alive, as the force behind poetry and its
locus (the subject), means maintaining the gap between reach and grasp.
Between a Lesbia "not content with Catullus alone" and Lesbia the radiant
goddess stretches the poetic imagination, fired by desire.

Consider the fact that these two portraits of Lesbia frame the long
and complicated excursus into love and loss; that structural detail graphi-
cally reflects the function of the two within the imaginative process of
desire. Finding our way from the one to the other involves an exploration

140

of creation, starting from its frustration in Laodamia and Protesilaus and ending with its fruition in the late-born grandson—and that exploration itself constitutes the basis of c.68 insofar as it provides most of its subject matter. The tense conflict felt in the elegiac treatments of this dichotomy (as in 72, 75, and 85) is not evident by the end of the poem. Reconciliation no longer matters: both levels of perception float one on top of the other, while the mind (and the poetry) moves in between. This is *Aufhebung* of the object—an abolition of it as concrete fact, while retaining its principles not for stasis but for a push forward into the next spiral of the dialectic of desire. It partially reconciles the *Symposium* and the *Phaedrus*. Like the *Phaedrus*, it retains the singularity of the object as an inspirational template for future instances of desire: the poems derived from meditating on the two Lesbias are *like* children she might have provided, bids for immortality. But like the *Symposium*, it reduces the importance to desire of the object's particularity: Catullus need no longer possess Lesbia; memory of her, however constructed, will do instead.

This fictive bridge between antinomies—narrative equivalent of Hercules himself—realized in the structure of the poem itself, spins out between the two contradictory poles of desire. The poem realizes, paradoxically, the two tendencies of desire at once: the preservation and abolition of difference—of which Woman is the guarantor and threat. But for once in the corpus, the two antinomies refuse to collapse into one another; rather, they are the basis for endless substitutions. Their suspension in mutual relation constitutes the basis of creation in c.68.

By ending on a point of sustained contradiction, I wish to emphasize that seeking to abolish such textual mobilities in "certainty" implies a conceptual framework too narrow to accommodate the poem—a framework that forces us to eliminate certain questions about the poem before we have properly assessed them. The unitarian/separatist controversy over c.68 paradigmatically represents this. While no amount of subtle mapping of c.68's interlaced correspondences can explain away its jarring anacolutha and anomalies, no concentration on the latter can surgically produce any text or texts free of such gaps and lines of fracture. To cleave strictly to either position involves selective blindness to basic data produced by the text.

The poem produces an undecideable uncertainty parallel to its unsettling of gender and identity categories. The possibility of determinate, transmissable meaning—as allied to phallic "knowing," and thus to masculine authority, and to gender position—here dissolves and seeps away through the gaps in the text, the gaps that are the sites of readerly delight,

141

of *jouissance*. Such dissolution invites us to try again—to close up the gaps, get behind the text, find out what Catullus "really meant." The play back and forth between these two moments—of thinking you have the message, and knowing you do not quite—is an oscillation basic to the activities of reading and interpreting Catullus. Thus does the text stage an unlimited interrogation both of itself and of the institutional positions (gender, identity, sexuality) it depicts. The very principle of its operation resides in its multiplying chains of meaning. The ultimate message of the poem is: "keep reading."

6

Some Final Reflections

Others taunt me with having knelt at well-curbs
Always wrong to the light, so never seeing
Deeper down in the well than where the water
Gives me back in a shining surface picture
Me myself in the summer heaven, godlike,
Looking out of a wreath of fern and cloud puffs.
Once, when trying with chin against a well-curb,
I discerned, as I thought, beyond the picture,
Through the picture, a something white, uncertain,
Something more of the depths—and then I lost it.
Water came to rebuke the too clear water.
One drop fell from a fern, and lo, a ripple
Shook whatever it was lay there at bottom.
Blurred it, blotted it out. What was that whiteness?
Truth? A pebble of quartz? For once, then, something.
                                               —Robert Frost[1]

I BEGAN THIS BOOK by looking at the Catullan corpus as a text that
will not stay still: because the poems offer just enough similarity to suggest
patterns, and just enough anomaly to refuse any definitive pattern, they
cohere and dissolve constantly before our eyes. The corpus lacks definitive
context or details that clearly indicate a dominant order; whatever order
there is to be, we, the readers, must provide it. Consequently the Catullan
text dramatizes in particularly stark fashion the reader's role in constructing

whatever text she reads. Like images reflected in a pool, the order we draw out of these poems will always be fragile—both organized and shattered by the fact of our looking and by our own partial reflections.

But short of being the most unembarrassable narcissists, we never look solely for ourselves: we also look for the author, desiring his presence as "something" hinted on the other side of the mirror, as the Other who addresses us. We seek the vestiges of his presence in pattern, motif, and design. That is why I have not scrupled, in describing the poems, to assign their features to Catullus' agency: when I say, for example, "Catullus adheres to Callimachean aesthetics, as exampled in such-and-such a poem," I view the author so invoked as a necessary fiction, even a helpful one: he gives me something to call the speaker and a frame to an open-ended inquiry. But his name tells me nothing in advance about him or his poetry and should never close off a question. If we say "Catullus was not the type to mean *this*," or "Catullus could not have thought *that*," we do too little justice to the complexity of human consciousness—his *and* ours.

I have brought Plato and psychoanalysis to bear upon the Catullan text precisely in order to explicate the complexity of that consciousness, whose seams and fractures this "little body of poems" reflects in exemplary fashion. I hope I have shown from their colloquy with Catullus not only how modern theory serves us well in investigating ancient texts, but that the very categories "ancient" and "modern" often used to sequester the one from the other are specious. We can no longer say, in a corporate version of the authorial fallacy, "the ancients were not the types to mean *this*," or "the ancients could not have meant *that*." Clearly, Plato crystallizes a way of thinking about desire and the subject that anticipates questions Freud and Lacan ask over twenty centuries later, and foreshadows many of their answers. To deny this possibility a priori implies that human thought lacks an idea completely until "discovered"—at which point it can be added to the discoveries upon which the course of thought builds, in a paradigm of accumulation. To the contrary, history (as I hope I have shown) indicates that determinations are advanced, withdrawn, and reconfigured with much greater fluidity than simple linear models imply; ideas perpetually rise to the surface and sink again into obscurity.

Small wonder, then, if comparable formulations of where and how desire fractures the subject and the text arise in "ancient" philosophy, "modern" psychoanalysis, and "classical" erotic poetry. And while I view this recurrent interest in divided subjectivity as intricately imbricated with historical circumstances, it would be selling our evidence short to point to such-and-such a historical event as "explaining" Catullus' poetry (or Plato's, Freud's, or

Lacan's writings). That would translate logical priority into temporal priority, a fallacy I have argued against repeatedly in this book. Rather, Catullus' poems are themselves among the best primary evidence we have for the way the Romans constructed contemporary historical circumstances in the Late Republic. We usually think of the Republic's last decades as a time in which various factors—increasing competition for political office; the slave revolts, and Social War; the power of rival military leaders and their armies—contributed to profound social displacements and radical upheaval in political institutions. But Catullus' poetry draws the connections between society and the subject both more subtly and sweepingly than the boldest historian. He connects the breakdown of social and political institutions—the failure of the "mystified" account of their origins, purposes, and efficacies—along a continuum to equally suspect authority enforcing gender relations, social allegiance, and identity.

Plato, Freud, and Lacan have all helped me trace these connections where they attach to subjectivity. But I have not sought to describe Catullus' poetry as yet another instance of psychoanalysis' or Platonism's general validity. I have striven to avoid either "Platonizing" or "psychoanalyzing" the text. Rather, all the theories of desire I have used enable me to describe with a concision and accuracy otherwise impossible *what Catullus' text is doing*—how it represents (rather than just embodies) the relations between gender and knowledge, desire and subjectivity, language and the object. As I indicated in chapter 1, I see Catullus' text as the dramatized insufficiency of prevailing modes of thought (of his time *and* ours) on self, gender, authority—and that in too principled a fashion to be mere happenstance. His myriad costume changes throughout the text motivate questions on the conceptual adequacy of *each* costume—such as "masculinity"; "femininity"; "rationality"; "*Romanitas.*" Where each category of thought begins to unravel, we are invited to ask whether it accurately reveals the world to us, or only re-presents our own circumscribed rounds of thought.

But we are invited as well to see what accommodation can be made with such inadequacy. Even with the failings of the structures that pretend to uphold the self mercilessly exposed, these poems produce the *effect* of a self— a fiction hard-won, though unsecured. However divided, dispersed, and undone, a voice addresses us from these verses, that always coalesces into shape and always dissolves into tangled threads—and with that very play between self-construction and self-undoing, demands from us continual rereading. If we attend carefully to this interplay of text—*and* reader—between self and subject, weaving and unweaving order, reading and rereading, we shall not only locate Catullus more accurately within the critical framework but see

145

how we and the framework must change to accommodate his reconfiguration(s). Then shall we indeed "think beyond our means."

I am convinced, naturally, that a textual methodology grounded in the divided subject of desire, as Plato and psychoanalysis reveal that subject to us, can and should be applied to the rest of the Catullan corpus besides the Lesbia cycle. But I have good hopes of it, as well, for clarifying the opacities of other Roman erotic verse—those places where we may have taken refuge too soon in lamenting classical literature's imperfect survival. Its logical gaps and rough joins perhaps indicate something other than attrition—another logic and other voices, that each era must construe for itself. Let us shift our perspective and gaze steadfastly there, just there, where the forgetful ages have wrapped the text most thickly in obscurity and oblivion.

With the thought of an apocalypse ardently desired and continually renewed, I shall end and suggest that Freud got it right when he chose Rome to model the Unconscious' timeless and all-preserving accumulation. His Eternal City waits for us patiently, there where the text is most unsaid and unthought, since it always depended but on *our* perspective to spring into view.

> Now let us, by a flight of imagination, suppose that Rome is not a human habitation but a psychical entity with a similarly long and copious past—an entity, that is to say, in which nothing that has once come into existence will have passed away and all the earlier phases of development continue to exist alongside the latest one. This would mean that in Rome the palaces of the Caesars and the Septizonium of Septimius Severus would still be rising to their old height on the Palatine and that the castle of S. Angelo would still be carrying on its battlements the beautiful statues which graced it until the siege by the Goths, and so on. But more than this. In the place occupied by the Palazzo Caffarelli would once more stand—without the Palazzo Caffarelli having to be removed—the Temple of Jupiter Capitolinus; and this not only in its latest shape, as the Romans of the Empire saw it, but also in its earliest one, when it still showed Etruscan forms and was ornamented with terracotta antefixes. Where the Coliseum now stands we could at the same time admire Nero's vanished Golden House. On the Piazza of the Pantheon we should find not only the Pantheon of to-day, as it was bequeathed to us by Hadrian, but, on the same site, the original edifice erected by Agrippa; indeed, the same piece of ground would be supporting the church of Santa Maria sopra Minerva and the ancient temple over which it was built. And the observer would perhaps only have to change the direction of his glance or his position in order to call up the one view or the other.[2]

NOTES
BIBLIOGRAPHY
INDEX

Notes

Preface

1. Syme 1956, 131.

2. E.g., Wiseman 1969; Quinn 1973a, 9–16; E. A. Schmidt 1973a; Dettmer 1988.

3. To be fair, the poor state of the manuscript tradition has been the object of much shrewd and perseverant scholarship (detailed in Thomson 1978, i–xvi, 1–42). Near the end of the twentieth century, we are the fortunate heirs of a greatly rehabilitated text of Catullus, in which a small—but significant—fraction of the original errors remain. These errors, however, staunchly resist emendation in some cases, editorial unification or division in others, and *both* reconstructive tools in still other instances. Similarly, the corpus as a whole resists an ordering of the poems universally satisfactory to all Catullus scholars. Part of my purpose in this book is to look again at individual textual *loci conclamati* in the context of the attempt to establish narrative order and unity within the corpus. Further, I propose to examine textual criticism on the one hand, and "plotting" on the other, as two facets of the same conceptual problem, which must be aligned with a third— the text's solicitation to the reader to reconstruct the writing and speaking subject(s) of the poems.

4. In formulating these issues, I have made use of H. M. Leicester, Jr.'s clear and trenchant discussion of subjectivity and conceptualization in literary criticism (Leicester 1990, 14).

5. A persistent source of unease to Catullus critics—including two of his earliest, Furius and Aurelius. In c.16, they accuse him of being "not much of a man" ("male marem") when he asks for "many thousands of kisses" ("milia multa basiorum") from Lesbia. (The reference might also be to kisses requested of Iuventius in c.48. But given that *milia multa* appears in identical metrical positions in c.5, to Lesbia, and c.16, I take the latter's barb to be more closely directed to Catullus' feminine infatuation. In this regard, see also the arguments of Fitzgerald 1992, 438n23. On the verbal and metrical symmetries of cc.16 and 5, see Winter 1973, 265n13.)

149

1. From Plato to Freud to Lacan: A History of the Subject

1. Merrill 1893, xii.

2. See, e.g., E. Havelock's astringent chapter on "The Canons of Catullan Criticism" (Havelock 1939, 79–85); Cherniss 1943; Rudd 1964; Rudd 1976, 145–81; Quinn 1972; Clarke 1976.

3. Perhaps the most egregious example of this practice of splitting Catullus along various axes is exampled in the tradition of the "two Catulluses"—ponderously learned Alexandrian and spontaneously lyric Romantic—attacked by E. Havelock (Havelock 1939). The axis of learning/spontaneity intersects the axis of variability I address, since behind it lurks a notion of Catullus as wavering between pedantic dispassion and wild excess. Moreover, Havelock's conspectus of the practice shows once more that the Catullan corpus regularly strikes readers as unable to represent a unified subject, and that they consequently propose various divisions to "make sense" of it.

4. For a judicious conspectus of gender slippage as an issue in Catullan criticism, see Adler 1981, 130–66.

5. Havelock 1939, 118.

6. The most incisive comprehensive evaluation of Catullus as divided is Adler 1981. She wisely focuses upon the vicissitudes of the personal pronouns and the dramatic stagings of the Catullan poems rather than (as most previous critics) a vague division drawn between each critic's estimate of what Catullus' "attitude" ought to be and the poet's words.

7. To which E. Schäfer eloquently objects: "Who knows the human heart so well, as to think it incapable of an anxious and hopeful return after a despairing refusal?" ("Wer kennt das menschliche Herz so gut, dass er ihm nicht nach der verzweifelten Absage an die Geliebte eine bangende, hoffende Rückkehr zutraute?" (Schäfer 1966, 49).

8. As Quinn considers c.11 subsequent in order to c.51 (Quinn 1973b, ad c.11).

9. Clausen 1964, 182.

10. Reported in Athenaeus ii.72a.

11. *Aetia* 1.3–4. All references to Callimachus are from Pfeiffer 1949–53.

12. By "cyclic epic," I refer to any of the poems included in the *epikos kyklos*—a collection of early Greek epics artificially arranged so as to describe serially a continuous narrative from the world's creation to the heroic age's end (thus far exceeding the scope of the *Iliad* and *Odyssey*). Callimachus makes no distinction in his contempt for the genre: "echthairō to poiēma to kuklikon"—"I hate the cyclic poem" (*Epigram* 28.1 Pfeiffer).

13. *Epigram* 28.3–4.

14. *Aetia* I.1.23–28; my emphasis.

15. *Epigram* 27.

16. *Aetia* I.1.19–20.

17. Fr. 460. Pf.

18. E.g., in Callimachus' epinikion to Sosibius (a victor in the Isthmian and Nemean Games), only a mastery of obscure mythology could gloss the periphrases "the two children, Learchus' brother, and Myrina's daughter's fosterchild" (Fr. 384.25–26 Pf.) as references to the cities Isthmia and Nemea, respectively.

19. Such as Cinna, whose painstakingly wrought masterpiece *Zmyrna* Catullus praises in c.95.

20. A concept William Levitan adduces in discussing the *technopaegnia* of Optatian Porfyry (Levitan 1985, esp. p. 255).

21. The division of opinion over c.8's interpretation is exemplary. Among those who see Catullus' portrait of his own amorous tortures as intentionally humorous are Wheeler 1934, 227–30; Klingner 1961, 220–25; Swanson 1963; Commager 1965; Gugel 1967; Khan 1968; Skinner 1971. Readers who, on the other hand, see c.8 as entirely serious and tragic are Fordyce 1961, ad loc.; Quinn 1959, 92–94; Fränkel 1961; Quinn 1973b, ad loc.; Dyson 1973. And now, even the sacrosanct c.51 has garnered a comic reading: see Newman 1983.

22. The efforts of a number of scholars have greatly aided the comparison between Plato and Freud in the following discussion. The results of their investigations into points of agreement between the philosopher and the psychoanalyst appear in the following works: Kenny 1973; Simon 1978; Preus 1982/83; Ferrari 1987, 156–60; Charlton 1988; Santas 1988; Price 1989, 215–22; Price 1990; Ferrari 1990.

Of these, Santas' book-length exposition is the most complete (though, curiously, he concludes by granting disproportionate weight to the differences between Plato and Freud and thereby discounting their similarities. I believe his own thoughtful and painstaking elucidation of the similarities belies his conclusion). Price and Ferrari's expositions, on the other hand, are particularly sophisticated despite their brevity, and raise a myriad of thought-provoking issues in short compass.

23. SXXIV. See esp. the sessions of 15 March–17 May 1977, "Vers un signifiant nouveau."

24. Examples would include *venustus; deliciae/delicatus; sal;* etc. See Seager 1974. On *deliciae/delicatus*, see Fordyce 1961, ad 50.3.

25. The wide historical fluctuations in evaluation of Catullus argue for the wisdom of this assumption—the history of c.68, the *"Schibboleth des Catullinterpreten"* in G. Jachmann's words, is instructive. Whereas in M.-A. Muret's 1554 edition of the Catullan corpus, he assesses poem 68 as "the most beautiful [elegy] in every way, and I do not know whether any more beautiful could be found in the whole of the Latin language," the two most widely circulated modern editions of the poems roundly excoriate the poem. K. Quinn labels 68 an "early experiment in stream-of-consciousness technique" that is "too obviously contrived" and guilty of "a good deal of shoddy workmanship" (Quinn 1973b, ad c.68), while Fordyce decries the poem's rhetorical descent from sublimity into "jarring prosaic phrases"

(Fordyce 1961, ad c.68). Not coincidentally, the beginning of these aesthetic reservations coincides historically with early Romanticism, into whose interpretive framework of unified, autonomous identities poem 68 resolutely will not fit because of the split addressee: one "Mallius," then an "Allius," with no explanation of the shift. I shall discuss more fully the problem of conceptualizing "unity" as it bears on aesthetics at the end of this chapter.

26. *Symp.* 206e5.

27. Cf. Price 1989, 38–42.

28. Halperin 1985.

29. Halperin (Halperin 1985) anatomizes the Platonic discussion of *erōs* between object and aim (172) but, unaccountably, does not draw attention to Freud's identical distinction in his analysis of the drive and cites a vaguer parallel to Freud's theories of transference (174).

30. On this see esp. Santas 1988, 99ff.

31. As noted by Vlastos 1973, 27.

32. *SE* 7:125–243.

33. Mitchell-Rose 1982, 14.

34. *Fides* = "trustworthiness"; *amicitia* = "friendship/partisanship"; *pietas* = "respectful observation of social, familial, or religious obligations." Here—as throughout this book—I offer translations of particular Latin words as roughly serviceable guidelines for the Latinless reader. However, such a reader should be aware that no English equivalents can adequately capture the words' full denotative and connotative range.

35. Santas 1988, 99, also notes Freud's advantage in explaining specific object choice but ties the question to the issue of idealization, not to the sexual "aberrations."

36. Mitchell-Rose 1982, 13.

37. "Some Psychical Consequences of the Anatomical Differences Between the Sexes," *SE* 19:252; my emphasis.

38. "Analysis Terminable and Interminable," *SE* 23:250–53.

39. Roughly, from *Three Essays on Sexuality* (1905—*SE* 7:125–243) to the *New Introductory Lectures on Psychoanalysis,* Lecture 23, "Femininity" (1933—*SE* 22:112–35).

40. See, e.g., *Outline of Psychoanalysis, SE* 23:201–4, and his last work, the unfinished essay on *Ichspaltung* ("The Splitting of the Ego in the Process of Defense," *SE* 23:273–78).

41. Felman 1987, 15.

42. Elaborated in SXXII. However, the concept of the three orders had long been in place in Lacan's thought before that seminar. Much of SXXII consisted of trying to represent the relations of the three orders by reference to mathematical topography (e.g., the Borromean knot). On the orders' emergence as concepts in the course of Lacan's career, see Macey 1988, 228–29.

43. E.g., "Mourning and Melancholia," *SE* 14:243–58, esp. 247, 249, and 255.

44. *Republic* 439–41.

45. Lacan discusses the Real most forcefully and imaginatively in SXI, chap. 5, "Tuché et automaton."

46. SI, 81–83/68–69.

47. SII, 122/97.

48. SXI, 49/49 ("Le réel est ici ce qui revient toujours à la même place").

49. "Dora's" persistent cough, for example, indicated to Freud that she knew her father, though impotent, to be carrying on an adulterous affair with Frau K. "Dora's" cough indicated the organ by means of which she concluded he gratified his lover (*SE* 7:47–48).

50. *Écrits* 93–100/1–7.

51. *Écrits* 101–24/8–29.

52. F. O. Copley pinpoints these self-divisions with great sensitivity (Copley 1949).

53. See chaps. 18–23 (esp. 18 and 20) in Benveniste 1971.

54. SXI, 127–30/138–42.

55. SXI, 127/139.

56. Bowie 1991, 92.

57. Borch-Jacobsen 1991, 205–7, analyzing Lacan's use of Freud's *Project for a Scientific Psychology* (*SE* 1:281–397) in SVII, 61ff.

58. The discussion on language that follows depends chiefly upon SIV and SVII.

59. *Écrits* 691/287.

60. *Écrits* 691/286.

61. The phallus is nearly a pandemic concept in Lacan's work. The crucial text, however, is "La signification du phallus" (*Écrits* 685–95/281–91).

62. Particularly clear in his essay "On Transformations of Instinct as Exemplified in Anal Erotism," *SE* 17:127–33.

63. A brief version of the story also appears in *The Interpretation of Dreams,* *SE* 5:461n1.

64. *Écrits* 317–22/102–7.

65. Illuminating discussions of the relationship between psychoanalysis and narrative—particularly of the fictionalization of the putative originary "event," or *fabula,* whose place is held by *da* in our example—can be found in Brooks 1979 and Culler 1980.

66. See, in this regard, *Écrits* 197–213.

67. SXI, 60/62; *Écrits* 276–78/65–67.

68. As Lacan calls it, borrowing Freud's phrase from *GW* 3:609; *SE* 5:603. Cf. Lacan, *Écrits* 173/526; 228/587.

69. See, e.g., SXI, 199/218. The primal Unconscious logically predicates the

operation of repression, which draws material into the Unconscious by attraction to material already repressed. Freud postulated the primal Unconscious as the very first repressed material, which anchors the whole chain of subsequent repressions. See, e.g., "Repression" (*SE* 14.148); "The Unconscious" (*SE* 14:181).

70. *Écrits* 503/154; SIII, 303–5.

71. *Écrits* 793–827/292–325; see also S. Žižek's lucid discussion of the subject's political *capitonnage* (Žižek 1989, 87–129).

72. See M. Nussbaum, who is eloquent in her exasperation with Diotima's combination of asperity and slippery reasoning used to bully the philosophic lover into abandoning bodies for Ideas ("The Speech of Alcibiades," Nussbaum 1986, 179–80).

73. Cf. Ferrari 1987, 39–45.

74. The fullest discussions of *objet a* are to be found in SX, SXI, and SXIV.

75. *Écrits* 614/251–52; 817–18/315.

76. *Écrits* 817–18/315.

77. Cf. Borch-Jacobsen 1991, pp. 227–31.

78. SXI, 129–30/141–42.

79. Miller 1984; Ragland-Sullivan 1991.

80. SXX, 70–71.

81. Just as in Freud's account of the little boy's *retrospective* construction of the castrated female body in "Some Psychical Consequences of the Anatomical Difference between the Sexes," *SE* 19:252.

82. *Écrits* 499–501/151–52.

83. *Écrits* 823, 825/320, 322–23.

84. Recent work by D. Halperin (Halperin 1990), J. J. Winkler (Winkler 1990), and E. Cantarella (Cantarella 1988)—all inspired by M. Foucault's *Histoire de la sexualité*—has emphasized the way in which gender positions in ancient Greece and Rome depended less on the anatomical sex of one's object than on that object's position of subordination to oneself. Thus "masculine" for Greek and Roman males could be glossed as "sexual penetrator"—of slaves, women, and (for Greeks) younger males (Roman law and mores, by contrast, forbade sexual relations with freeborn Roman youths). "Feminine" is "that which is penetrated"—including the anatomically male. Penetration of males did not (as in twentieth-century constructions of homosexuality) undermine one's masculinity; rather, it reinforced it.

This work is, to a degree, welcome news to a Lacanian such as myself, insofar as remapping ancient sexuality between the poles of penetrator/penetrated, rather than male/female, approaches the flexibility of Lacan's conceptual categories Man/ Woman in the latter's entire indifference to anatomy. The work of Foucauldian classicists thus supports the application of Lacanian theories of gender to the ancient world. However, by focusing almost exclusively on behaviors and actions, the Foucauldians have avoided theorizing a consistent *subjectivity* of sexuality. They thus lack a conceptual basis from which to address important historical continuities between ancient and modern sexualities—such as the subordinate position of women in each. (See, in this regard, my review of Halperin 1991 [Janan 1991]; Richlin 1992a, esp. pp. xiii–xxviii; Richlin 1993). I believe, and shall demonstrate, that Lacanian psychoanalytic theory can remedy this lack.

85. SXX, 31.

86. See, e.g., SXX, 75.

87. SXX, 46.

88. *Écrits* 817–27/315–24.

89. *Symp.* 202a2–9.

90. *Phaedrus* 229c6–230a6.

91. *Phaedrus* 230d3–5.

92. Anthony Giddens' felicitous coinage (Giddens 1979, 52). See his illuminating discussion of the consequences of emphasizing structural determination of the subject over any possibility of her agency or transformation in chap. 2, "Agency, Structure."

2. Poems One Through Eleven: A Fragmentary History of the Affair

1. Parker 1936, 181.

2. On c.1 as poetic manifesto, see Elder 1966a. See also: Wiseman 1979, 169–70 and 174; Skinner 1987a.

3. My arguments do not depend upon the order of cc.2–11. The points they touch upon are interrelated; they suggest a narrative of the affair; and both these facts would be true even if they were scattered throughout the corpus. For interpretations of these poems as forming a coherent narrative sequence, see Barwick 1958; Williams 1968, 469ff.; Segal 1968b; Rankin 1972; Schmidt 1973a, 217–19; Westphal 1870, 5; Offermann 1977, 270–73; Skinner 1981, 39–43.

4. The proportions and ordering of the original *libellus*—if anything of either survives in the modern *Catulli Veronensis Liber*—have formed a subject of interest in the nineteenth century, of fierce controversy and considerable speculation in the twentieth. The point of common ground is that c.1 points to the publication of some volume of verse arranged by Catullus himself. The question is, which poems of the present collection were included in that *libellus*, and in what order? Estimates range from the unusually conservative claim of T. K. Hubbard (Hubbard 1983) that only the first fourteen poems compose the *libellus* to the reckless expansiveness of those who see the whole collection of poems as we now have it as the result of Catullus' own editing and publishing (in one volume or in three). Among the proponents of the latter view are Wilamowitz-Möllendorff 1913, 292; Wiseman 1969, 1–31; Quinn 1973a, 9–20; Offermann, 1977; Schmidt 1979; Most 1981; Dettmer 1988. A middle ground is defined by those critics who see the present collection as the result of a posthumous editor combining the original *libellus* referred to in the dedicatory c.1 with subsequent *libelli* (even Hubbard concedes a second *libellus* beginning with 14a, though "the polymetra of the second collection

seem not to be as closely organized as those of the *libellus*" [Hubbard 1983, 255])
and/or with various single poems. Proponents of this view include Ellis 1889, 1–
3; Friedrich 1908, 71–76; Schmidt 1914; Wheeler 1934, 4–32; Ullman 1955,
102–4; Fordyce 1961, 409–10; Coppel 1973, 141–84; Giardina 1974; Clausen
1976; Skinner 1981. Arguments are based on statistics, such as the capacity of
the average papyrus roll or the number of verses contained in the average published
libelli of other poets (such as Propertius or Tibullus), as well as on perceived formal
and thematic correspondences between groups of poems of various sizes. These
methods of analysis can hardly be called exact and have so far yielded no general
consensus. I therefore will not base any of my arguments on the idea that Catullus
himself is responsible for the order of the poems as we have them, in part or as
a whole.

5. G. P. Goold (Goold 1974 and 1981) has recently drawn renewed attention
to Th. Bergk's emendation of 1.9 to read as follows:

> quare habe tibi quidquid hoc libelli,
> qualecumque *quidem est, patroni ut ergo*
> plus uno maneat perenne saeclo.

The proposed emendations are both ingenious and interesting—but not compel-
ling, especially since I do not share Goold's stylistic dissatisfactions with the text
when minimally amended by the addition of an *o*. (Rather, I believe G. Williams'
praise describes the poem aptly: "careful artistry is combined with an impression
of live informal immediacy" [Williams 1968, 41]). Against Goold's argument, see
Wiseman 1979, 167–74; Mayer 1982. For a supporting opinion, see Skutsch
1982.

6. Quinn 1973b, ad loc.

7. See Fordyce 1961, ad loc.

8. As is true of the poet Caecilius' adoring fan and lover, "Sapphica puella" /
"musa doctior" (35.16–17). Catullus admires Caecilius, too—because, the poem
implies, the two men share the aesthetic principles whose effects so dazzle Caecilius'
puella. Quinn notes the analogy (Quinn 1973b, ad loc.).

9. Todorov 1971a.

10. Todorov 1971a, 238–39.

11. The French text reads: "La simple relation de faits successifs ne constitue
pas un récit: il faut que ces faits soient organisés, c'est-à-dire, en fin de compte,
qu'ils aient des éléments en commun. Mais si tous les éléments sont communs, il
n'y a plus de récit car il n'y a plus rien à raconter. Or la transformation représente
justement une synthèse de différence et de ressemblance, elle relie deux faits sans
que ceux-ci puissent s'identifier. Plutôt qu' «unité à deux face», elle est une opération
à double sens: elle affirme à la fois la ressemblance et la différence; elle enclenche
le temps et le suspend, d'un seul mouvement; elle permet au discours d'acquérir
un sens sans que celui-ci devienne pure information; en un mot: elle rend possible
le récit et nous livre sa définition meme" (Todorov 1971a, 240).

12. G .R. F. Ferrari (Ferrari 1987, 19–20, 61–64) is particularly lucid and illuminating on the issue of collection and division as a principle of philosophic investigation and evaluation.

13. Citing Plato's own pupil, Aristotle. See Brooks 1984, 91.

14. Todorov 1971b, 42.

15. Refining Roman Jakobson. See "Two Aspects of Language and Two Types of Aphasic Disturbances," in Jakobson 1956.

16. Laplanche-Pontalis 1973, 82.

17. Laplanche-Pontalis 1973, 121.

18. On recombinatory poetics and the exhaustion of literary possibilities, see Levitan 1985, esp. 249–50, 253, 267n37, and 267–69.

19. "Act whose explicit goal is not attained; instead, this goal turns out to have been replaced by another one. . . . parapraxes, like symptoms, are compromise formations resulting from the antagonism between the subject's conscious intentions and what he has repressed." (Laplanche-Pontalis 1973, 300).

20. On the poem's irony, see Lateiner 1977, 15ff., and Skinner 1981, 53–55, both of whom emphasize the distance the poem draws between the poet and his poetry. But A. Richlin rightly draws attention to the poem's self-deconstruction: ✓ "the poem itself in reality achieves a kind of public verbal rape, even if it is a joke; so much for the actual chasteness and *pietas* of the poet/Catullus" (Richlin 1983 and 1992a, 13). Martin 1992, 76–79, and Fitzgerald 1992 pursue both lines of interpretation by arguing (as do I, but from a somewhat different theoretical framework) that uncertainty about the poet's honor is part of an elaborate game with the audience kept unresolvably in play by the poem itself.

21. For a fascinating study of c.63 proceeding from similar premises, see Skinner 1993.

22. The most recent partisans of this view are Nadeau 1980; Genovese 1974; Giangrande 1975. (And now, Hooper 1985, who adds nothing of substance to previous arguments). Nadeau and Giangrande (but not Genovese) extend their argument for reading cc.2 and 3 as extended allegories for the sexual play between Catullus and Lesbia, to reading 2b as a reference to a substitute for that play—to masturbation. H. D. Jocelyn (Jocelyn 1980) summarizes the opposition view to taking *passer* as equivalent to "penis" and therefore to the masturbation idea as well. As Jocelyn notes (422–26), the penis/*passer* equation stretches from Politian through Isaac Voss, the seventeenth-century editor and commentator on Catullus, to Forcellini in the eighteenth century (Forcellini 1771, s.v. *passer*).

The arguments of these allegorists center upon the sexual significance of certain words in the poems. For example, as Jocelyn notes: "in some contexts *sinus* could function like *cunnus, noscere/cognoscere* like *futuere* and *vorare/devorare* like *fellare*." But "there is no reason . . . to suppose a regular usage of the spoken language behind any of the sporadic literary examples. Literature moreover applied all the words in question regularly and commonly to non-sexual things and non-sexual acts" (Jocelyn 1980, 427–28). Moreover, the equation upon which the allegorical arguments chiefly rest—*passer* = "penis"—has no Latin evidence (Jocelyn 1980, 427). Genovese bases the equation partly on the late third-century C.E. evidence of Festus as to the obscene meaning of *strutheus,* a term based on the Greek word for sparrow (*struthos*), "which is what the Greeks call the *passer*" (Genovese 1974, 121–22). That hardly confirms that the word *passer* itself meant "penis" in the 200's C.E., much less the first century B.C.E. Giangrande, on even weaker ground, resorts to modern vulgar Italian usage (*passero* = penis) as evidence for the Latin of Catullus's day (Giangrande 1975, 137).

Those who interpret 2a and 3 as alluding to masturbation rest their analyses chiefly upon myth's constructions of Atalanta's sexuality. Voss (taking *malum* as referring to the testicles and amending the *possem* of 2.9 to *posse*) interprets 2b as saying, in effect, "to play with the *passer* (i.e., to masturbate) is as grateful to me as the sight of Hippomenes' genitals was to the virgin Atalanta." Giangrande and Nadeau (neither of whom amends the text) construe the myth of Atalanta, and thus the tone and alignment of the passage, slightly differently. Giangrande adduces modern (e.g., Licht 1926) rather than ancient evidence to the effect that Atalanta was thought of as disliking sexual penetration and therefore as practicing fellation in order to *keep* her "zonam diu ligatam." Therefore, he reasons, the apple that made her suffer sexual penetration would be odious to her. Nadeau, on firmer ground, simply points to her myth's emphasis on preserving her virginity (hence the bridal contest and its fatal consequences for most suitors) and to the apple as "symbolum rei venereae" as proving a relationship of antipathy. Both then go on to interpret 2b as saying, "to masturbate would be as grateful to me as the apple was to Atalanta"—i.e., not at all grateful, but rather a matter of distaste.

The evidence upon which these interpretations rest is, to say the least, weak. Jocelyn adduces many more arguments against this interpretation, which I will not rehearse here. The most telling count against such narrow allegory is the sense (or rather, nonsense) it would make of the poems. I do not deny (in fact, I argue in favor of) the erotic resonance of cc.2 and 3's vocabulary and imagery. However, to read these poems as if each word had a one-to-one correspondence with an obscene denotation is to miss (as I argue in my text) a much more subtle Catullan construction of sexuality and its signification.

23. The species of bird referred to as *passer* is controversial: it is not a sparrow, as often translated. The preponderance of opinion leans toward the rock thrush—but since I find this name both clumsy and ugly, I have preferred to leave the Latin term untranslated.

24. As Quinn notes (Quinn 1973b, ad loc.). See also Korzeniewski 1978–79, esp. 230–37.

25. Or so I infer from Politian's sexual interpretation of Martial's reference (11.6.16) to Catullus' *passer* (Politian 1489, cap. vi). J. Sannazaro, in castigating Politian for the suggestion, made the straightforward assumption that Politian had in mind Catullus' own *passer* poems as well as Martial's allusion to it (Sannazaro 1535). Other sixteenth-century commentators followed Sannazaro's construction

of Politian's comment (see Guarini 1520, ad loc.; Realinus 1551, 54–55; Muret 1554, 2; Scaliger 1577, 6). Whatever Politian intended, later tradition read him as *pater logou*.

For a balanced and subtle assessment of *Martial*'s own use of *passer* as less unambiguously sexual than often assumed, see Pitcher 1982.

26. See, e.g., Riese 1884; Baehrens 1885; Ellis 1889; Merrill 1893; Friedrich 1908; Lenchantin de Gubernatis 1928; Kroll 1929; Fordyce 1961; and Quinn 1973b, ad loc.

27. In the context of Roman erotic poetry, *dolor* usually refers to "love pangs"; *ardor* means "passion"; and *curae* denotes "the cares of love."

28. "On Transformations of Instinct as Exemplified in Anal Erotism," *SE* 17:127–33.

29. Fenichel 1949.

30. See, e.g., *Écrits* 733.

31. K. J. McKay explores the element of witty and comic play in his study of Callimachus' Fifth and Sixth Hymns (McKay 1962). His favorite characterization for Callimachus and his poetic practice is "mischievous," but specifically defined in a context of mental challenge: "if this study establishes anything, it draws attention to Kallimachos as 'the mischievous poet', who delights in the ebb and flow of images and challenges us to detect when his semantic tide is on the turn" (12). See also McKay's comparison of Hymn Six with the conventions of Doric comedy (117–24). More recent treatments of the comic in Callimachus include Hutchinson, 1988, 26–84 passim; Bing 1988, passim, but esp. 91–143. C. Martin devotes an interesting chapter to the subject of playfulness in Catullus, that I find parallels some of my own thinking about his poetry, but from a quite different theoretical viewpoint. Martin draws upon G. Bateson's "Notes Toward a Theory of Fantasy and Play" in order to analyze Catullus' poetry as "metacommunicative discourse" (Martin 1992, 67–91).

32. *Aetia* I.1.5–6.

33. E.g., J. Ferguson (Ferguson 1970) translated Epigram 19, commemorating a fictitious "Nicoteles" ("finishes the winner") son of "Phillip" ("horse lover") so as to reveal Callimachus' droll twist on a traditionally lugubrious form—the funeral epitaph.

Δωδεκέτη τὸν παῖδα πατὴρ ἀπέθηκε Φίλιππος
ἐνθάδε, τὴν πολλὴν ἐλπίδα, Νικοτέλην.

Mr. Ryder senior retired
his twelve-year-old son
here, the favorite,
Victor.

34. E.g., c.36:

Annales Volusi, cacata carta,
votum solvite pro mea puella.

nam sanctae Veneri Cupidinique
vovit, si sibi restitutus essem
desissemque truces vibrare iambos,
electissima pessimi poetae
scripta tardipedi deo daturam
infelicibus ustulanda lignis,
et hoc pessima se puella vidit
iocose lepide vovere divis.

(36.1–10)

Annals of Volusius, shit-shotten sheets, fulfill a sacred vow on behalf of my girlfriend. For she vowed to holy Venus and to Cupid that if I were restored to her and ceased to brandish my bitter verses, she would give the choicest scribbles of the worst poet to the lamefooted god, to be burned by accursed wood. And so this plague of a girlfriend thought herself pretty clever to make such a charming vow, in jest, to the gods.

"Iocose" and "lepide" assess Lesbia's vow as "up to snuff" according to Callimachean standards—

acceptum face redditumque votum,
si *non illepidum neque invenustum est*

(36.16–17)

—"acknowledge the receipt of the vow and pay it back" / "*as truly as it is a witty and charming one*" (Ellis 1889, 130; my emphasis. On *lepidus* as a neoteric stamp of approval, cf. c.1.1: "cui dono *lepidum* novum libellum . . . ?" and c.6.17: "volo te ac tuos amores" / "ad caelum *lepido* vocare versu"). One can easily see why: to consider just a few points—

a. The votive hymn parodies the serious form, twisting the conventions just enough to be witty. Quinn 1973 points to 36.6, "electissima"—"only the best is good enough for a god." But "pessimi poetae," as he notes, deflects the "hymn's" trajectory: "even the best in this case is not up to much." Fordyce 1961 cites Euripides *IT* 20 (Agamemnon's vow) as a serious paradigm of divine address, molded around excellence sacrificed to divinity: "He promised *the most beautiful thing* that the year should give birth to to the light-bearing goddess."

b. It uses learned periphrasis to refer to fire, 36.7: the "tardipedus deus" = "Vulcan" = "fire." Cf. 27.7: "hic merus est Thyonianus" = "here is the god sometimes addressed as 'Thyone' (i.e., Bacchus) undiluted" = "this is straight wine." Deciphering the epithet *Thyonianus* requires considerable erudition on the reader's part. As Fordyce notes, "Thyone" is an alternative name for Semele, Dionysus' mother (Fordyce 1961, ad 27.7, citing *Homeric Hymn* 1.21).

Such allusions to mythical and textual variants within the literary tradition are a quintessentially Callimachean feat of *sprezzatura*. As D. Clayman notes,

Callimachus' tale of Acontius and Cydippe describes his heroine as partipating in "the dance of sleeping Ariede" (Fr. 67.13 Pf.). "Ariede" was Zenodotus' reading in *Il.* 18.592; all other editions read "Ariadne." Callimachus' reference to the minority reading thus flaunts his acquaintance with the latest textual criticism (Clayman 1982, 1.469). Again (in an instance closer to the present Catullan example), Callimachus refers to Dawn as *Tito* rather than *Eos* (*Aetia* 1.21.3). This title for the goddess only he and Lycophron, the fourth-century tragedian, share. Choeroboscus explains the title as a shortened feminine version of *Titan*—thus a reference to her status as one of the oldest generation of gods, as opposed to the Olympians (Choeroboscus, *Peri orthographias*, II.263.30 in Cramer 1835).

35. *Jokes and Their Relation to the Unconscious, SE* 8:102–15.

36. Thomson capitalizes "somnus;" I consider the implied personification unnecessary, and have therefore followed Mynors' punctuation in this instance.

37. I owe this *trouvaille* to Professor Francis Newton.

38. The word *Romanitas* is admittedly postclassical (from Tertullian, *De Pallio* 4)—but I follow C. N. Cochrane's example in using it to mark succinctly the powerful ideology of "the Roman way" so evidently at work throughout Roman history (Cochrane 1944).

39. On Catullus' use of erotic imagery here, see Scott 1969.

40. On the erotic force of Licinius' wit, see Segal 1970, 27.

41. Segal 1970. For other discussions of *otium* in Catullus, see Borzsak 1956; Pucci 1961, 249ff; Woodman 1966; Wills 1967, 193; Frank 1968; Laidlaw 1968; Lejnieks 1968; Rosenmeyer 1969, chap. 4; Finamore 1984.

For an exhaustive evaluation of *otium*'s connotations and denotations in Latin culture as a whole, see André 1966. See also J. Fontaine's thoughtful review of André's work (Fontaine 1966).

42. Cf. c.61.204–5:

> *ludite* ut lubet, et brevi
> liberos date . . .

43. Cf. Ipsitilla, addressed as "mei lepores," when she is being asked for an assignation (32.2); the "lepidissima coniunx" and "lepidus filius" whom Gallus joins in c.78 as lovers, "ut bello bella puella cubet" (78.4).

44. Such as Catullus' own poetry: his *libellus* is *lepidus* in 1.1; his *versiculi* have *lepos* in 16.7.

45. See Fordyce 1961, ad 50.3.

46. Cf. c.68, where Catullus explains his inability to write poetry as stemming from the same source that quelled all his pleasure in love—his brother's death, which caused him to flee "haec studia atque omnes *delicias* animi" (68.26). I will discuss the meaning of this phrase in greater detail in chap. 5.

47. On the close connections among play (*ludus*), *otium*, and nugatory verse, see Wagenvoort 1935.

48. Cf. Cicero, *Pro Sestio* 66.138–39; also Balsdon 1960.

49. Cicero oddly resembles Catullus: he is also an outsider to Rome, as a *novus homo;* also ambitious in his chosen arena; also one who reinvents the Latin language for his own purposes. Yet Cicero's conservative allegiance to Rome's dominant political and social order makes him useful to set against Catullus, as a way to measure Catullus' particular inflection of terms central to Roman social norms. (For Cicero's conservatism, see Wood 1988.) C.49's praising Cicero as "dissertissime Romuli nepotum," in contrast to Catullus as self-styled "pessimus omnium poeta," has generally been taken as ironic. Whether ironic or not, c.49 does show Catullus himself constructing Cicero as his polar opposite. (For a view of the poem as sincere praise of Cicero, see Thomson 1967.)

50. Cf. **68.**145, which describes his meetings with Lesbia as "dear, stolen gifts" ("furtiva . . . munuscula").

51. Controversy has raged over whether 2.11–13—usually printed separately in editions of Catullus and labeled "2b"—belong to poem 2a. K. Lachmann (Lachmann 1829) printed 2.1–10 separately from 2.11–13 and was followed suit by a number of editors, including Ellis 1878; Riese 1884; Baehrens-Schulze 1893. The tradition continues among modern editors (e.g., Schuster-Eisenhut 1958; Mynors 1958). Among those who accompany their editions with an explanation of their separatism are: Kroll 1929; Quinn 1973b; Fordyce 1961. W. Eisenhut (Eisenhut 1965), although he concentrates for the most part on undermining textual arguments for a unified c.2, adduces additional thematic and grammatical points against uniting 2a and 2b (Eisenhut 1965, 304n1). Among the various separatist arguments are the following points:

 a. The grammatical connection between 2.9–10 and 2.11–13 is difficult.
 b. The myth of Atalanta is an inappropriate cap to a poem about a game with a *passer.*
 c. Although the manuscripts run all thirteen lines together, they also combine them with c. 3, which is clearly a separate poem; inaccurate combinations are present throughout the manuscripts (as are false distinctions).

Among the unitarians are Dornseiff 1936; Dornseiff 1953; Barwick 1958, 313; Salvatore 1953, 420; Wagenvoort 1940; Ghiselli 1953; Lieberg 1962, 99–110; Gugel 1968; Pearcy 1980; Dettmer 1984; Wirth 1986. Lenchantin de Gubernatis prints 2a and 2b as one poem but evidences some discomfort over his decision (Lenchantin de Gubernatis 1928, 5). Pearcy rearranges the order of the lines but accepts them all as one poem. Unitarian arguments center on the following points:

 a. The grammatical connection can be made in various ways: R. Ellis (Ellis 1889, 9) suggests taking "possem" as conditional, even though followed by the indicative in "tam gratum est," so that the sense of 2.9–13 would be "could I but play with you, *passer,* it would be as grateful to me as was the apple to Atalanta," and cites Plautus, *Poenulus* 4.2.99, and Martial 2.63.3 as parallel unexpected conjunctions of indicative and subjunctive. R. Kent picks up Ellis' suggestion and expands on it, suggesting that the present indicative "has reference to a possible future realization. Anything but the present indicative would seem to me utterly out of place; Catullus could not here admit the unattainability of his desires" (Kent 1923, 353). A. F. Braunlich argues, not very convincingly, for the same grammatical construction, but assumes as the subject of "est" in 2.11 "Lesbia's encouragement of the poet's suit" (Braunlich 1923, 351). Other editors resort to changing the text: to *possum* in 2.9, for example (so Birt 1895, viff.; Giri 1894, 55ff.); to *posse* (Voss 1684).

    b. A connection to Atalanta can also be drawn. As playing with the *passer* makes the bird an amorous connection between Lesbia and Catullus (actual for Lesbia, hoped-for by Catullus), so the apple was a vehicle that evidenced Hippomenes' love for Atalanta. As H. Gugel puts it, "der Apfelwurf bedeute für Atalante die Gewissheit, von Hippomenes geliebt zu werden, das Spiel mit dem Vogel folglich dasselbe für Catull" (Gugel 1968, 818–19). (The same equation of play with the *passer* and the throwing of the apple is made by Lieberg 1962, 102; Gallavotti 1929; Wagenvoort 1940, 294ff.)

    c. Although (as Eisenhut 1965 demonstrates) the manuscript tradition is no argument *for* unity, neither is it (as Gugel 1968 remarks, 811) any argument *against* unity. Gugel rightly points out that the only reasonable criteria for unity, given a manuscript tradition so corrupt and unreliable, must be internal and not textual (Gugel 1983, 813).

I take the whole thirteen lines to be one poem. I am convinced by the numerous structural, thematic, and formal parallels between 2a and 2b (most fully enumerated by Lieberg and Gugel) that the two belong together.

52. Such as animates the character of Diotima. See D. Halperin's subtle reading of her speech in the *Symposium* (Halperin 1990, 113–51).

53. On *zonam solvere* as sexual consummation, see Kroll 1929, ad loc.

54. *Symp.* 203b-c.

55. The poems have not been read together often, though Merrill 1893 and Quinn 1959 both note (briefly) that the two are closely connected. L. Ferrero (Ferrero 1955, 170ff.) and C. Segal (Segal 1968a) are exceptions. Segal's reading is a particularly sensitive one, to which I am indebted for many of the details of my discussion, though I have placed them in a different framework. He also includes helpful bibliography on previous readings of 5 and 7 as independent poems.

56. "The question of Seven comes from Lesbia; the poem, while answering that question, is in a sense a reproach to her for having asked it" (Segal 1968a, 301).

57. See Moorhouse 1963.

58. On the association of stars, thievery, night, and love, see Ramminger 1937, 68–71; Segal 1974.

59. Strabo (xvii.837) says, "Cyrene is said to be the creation of Battus, and Callimachus alleges that he [Battus] is his ancestor." The Suda, on the other hand,

says that Callimachus' father was named Battus but says nothing to support any connection with the Battiads, the founding family of Cyrene. Both Strabo and the Suda may be basing their biographical details upon divergent interpretations of Callimachus' own epithet for himself, Battiades.

> Βαττιάδεω παρὰ σῆμα φέρεις πόδας εὖ μὲν ἀοιδήν
> εἰδότος, εὖ δ' οἴνῳ καίρια συγγελάσαι.
>
> (*Ep.* 35 Pf.)

You are passing by the tomb of Battiades, who knew well how to sing, and how to laugh a bit over the wine, when the time was appropriate.

J. P. Elder (Elder 1951, 108) notices the reference to Callimachus.

60. *Symp.* 202b10–202d7.

61. *Symp.* 202e3–203a8.

62. The next Lesbia poem in the cc.2–11 subcycle would be c.8. However, I see c.8's principal importance to our analysis as that of a "renunciation poem"— like c.11. Rather than dilute my discussion of renunciation by dividing it between two poems, I have chosen to concentrate on c.11 as the stronger exemplar of Catullus' emotional divorce from Lesbia.

63. Recent essays on c.11 include Bright 1976a; Yardley 1981; Fowler 1983; Scott 1983; Fredericksmeyer 1983; Blodgett-Nielsen 1986; Sweet 1987 (who includes an overview of the major interpretive cruxes in his discussion, along with previous bibliography. I find his discussion of the poem, and that of Blodgett and Nielsen, particularly sophisticated).

64. A seemingly awkward detail whose implications for the artistic coherence of the poem have been much discussed. See the interpretations of Kinsey 1965a; Ross 1969, 173–174; Putnam 1974; Duclos 1976; Mulroy 1977/78; Woodman 1978; Fredericksmeyer 1983, 39–40; Heath 1989.

65. For the plow as a male sexual symbol, cf. Sophocles' *Antigone* 569. For the more general image of cultivating a field as a metaphor for sexual relations between male and female, cf. Sophocles, *OT* 1256, 1458; Aeschylus, *Sept.* 753; Lucretius 4. 1107. These passages compare the female to the cultivated field or furrow, and the male, by implication, to whatever cultivates that ground.

The gender reversals implicit in both images of c.11's final strophe have been noted in Segal 1968b, 317; Duclos 1976, 86.

66. The flower traditionally symbolizes feminine sexuality in Graeco-Roman poetry. Cf. Sappho 105c (LP) on nubile women as flowers; also Catullus' own epithalamia, 61.188, 62.39–47. For the flower as representing female virginity, cf. Archilochus PC7511 (where Neoboule has "lost her virgin flower"); Hesiod 132 Merkelbach-West; Catullus 62.46. For the flower as, more generally, female sexuality, cf. Aeschylus, *Ag.* 743, where Helen comes as a bride (though not a virgin) to Troy and is called "erotos anthos"; also Catullus 64.401–2: "optavit genitor primaevi funera nati," / "liber ut innuptae poteretur *flore* novellae."

67. For a more general view of Catullus' implied political commentary, see Skinner 1980.

3. Poems Eleven and Fifty-one: Repetition and *Jouissance*

1. From *Alcestis,* translation by R. Lesser (Lesser 1975, 13).

2. This hope applies as much to homosexual relations as it does to heterosexual relations. Woman is, as I said in chap. 1, a position of fictive complementarity founded on the signifier, not on anatomy.

3. Note Catullus' repeated insistence that Lesbia's existence is the essential complement to his own: he habitually calls her *mea vita* (109.1, 104.1) and says further that she makes his life worth living (68.160). Consider also that in the idealized allegory of his love for Lesbia, Laodamia is said to lose a union "sweeter than her own life and breath" ("ereptum est vita dulcius atque anima" / "coniugium," 68.106–7).

4. Padel 1983.

5. Sissa 1990.

6. Sissa 1990, 10.

7. Such as the college of augurs and the *ordo haruspicum LX.*

8. In *De Divinatione,* Cicero puts arguments for belief in the Sibyl's inspired power in his brother Quintus' mouth (*De Div.* 1.79), who says of his whole conspectus on divination, "there is nothing new or original in my beliefs" ("Nihil . . . equidem novi, nec quod praeter ceteros ipse sentiam," *De Div.* 1.11). Cicero's refutation makes Quintus look credulous, but neither stupid nor outlandish, for holding such beliefs. Indeed, Cicero would not have had to expend so much energy on his rebuttal in if Quintus' beliefs were the opinion not only of the *maiores,* as Cicero admits (*De Div.* 2.110–12), but also of many of his contemporaries.

9. The final work of H. W. Parke's life, his illuminating study on the Sibyls, has been edited by B. C. McGing and published posthumously (Parke-McGing 1988). I have been greatly assisted in the discussion that follows by Parke's and McGing's judicious scholarship.

10. Anomalous, but hardly inconsequential. The importance of the Sibylline prophecies can be measured by Roman reaction to the burning (in 83 B.C.E.) of Jupiter Optimus Maximus' Capitoline temple, which housed the books. As soon as the chaos of the civil war between Sulla and Marius was sorted out, a diligent search eventually spanning much of Italy, some of the Greek islands, and Africa was set in motion to replace the prophecies with a fresh collection (the first search yielded only about a thousand replacement verses, apparently judged insufficient to replace the former collection of over three thousand. Parke-McGing 1980, 138–39, examines the evidence for more than one search expedition).

Though he postdates Catullus, Augustus' assessment of the potential insurrectionist power of the Sibylline prophecies may offer an additional clue to their importance. Augustus reorganized the observances surrounding the texts to shore up the power of his principate. He moved the books from the temple of Juppiter Optimus Maximus (identified with the Republic) to the temple of Apollo (tutelary god of the Princeps). He also gathered up all the Sibylline prophecies circulating illicitly in *fatidici libri* and submitted them to the editorship of the *quindecemviri,* as the appropriate judges of which were truly Sibylline—meaning, presumably, those that could not be read as anti-Principate, among other criteria. One would assume that if Augustus considered the Sibylline prophecies an insignificant part of the religious tradition he inherited, he would not have bothered tampering with the traditional observances. Parke-McGing offers a full account of Augustus' innovations (141–42).

11. Obviously, I do not accept the thesis advanced by U. Wilamowitz-Möllendorf that an Alexandrian model stands behind c.63 (Wilamowitz-Möllendorf 1879; see also Wilamowitz-Möllendorf 1924, 2.291–95). J. P. Elder reviews the evidence for such a position and convincingly rejects it (Elder 1947, 394n2).

12. As noted by Weston 1919/20; Lieberg 1962, 85–92; Wirshbo 1980; Fredericksmeyer 1970, 436; Adler 1981, 163–66.

13. As argued by Fortenbaugh 1966.

14. Mitchell-Rose 1982, 52 and 52n18.

15. Teresa of Avila 1980, 2:216.

16. See Ferrari 1991, esp. 141–48—though I think he overstates the case for Plato's sternly disciplined allegiance to rationality over poetry.

17. "The Speech of Alcibiades," Nussbaum 1986, 165–99, esp. 184–95.

18. See M. Nussbaum, "This Story Isn't True: Madness, Reason, and Recantation in the *Phaedrus,*" (Nussbaum 1986, 200–233). She cogently argues that the *Phaedrus* is a palinode to Diotima's disdain for passionate love of the individual, as expressed in the *Symposium.*

19. A. Carson's translation (Carson 1986, 161).

20. A. Carson is clearest on the problem: "the verse is a dactylic hexameter and scans fine except for the word *de,* which precedes the divine name Pteros. *De* is by nature a single short syllable and stands at a position in the line that requires a short syllable; the rules of Greek prosody, however, regularly call for a short syllable, when it is followed by two consonants, to become a long syllable. Thus the *pt-* with which the gods enlarge *erōs* forces this verse into a metrical dilemma." See also her interesting and sensitive expansion on what the verse implies for the *Phaedrus'* view of desire (Carson 1986, 160–62).

G. R. F. Ferrari (Ferrari 1987, 169) notes the point briefly ("a whiff of the grotesque will always accompany such large philosophic aspirations as are here evoked; the god, with all those extra consonants, is just too big a name to fit mere human measures").

21. A tactic of mystification that characterizes both Platonic and Freudian accounts of love as well. Alcibiades elevates Socrates to the position of Woman, whose hidden *agalmata* constitute a powerful, but completely unavailable, lure. And Freud's own construction of Woman as the "Dark Continent" ("The Question

of Lay Analysis," *SE* 20:212), whose mysterious desire was a matter for his persistent investigation, casts him in the posture of beseeching courtly lover before an enigmatic and unresponsive Lady.

References to instances of these attitudes in Catullus' contemporary culture could be multiplied ad infinitum, and would far exceed the scope of the present study. Several conspectuses exist, however, useful both in themselves and for their bibliographical guidance to further sources. See Hallett 1989; Richlin 1983; Richlin 1992a, esp. pp. xiii–xxxiii; Richlin 1992b; Culham 1987; Hillard 1989. In addition, G. Lieberg has written the definitive study of one pole—the icon of the "divine" mistress (Lieberg 1962).

Of particular interest is M. Nussbaum's recent study demonstrating Lucretius' awareness of these two illusory poles as constructions of Woman, and his philosophical impatience with the repetitive cycle of infatuation and revulsion they underwrite (Nussbaum 1989). Lucretius' summation of the Graeco-Roman erotic tradition in *DRN* 4.1154–70 is particularly illuminating insofar as it draws the clichés it ridicules largely from the ancient poetic tradition—particularly from Hellenistic epigram, whose heir Catullus styles himself (see Kenney 1970; Kenney tentatively advances the hypothesis that Catullus himself is a particular tangential target of Lucretius' satirical summary). The Lucretius passage demonstrates clearly that Catullus did not invent the organizing poles of his love poetry *ex nihilo* but drew upon material already abundantly present in the poetic and cultural tradition he inherited.

22. As Quinn notes: "the word is too unusual for the repetition to be fortuitous" (Quinn 1973b, ad c.11).

23. For the purposes of my analysis, I am considering Sappho's poem *only* as Catullus' conscious foil, and not as a poem composed by a woman (or a man, for that matter). My discussion of gender and *jouissance* in previous chapters and in this one should make it clear that gender positions are mobile, assumed only in and through signification. To try to investigate, then, whether Sappho "composed as a man" or "composed as a woman" in *Phainetai moi,* while simultaneously trying to analyze Catullus' poem, would complicate the investigation exponentially; and to *assume* she composed as either would be logically indefensible, given my stated premises.

24. For a painstaking analysis of the differences in detail between c. 51 and *Phainetai moi,* see also Ferrari 1938.

25. "Erotikai maniai," *On the Sublime* 10.1.

26. Text of Sappho taken from Lobel-Page 1955, amended to include Page's later reconsideration of the poem's form as evidenced in Page 1968. Page's 1968 edition was able to take into account papyrological evidence published in 1965.

27. Cf. c.51 in which Catullus writes poetry and becomes enthralled with Licinius when they were both *otiosi.*

28. Mitchell-Rose 1982, 52n17.

29. Among the modern critics who have argued against construing the fourth

strophe with the rest of c.51 are Fordyce 1961, ad loc.; Jensen 1967; Wormell 1966; Richmond 1970; Wilkinson 1974; Copley 1974.

Among those who argue for the fourth strophe's construction with the rest of c.51 are Ferrari 1938; Lattimore 1944; Borzsak 1956; Stark 1957, 330–33; Commager 1965, 89ff.; Fredericksmeyer 1965; Elder 1966b, 202–9; Wills 1967; Lejnieks 1968; Schmidt 1973b; Kinsey 1974; Shipton 1980; Adler 1981, 30–34; Baker 1981, 317–24; Itzkowitz 1983; Knox 1984; Finamore 1984; Russell 1986, 123–34. Note particularly the contribution of Itzkowitz, who sees the significance of the fourth strophe as inhering in its anomaly (as I do). He explains this, however, as designed to dramatize reflection on the act of creating the poem's first three strophes.

4. The Epigrams: "I Am Lying"

1. "Jokes and Their Relation to the Unconscious," *SE* 8:62.

2. Proust 1970, 109.

3. A term *not* to be reduced merely to the "sexual act"; it encompasses social, political, epistemological relationships between those who align themselves with the positions of Man and Woman, respectively. Lacan's investigation of these positions takes on nothing less than an entire structure of institutionalized oppression. See E. Ragland-Sullivan's discussion of Lacan's implications for feminism (Ragland-Sullivan 1991).

4. For c.51 as marking the beginning of the affair, see Wilamowitz-Möllendorf 1913, 58n2; Kroll 1929, ad loc.; Fordyce 1961, ad loc.; L. P. Wilkinson in Bayet et al. 1953, 47–48; Quinn 1973a, 57–59.

5. Mythical because, even if it exists, it cannot ultimately be known by speaker or listener. The existence of motivating forces unavailable to the speaker's or listener's Conscious obviate the possibility—forces such as the Unconscious (which functions both intrapsychically *and* in the "repressed" values of any cultural milieu) and the Real.

6. *Fides* = "good faith"; *veritas* = "truth"; *pietas* = "respectful observance of reciprocal obligations."

7. *Foedus*, "agreement"; *amicitia*, "friendship/partisanship."

8. S. Commager also draws attention to the tradition of funeral epigrams as a possible influence on Catullus' adaptation of the form: "the primary function of an epitaph is to present in the smallest possible compass the essence of a life . . . . Catullus here further compresses the epigram's natural tightness" (Commager 1965, 93).

9. Possible because of elegy's structural peculiarities. The hexameter's principal caesura, and the pentameter's diaeresis, each customarily mark off equal metrical units of two and one half feet. Thus these distinct initial sections of each line can share metrical patterns; metrical repetition between them would urge the reader

to juxtapose their contents in her mind, above and beyond the way hexameter and pentameter unfold a message in sequential reading.

10. The latter phrase set off by the *logical* caesura—though a caesura obviously bridged by elision.

11. Saussure 1966, 113.

12. *Écrits* 506–9/156–58.

13. See *Rhetoric* 1406b20–22; 1410b13–1413b2; *Poetics,* 21.

14. Recent readings of c.70 include de Venuto 1966; Laurens 1965; Konstan 1972; Miller 1988.

15. See Laurens 1965.

16. Note the repetition of "he swore," parallel to c.70's repetition of "she says." Laurens 1965 notes the parallel (545).

17. Ὤμοσε Καλλίγνωτος Ἰωνίδι μήποτ᾿ ἐκείνης
ἕξειν μήτε φίλον κρέccονα μήτε φίλην.
ὤμοcεν· ἀλλὰ λέγουcιν ἀληθέα τοὺc ἐν ἔρωτι
ὅρκουc μὴ δύνειν οὔατ᾿ ἐc ἀθανάτων.
νῦν δ᾿ ὁ μὲν ἀρcενικῷ θέρεται πυρί, τῆc δὲ ταλαίνηc
νύμφηc ὡc Μεγαρέων οὐ λόγοc οὐδ᾿ ἀριθμόc.

Ep. 25 Pf.

18. Miller 1988 notes the inversion (129).

19. Fragment 811 Snell; noted by Fordyce 1961, ad loc. (as "Nauck 741"; the fragment is in fact Nauck 742). For an interesting deconstructive reading of c.70 that also draws upon the question of gender reversals between c.70 and its principal source in Callimachus, see Miller 1988.

20. Cf. also 62.36–7, in which the boys' chorus similarly dismisses maiden resistance to marriage and the wedding night as a sham.

21. Cf. Žižek 1989, 112.

22. C.72 has received attention in the following recent essays: Harmon 1970; Davis 1971; Kubiak 1986. Kubiak provides a thoughtful overview of previous interpretations, together with bibliography (Kubiak 1986, 1–2).

23. To review just a few of the reactions among accomplished Latinists: Lenchantin de Gubernatis' edition takes "nosse" as independent of the modal "velle" in the pentameter, while E. Baehrens, E. Benoist with E. Thomas, and W. Kroll maintain, in their respective editions of Catullus, that "velle" is to be supplied to the hexameter from the pentameter. Neither construction, however, resolves the problem of whether Lesbia's knowledge of Catullus, or his of her, is in question. Quinn (Quinn 1973b, ad loc.), supplying both "dicebas" and "te" to 72.2 from 72.1, and taking the grammatical function of "te" as being the same in both lines, construes the two lines together as reporting, "I wish to know Catullus alone, and do not [wish] to have Jove before Catullus."

24. For a brilliant and meticulous study of rereading as a phenomenon of interpretation, see Winkler 1985. The measure of Winkler's ingenuity is the sophis-

ticated critical apparatus he puts together from sparse resources—chiefly, Genette 1980; Barthes 1974; and an occasional glance at Todorov 1973 and 1977. Winkler supplements these with works directed specifically at the mechanics of the "unrereadable" ratiocinative novel—detective novels, mystery novels, and other varieties of suspense fiction—because such fiction models a narrative whose conclusion necessarily forces all but the cleverest readers to revise previous interpretations of narrative data. (Noteworthy among these ratiocinative analyses are the sophisticated anthology of essays on suspense fiction edited by G. W. Most and W. W. Stowe [Most-Stowe 1983] and S. Tani's meditation on the avant-garde detective novel [Tani 1984, esp. chap.5, "The Metafictional Anti-Detective Novel"].)

The paucity of theoretical support Winkler derives from the criticism of mainstream literature indicates the degree to which rereading (the sine qua non of criticism, given that few critics would catch the textual details they discuss on a first reading) virtually disappears as an acknowledged activity in critical discourse. Even reader response and reception theories, which strive to recover the reader's experience of the text for scrutiny, usually present it either as a monolith (the idealized sum of all rereadings) or as a transindividual series of "receptions" stretching over large expanses of historical time (cf. e.g., Jauss 1969). Two recent anthologies of reader-response criticism show this: Tompkins 1980 and Suleiman-Crosman 1980. Of the critics whose essays appear in these two volumes, only S. Fish closely pursues the temporality of reading, scrutinizing the process as it unfolds for an individual reader, and reconstructing each successive revision of the sentence/verse/line, as word succeeds word before one's eyes.

Fortuitously, both Fish's inflection of reader-response criticism, and Winkler's foray into ratiocinative narratology, parallel a Lacanian model of the reader and the reading process in several respects. First, Fish's attention to the unfolding line matches Lacan's idea of *capitonnage* supplying provisional punctuation. Fish explains his method as "*slow[ing] down* the reading experience so that 'events' one does not notice in normal time, but which do occur, are brought before our analytical attentions. It is as if a slow motion camera with an automatic stop action effect were recording our linguistic experiences and presenting them to us for viewing" (Fish 1970, 128). He thus points to the various meanings produced by shifting the *point de capiton* as one reads.

Second, Winkler's analysis depends upon the Lacanian distinction between the speaking subject and the subject of the speech, raised to the status of narratological theory. Winkler uses the example of "I ran" to point the difference between the two "I's," the one who ran, and the one who tells you about her running (the same schism Lacan illustrates with the sentence, "I am lying"). "The double I of any narrating easily becomes the duplicitous I" (Winkler 1985, 97), which leads Winkler to choose the ratiocinative tale as governing narratological model for the *Asinus Aureus*. Apuleius' novel solicits the reader to establish the events behind its deceptive narrative. However, the ratiocinative process (as I have been stressing in our discussion of the Catullan text) inheres in any narrative. We *all* want to know "what happened?" (between Lesbia and Catullus, Catullus and his brother, Catullus and Caesar, and so on). Winkler's discussion simply foregrounds the issue (albeit brilliantly) and equally foregrounds the way in which narrative, whether in prose or poetry, continually solicits successive revisions of the answer. (For specific—and rare—applications of reader-response theory to Catullus, see Pedrick 1986, and the particularly sophisticated account of Fitzgerald 1992.)

25. Cf. his telling description of their meetings as "*furtiva . . . munuscula . . .*" / "ipsius ex ipso dempta viri gremio"—"dear gifts, *stolen* from the very lap of her man himself" (68.145–46).

26. Ross 1969, 80–95.

27. *Benevolentia,* "goodwill"; *benefacta,* "benefits, good deeds"; *gratia,* "gratitude (for services rendered)"; *officia,* "a service done in the fulfillment of an obligation." But see Ross 1969, 80–95, for a fuller discussion of their Late Republican usage.

28. Ross 1969, 90.

29. Ross 1969, 84, 85.

30. Brunt 1965, 6.

31. Ross 1975, 10.

32. Brunt 1988, 351–81.

33. Konstan 1972, 102–4.

34. Konstan 1972, 103.

35. See Fordyce 1961; Quinn 1973b; Lenchantin de Gubernatis 1928, ad loc.

36. Quinn notes the echo (Quinn 1973b, ad c.75).

37. Partially noted by Kroll 1929, ad loc.

38. For an exhaustive anatomy of the antitheses, see Colaclides 1981.

39. For a painstakingly analytical reading of c.76, see Pietquin 1986. Pietquin includes an overview of previous bibliography (see esp. 3n12). (And now add Skinner 1987b.)

40. Ellis 1889, ad loc.

41. ἀξιῶ δὲ μὴ διὰ τοῦτο ἀτυχῆσαι ὧν δέομαι, ὅτι οὐκ ἐραστὴς ὤν σου τυγχάνω. ὡς ἐκείνοις μὲν τότε μεταμέλει ὧν ἂν εὖ ποιήσωσιν, ἐπειδὰν τῆς ἐπιθυμίας παύσωνται·

I do not think that I should fail to get what I want because I do not happen to love you. For lovers, when they leave off desiring, regret whatever good things they have done. (Phaedrus 230e7–231a3)

42. Quinn notes the parallels with c.51 (Quinn 1973b, ad loc.)

43. Skinner 1987b is illuminating on the disease imagery that partially controls c.76.

5. The *Carmina Maiora:* Hercules and the Engineering of Desire

1. *Maud; a Monodrama,* I.22, 10–11 (collected in Tennyson 1969).

2. Wheeler 1934, 172.

3. In his review of Kroll's edition of Catullus (Jachmann 1925, 209).

4. For an exhaustive structuralist study of c.63's thematic oppositions, see Rubino 1974. Rubino includes previous bibliography. See also Skinner 1993. Skinner provides bibliography postdating Rubino's overview.

5. I am grateful to Professor Diskin Clay for drawing this detail to my attention.

6. See my discussion of *"che vuoi?"* in chap. 4, on the epigrams.

7. On beast imagery, see Sandy 1968, 390–95; on Cybele's land as uncivilized, see Rubino 1974, esp. 156ff.; Wiseman 1985, 181.

8. Freud's image for "unknown" female sexuality ("The Question of Lay Analysis," *SE* 20:212).

9. Putnam 1974.

10. Cf. 7.10 ("vesano . . . Catullo") as well as Catullus' bitter retrospective on the Lesbia affair ("cum *vesana* meas torreret *flamma* medullas," 100.7) in relation to Attis' mental state ("stimulatus ibi *furenti rabie, vagus animis,*" 63.4; *"furibunda,"* 63.31, etc.).

11. Putnam 1974, 80.

12. For an interesting reading of c.64 that includes a thoughtful and exhaustive review of previous bibliography, see Duban 1980. Note particularly the contributions of Putnam 1961; Bramble 1970; Konstan 1977 (all cited by Duban). Add now: Forsyth 1980; Wiseman 1985, 176–80; Martin 1992, 151–71; and especially Fitzgerald forthcoming, which breaks new theoretical ground in assessing c.64.

13. Harkins 1959, 113.

14. *Isthm.* 8.30ff.

15. Quinn (1973b, ad loc.) notes the difference in the modes of time's passage in the two narratives. The thematic implications of another temporal contradiction—Peleus' journey being defined as the first sea journey, a claim contradicted by Theseus' appearance in a boat in 64's *ekphrasis*—are explored by Weber 1983. Weber includes previous bibliography on the problem.

16. For the most recent assessments of the heroic age in 64—largely negative— see: Putnam 1961; Kinsey 1965b; Curran 1969; Bramble 1970; Forsyth 1975; Konstan 1977; Duban 1980; Zetzel 1983. For more positive views, see Giangrande 1972; Harmon 1973; Dee 1982; Cairns 1984.

17. Pindar, *Isthm.* 8.34ff; Aeschylus, *P.V.* 768; Apollonius Rhodius, 4.790ff.

18. *Theogony* 126–89, 453–500.

19. C.64.38–42, describing the effect on the countryside of Peleus' and Thetis' wedding celebration, has disturbed more than one reader. As far back as the sixteenth century, B. Realinus (Realinus 1551) noted the unrealistically swift degeneration of the countryside on the day of the wedding, though he goes on to refute his own objection with Catullus' "poetic license." R. Ellis (Ellis 1889, 291) notes a "want of proportion" in these lines and says "there is a *nescio quid nimii.*" And G. Williams says "the gathering of the people of Thessaly and the portrait of something like a Golden Age (38–42) are surprising" (Williams 1968, 226), though he does not state specific reasons for his judgment.

Williams notes the parallel with the Golden Age that G. Pasquali (Pasquali 1920, 17) is, to my knowledge, the first to detect. Pasquali considers the passage not only incongruous but evidence for his thesis that c.64 is an unskillful conflation of two Hellenistic models. Pasquali's comparison to the Golden Age is noted, but his argument for conflation refuted, by F. Klingner (Klingner 1956, 27–30). L. Ferrero (Ferrero 1955, 396–97), on the other hand, both notices the parallel and integrates it into the poem's interpretation as foreshadowing the unhappy outcome of Peleus and Thetis' marriage. He says of the passage that "alla convenzionale rievocazione dell'età dell'oro conferisce un significato umano, sottolinea la provvisorietà di quel momentaneo ritorno di un'età felice, e suggerisce con discrezione alcuni aspetti negativi quasi a ritrarre il lettore indietro dal lasciarsi afferare dal generale tripudio."

The parallels between 64.35–42 and the Golden Age, and the darker aspects of the poem as a whole, have not gone unnoticed by more recent critics. However, of late, the two observations have not often been integrated. This is all the more suprising in that two relatively new works have thoroughly and skillfully documented both the parallels and their negative implications. The earlier work is J. C. Bramble's (Bramble 1970, 38–39); his article is followed by D. Konstan's even more detailed discussion in his chapter "The Golden Age" (Konstan 1977, 31–38).

For example, among recent critics, D. P. Harmon (Harmon 1973, 314) notes the parallel with accounts of the Golden Age, but, like Williams, interprets it positively. V. Bröge (Bröge 1976, 180) even says, "important for our purposes here [interpreting 64] is Hesiod's version of the five ages of man's history," but then steadfastly ignores the Golden Age imagery of 38–42. S. E. Knopp (Knopp 1976, 211) both argues for a negative interpretation of the poem as a whole and of the passage *and* specifically praises Bramble's article. Yet he does not exploit Bramble's interpretation of the passage as a parodistic Golden Age, though it would seem to serve his argument. J. Duban (Duban 1980) cites Konstan repeatedly but again refuses to integrate Konstan's observations on the Golden Age into his own dark interpretation of the poem.

I cannot account for this reluctance to use or build on Bramble's and Konstan's work except to say that perhaps the intricacy of their interpretations works against the desire for a smoother, more integrated and univocal reading of the poem.

20. *WD* 42–50.

21. Euripides, *IA* 1040ff. Fordyce notes the change (Fordyce 1961, ad loc.)

22. This accords with J. E. G. Zetzel's view, expressed in connection with cc.68 and 101, that Catullus regards "the Trojan War as the death, not the apex, of the heroic age" (Zetzel 1983, 255).

23. Thomson prints "liber uti nuptae poteretur flore novellae," accepting Maehly's and Baehrens' suggested emendations. The line thus produced makes smoother sense, but I do not find the difficulties of the manuscript readings insuperable, nor the suggested emendations compelling. I have therefore hewed more closely to the manuscripts.

24. Loraux 1990. Her essay will be discussed in more detail below.

25. "Why Is Diotima a Woman?" Halperin 1990, 113–51. Halperin points out that among other things Diotima conceives of desire and reproduction as inextricably interdependent—true for male biology but not for female biology.

26. The unity, or separateness, of poem 68 has long been a critical issue in Catullan scholarship. Separatists generally divide the poem into at least two, sometimes three, parts (1) 68a, comprising lines 1–40; (2) 68b, comprising lines 41–148; (3) 68c, comprising lines 149–60. The divisions are structurally distinguished by the fact that in sections a and c Catullus addresses his friend and interlocutor in the second-person singular, whereas in b, he refers to the deeds of a friend in the third-person singular. The difference in names, which I have discussed in the body of the chapter, is also a structural distinction, but one that marks off only two sections within the poem, 68a from 68b + c.

There are a number of interpretive and textual cruxes in the text of 68. None of these is, by itself, incontrovertible evidence either for or against the unity of 68. However, one's stand on the unity or disunity of the poem will tend to decide the cruxes in such a way as to support that overall position. If you believe, for example, that the poem is an integral whole, then you are likely to explain the Mallius/Allius dichotomy in a way that assimilates these two names to the same addressee. If you do not believe in the poem's unity, you will point to the name discrepancy as evidence in your favor.

The question of names is in fact the crucial factor; I doubt that anyone would have made a case for the disunity of 68 had the manuscript variation in appellatives not existed. Other cruxes that *can* be interpreted as non sequiturs are too minor by themselves to signal disunity. For that reason, I have devoted most of my attention to reviewing the literature on the name controversy. For other problematic issues that might be adduced to support or argue against unity, I have merely named a representative selection of opinions.

The case for unity has been argued in the last few decades by J. Vahlen (Vahlen 1902, 1043); G. Jachmann, in his review of Kroll (Jachmann 1925, 209); H. W. Prescott (Prescott 1940); F. Della Corte (Della Corte 1951, 40–42); E. Fränkel, in his review of Fordyce's edition (Fränkel 1962, 262); G. Lieberg (Lieberg 1962, 152–63); G. Williams (Williams 1968, 229–30); C. Witke (Witke 1968, 33n1, 49); F. Solmsen (Solmsen 1975, 260n1); P. Levine (Levine 1976); A. Sorci (Sorci 1980/81); G. Most (Most 1981, 122). I count as unitarians those who consider 68b–c to have been composed prior to 68a, the latter being a "cover letter" for the longer section of the poem.

The case for disunity has recently been argued by K. Vretska (Vretska 1966); T. E. Kinsey (Kinsey 1967); B. Coppel (Coppel 1973, 97–140); T. P. Wiseman (Wiseman 1974, 77–103); G. Milanese (Milanese 1988).

The problematic points most frequently raised in connection with the issue of unity or disunity are:

a. The name of the addressee/addressees, on which the manuscripts differ (for lists of the manuscript readings, see: Prescott 1940, 494; Wiseman 1974, 88; Most 1981, 116–17.)
b. The nature of his distress and the *munera et Musarum et Veneris* that he requests
c. The identity of the subject of 157–58
d. The structural pattern of the poem as a whole

The unitarians argue that:

a'. The addressee of 68a and 68b–c are the same. Several scholars have proposed that V's *mali* is a corruption of an original *mi Alli* (whether one takes *mi* to be dative—a possibility at 68.30—or vocative). Among these are F. Schöll (Schöll 1880, 472–73; H. Diels (Diels 1918, 936n1); F. Vollmer (Vollmer 1919, 7–8); G. Perrotta (Perrotta 1927, 135–37); H. W. Prescott (Prescott 1940, 493–97); C. J. Fordyce (Fordyce 1961, ad loc.); G. Lieberg (Lieberg 1962, 153–54); D. F. Bright (Bright 1976b, 88–90).

Others have argued that Catullus uses the addressee's *praenomen* at one time, at another his *nomen gentile*—though that is unparalleled in Catullus' corpus. This solution was first proposed by K. Lachmann in his edition of the poems (Lachmann 1829) and is supported by H. Magnus (Magnus 1875, 850); A. Kiessling (Kiessling 1877, 15); J. Vahlen (Vahlen 1902, 1024–25); L. Jus (Jus 1927, 79–84); R. A. B. Mynors (Mynors 1958); C. Witke (Witke 1968, 33n1); B. Coppel (Coppel 1973, 133–35).

In a slight modification of this solution, Ellis (Ellis 1889, 401–2) argues that Mallius may have been a *nomen gentile* serving as a *praenomen* without actually being one, with the same consequences: one man is addressed by two different names.

G. Pennisi (Pennisi 1959, 235–36) sees Mallius as Manlius and the same as Manlius Torquatus of c.61. He amends Allius out of existence, taking *ali* in 68.50 (X's reading) and *alii* in 68.150 (V's reading) to be corruptions of an original *ille*.

P. Levine suggests a solution with which I concur, partly because it requires the least amount of textual manipulation and explanation as to why Catullus might have addressed the same person by two different names. He accepts the different identities of Mallius in 68a and Allius in 68b–c, proposing that the latter "is not about Mallius but for Mallius" (Levine 1976, 71).

b'. The separatists (e.g., E. Baehrens [Baehrens 1885, 2.493–95, 501–3]; W. Kroll, [Kroll 1929, ad loc.]) point out that Catullus declares himself utterly unable to fulfill Mallius' request for *munera Musarum et Veneris* in 68a. (For an exhaustive analysis of the various proposed interpretations of this phrase, see Coppel 1973, 35–86). If Mallius requests poetry from Catullus (as most take the sense of *munera Musarum* to be), it makes no sense for Catullus to say "I cannot" and then provide a poem (68b–c).

However, interpretation of this phrase does not quite so neatly divide the separatists from the unitarians as does the name controversy in general. Prescott, for example, considers 68 a single poem—yet he reads Catullus' refusal to provide *munera et Musarum et Veneris* as do the separatists Baehrens and Kroll. He does not see this refusal as absolute, however. "Surely it is not reading too much into the Latin to understand [Catullus] as meaning that, in spite of his inability to grant adequately the favors asked of him, he must at least record his indebtedness to his friend for services rendered (Prescott 1940, 487)." J. Sarkissian (Sarkissian 1983, 13) concurs in that he, too, reads 68b–c as a reconsideration of the refusal, but one that he carefully assigns to Catullus the *persona* of the poem, and not to the poet Catullus ("observation of the distinction [between poet and persona] permits us to regard the speaker as a less than omniscient voice, one not necessarily reliable at all times" [Sarkissian 1983, 1]).

On the whole, the resolutely bipartite structure of 68a and the "utriusque" of 39 argue against taking *munera et Musarum et Veneris* as hendiadys—standing for "love and poetry" = "love poetry." (Cf. Birt 1890, v–ix; on the bipartite structure, see Skinner 1972, 497–500, 500n13, and her particularly subtle elucidation of the principle throughout her essay. Skinner, however, argues against hendiadys by saying "all attempts to interpret *munera Veneris* as erotic pleasure of some sort, and *munera Musarum* as poetry of some sort, come to grief in trying to explain how erotic pleasure could even be requested, much less sent as a gift" [Skinner 1972, 500n13]. Mallius, however, has not specified that Catullus must *send* the *munera*—he might have wanted Catullus to come in person. Moreover, to object that erotic pleasure cannot be requested seems puzzlingly naïve for so sophisticated a critic.) Seeing the request as for two separate favors allows us to read 68.39 as the refusal of only *one* favor. And although, on the basis of his interpretation of the context, Kroll himself decides in favor of "non" negating the whole sentence, he admits that grammatically, "non" could negate only one of the two requests. Read that way, 68b would answer the other of the requests— presumably for the *munera Musarum,* "poetry."

Some ingenuity has been expended on trying to determine what misfortune Mallius is suffering, and whether 68b–c would adequately assuage his distress, therefore whether it can appropriately be assimilated to 68a. Kinsey (Kinsey 1967, 40) and Most (Most 1981, 121n47) both argue that love poetry is no consolation to one suffering distress in love. Besides depending on dubious psychology, this conclusion does not dictate the limits within which a poet may invent a situation (or a request) in order to preface a poem.

c'. The argument for the separateness of 68c from the rest of the poem has been supported by the confusion over the identity of the "qui" who is included in the final general benediction of the poem:

> et qui principio nobis †terram dedit aufert†,
> a quo sunt primo omnia nata bona
>
> (68.157–58)

Mynors' comment on the daggered section—"locus conclamatus"—sums up the major part of the problem. Suggestions have been made that "qui" is Jupiter (Pennisi 1959, 224ff., reading *dat et aufert* in 157); the brother (Kinsey 1967, 45); Allius again (Oksala 1965, 87ff., amending "aufert" to *auspex*). Yet the question cannot be satisfactorily answered when the text as it stands is so damaged as to admit of no absolutely provable interpretation, only many different, and equally plausible, speculations. Most of the proposed emendations make the lines cohere quite satisfactorily with the rest of the poem. T. E. Kinsey, for example, suggests an emendation referring to the brother that would make perfect sense and smooth any apparent disjunction.

> et qui principio nobis erat omnia frater
> a quo sunt primo dulcia nata bona.

"The corruption would begin with the interchange of *omnia* and *dulcia*" (Kinsey 1967, 45).

d'. Various proposals have been put forward to explain the structural schema of 68. To advance such a schema is not peculiar either to the unitarians or the separatists; but where one draws the lines, whether one considers them absolutely divisive or simply transitional, and what interpretation one places on the structure so realized assign the critic to one camp or the other.

For example, various critics (e.g., Barwick 1947, 4; Skinner 1972) have analyzed 68a as an *omphalos* structure resembling the organization of 68b–c. Skinner sees this as evidence that 68a is a separate poem, while by contrast 68b is a "meandering flow of associations" (510). In the body of this chapter, I have discussed the rationale underlying the sometimes suprising associations of 68b and I disagree that in 68b "the poet's attention seems to wander far away from his immediate topic" (Skinner 1972, 510). Skinner concludes that "it is unlikely that Catullus incorporated these forty lines [of 68a] into poem 68 as the prologue to his *avant-garde* elegy. Such a conflation of schemata would certainly violate basic principles of unity and consistency. The jarring discrepancy would annoy any reader sensitive to the formal design of poetry; and the Roman audience capable of appreciating intricate patterns of arrangement in Hellenistic literature would be quick to note structural anomalies in a contemporary production" (Skinner 1972, 511). To my mind, however, Skinner unduly minimizes the structural intricacy of 68b—all the more surprising in that she aptly cites Wheeler's comparison of c.68 as a whole to "those nests of boxes cunningly wrought by some Chinese workman" (Wheeler 1934, 172). Wheeler's proposed governing schema for the *entire* poem (upon which many other critics have elaborated) closely parallels that which Skinner proposes for 68a alone; such a double *omphalos* structure for c.68 would *not* "violate basic principles of unity and consistency."

Both separatists and unitarians have proposed specific organizational schemata for 68a and 68b. The major division in approach is whether one divides the groups around a central *omphalos* strictly according to theme (so Kroll 1929, 219; Fordyce 1961, 344), or whether one tries to make these groups contain equal numbers of lines (so Skutsch 1892; Witke 1968, 31).

The mirror structure of 68a and 68b, as two *omphaloi*, seems to me to tip the scales in favor of unity. However, seeing structure certainly does not decide the case for unity one way or the other. Kroll, Fordyce, and Skutsch are separatists; Witke is a unitarian. (For an overview of the various schemata, see McClure 1974).

27. Starting with F. Schöll (Schöll 1880, 472–73).

28. For a somewhat similar reading of the text as a "double inscription" that proceeds from deconstructive principles, see Hubbard 1984. Hubbard also includes a thoughtful overview of previous bibliography on 68, regarding cruxes I have chosen not to address.

29. The exact spelling of the addressee's name is not germane to my arguments, so I will accept the form offered by the manuscripts closely related to V (give or take an "l").

30. The question is whether *munera et Musarum et Veneris* refers to a request for one thing or two; and if two, what, besides poetry, does Mallius want? See my discussion above in the context of the separatist/unitarian controversy over c.68; and for an overview of the interpretive debate less specifically focused on implications for the poem's unity/disunity, see Forsyth 1987.

31. The crux rests upon whether Catullus quotes Mallius in indirect or direct discourse. If the former, the "hic" in 68.28 = where Catullus is, Verona; if the latter, then "hic" = Rome, where Mallius wrote the observation. See Fordyce 1961, ad loc., for a full discussion of the problems involved in either reading.

32. I have printed *Malli* for the sake of clarity, since my compromise appellative for 68a's addressee is "Mallius"; Thomson prints *Manli*, the reading of Bibl. Riccardiana 606 and the group of manuscripts he designates "ε"; V's reading is *mali*.

33. Stated, without argument, by Quinn (Quinn 1973b, ad loc.)

34. *Phaedrus* 256a7–256e2.

35. As D. Halperin argues (Halperin 1985, esp. 163–66).

36. "The Speech of Alcibiades," Nussbaum 1986, 165–99.

37. Reading, with Fordyce, the G and R manuscripts' "hic" at 68.63 instead of the suggested emendation *ac*. I find his analysis of the reasons for doing so compelling:

> With the punctuation of the Oxford text and the reading *ac* in l.63, the simile of the mountain stream relates to Allius' service in l.66. In favour of this it can be urged that the point of the simile lies in the solace brought by the stream to the thirsty traveller and that *qualis* (57) corresponds to *tale* (66). On the other hand, (i) this leaves an abrupt transition between 56 and 57, where some explicit connexion might be expected; (ii) the insertion of another comparison for Allius in 63–65, this time with the welcome breeze sent by Castor and Pollux, the sailor's friends, makes the structure awkward and

unwieldy; (iii) elsewhere in Catullus a simile introduced by *qualis* relates to what precedes: compare 64.89, 65.13, and especially 109–16 of this poem, where *quale* adds a comparison even longer, and in its detail more irrelevant, than the present one. It is possible that the lines should be punctuated with comma after 56 and colon after 62, *hic* ('thereupon') read in l.63, and the simile related to the poet's tears in the preceding lines 53–56. So taken, the simile has precedent in Homer, *Il*.ix.14f. (repeated in xvi.3f.) ἵστατο δάκρυ χέων ὥς τε κρήνη μελάνυδρος/ ἥ τε κατ᾿ αἰγίλιπος πέτρης δνοφερὸν χέει ὕδωρ·, and it is reasonable to think that Catullus had these lines in mind. There, in the epic manner, the simile is expanded beyond the point of relevance in the detail of steep crag and dark water: so here Catullus develops the image for its own sake in a vivid picture. *hic* in 63 then makes the transition from Catullus' distress to Allius' comfort, and *tale* (66) takes up *velut* (63). (Fordyce 1961, ad 68.57)

I disagree, of course, with the idea that "the simile is expanded beyond the point of relevance" in Catullus, as my analysis of the imagery shows.

38. On the simile's general movement from negative to positive in tone, see Solmsen 1975, 263–64; Phillips 1976.

39. For discussions of the ancient accounts of the Laodamia myth, see Baehrens 1877; Roscher, *Lex.* ii.1827–28; Lieberg 1962, 209–18; Jacobson 1974, 195ff. For interesting discussions of the myth's application to c.68 itself, see Macleod 1974, 82–88; Sarkissian 1983, 17ff.

40. *Iliad* 2.701–2.

41. Eustathius 325, ad *Iliad* 2.701.

42. Both T. E. Kinsey (Kinsey 1967, 50) and E. Adler (Adler 1981, 114) remark upon the choice of Laodamia, a passionate heroine who sustains the grievous loss of a loved one at Troy, as effectively linking Lesbia *and* the brother in one mythological figure.

43. On the marriage imagery, see Quinn 1973b, ad loc.; Sarkissian 1983, 18ff., esp. 31. (More generally, on Catullus' view of the relationship *as* a marriage, see Mayer 1983.) On the "marriage" as doomed, see Baker 1960. J. Marquardt (Marquardt 1886, 29–80) reviews and assesses the evidence we have on the details of Roman marriage ceremonies.

44. Noted as a significant detail by Hubbard 1984 (34).

45. For an interesting intertextual reading of this moment, see Brenk 1987.

46. Moreover, "*uno* non est contenta Catullo" again dramatizes, in slightly different terms, the impossibility of *one* glimpsed in cc.5 and 7, and c.72. Lesbia's "not being content with *one* man" should mean that she is not content with her husband; but Catullus—who by definition is the "other man"—appropriates this term as if he were her *primary* attachment (the allure of c.72's enigmatic "dicebas quondam *solum* te nosse Catullum"). Yet his own rueful acknowledgment of her *furta* shows that he fails anyway: no matter how he reconfigures the relationship, he cannot attain the status of *one:* he can be neither her *only* man nor even her *primary* man.

47. E. Havelock argues for the direct identification of Catullus and Laodamia (Havelock 1939, 118–19); he is partially anticipated by R. Ellis (Ellis 1889, 402). Most critics have trouble smoothly aligning Lesbia, whose multifocal desire c.68 itself acknowledges and who has suffered no disappointment in love, with Laodamia, whose devotion to, and suffering because of, her love the poem pointedly emphasizes. Aligning Catullus with Laodamia has therefore become fairly commonplace. More recent critics who argue for this match are Harkins 1959, 103–4; Kinsey 1967, 49–50; Bright 1976b, 99–106; Tuplin 1981, 117–18; Ferguson 1985, 229–30.

48. Elsewhere in the corpus, *alo* occurs only in the context of female nurturing: Ariadne as a child in her mother's embrace ("quam suavis exspirans castus odores" / "lectulus in molli complexu matris *alebat*," 64.87–88); in 68 again, the only daughter nursing the grandfather's heir ("una caput seri nata nepotis *alit*," 68.120).

49. The *Oxford Latin Dictionary* defines *lumen* (entry 3) as: "the light enjoyed by living creatures (opp. the darkness of the Underworld); (hence, also *[lum]en vitale* or sim.) life (esp. in such phrs. as *[lum]en linquere*)" and cites, as instances of this usage preceding or contemporary with Catullus: Ennius, *Annales* 114; Lucretius 1.170, 3.1033; Plautus, *Truculentus* 518; Cicero, *De consulatu suo* fr.2.24. Under *lux* (entry 6a), the *OLD* gives as a denotation "the light of the sun (as enjoyed by all living creatures); hence, life" and adduces the following examples preceding, or contemporaneous with, Catullus: Plautus, *Captivi* 1008; Cicero, *Pro S. Roscio Amerino* 150, *Tusculanae disputationes* 3.2; Terence, *Hecyra* 852; Lucretius, 2.525. See also Sarkissian, who notes the link light imagery affords between the brother and Lesbia (Sarkissian 1983, 31).

50. E. Adler notes the opposition (Adler 1981, 175n45).

51. The repeated motif of theft was brought to my attention by Professor Francis Newton.

52. For a detailed intertextual reading of the *barathrum* image, see Tuplin 1981.

53. Plautus, *Bacchides* 149, *Rudens* 570; Lucretius 3.966.

54. C. W. Macleod notes the link between water images (Macleod 1974, 83). More generally, see Granarolo 1983.

55. Loraux 1990, 21–52.

56. Loraux 1990, 25.

57. On the logic of reproduction as one of the controlling metaphors Catullus employs to portray his artistic activity, see Hallett 1988.

58. "The ludicrous tastelessness in comparing the depth of Laodamia's love to oozy soil or possibly a drainage channel" (Elder 1951, 103); "a style bordering on the grotesque" (Copley 1957, 31); "in an extreme instance of the characteristically Alexandrian taste for the parade of mythological detail, Catullus . . . piles up a whimsically precious mythological excursus" (Fordyce 1961, ad loc.); "farfetched" (Witke 1968, 48); "almost impossible to take seriously" (Quinn 1973a, 188); "the excursus on Hercules . . . smells of the lamp" (Quinn 1973b, ad loc.).

59. The importance of this moment as categorically different from all other moments in the affair, and thus the one whose power in memory is greatest (the poem says nothing about its effect on Catullus or his poetry at the time) is marked by the images of *marriage* with which Catullus surrounds their first tryst, as I have discussed them in the text—the swinging torch, saffron yellow dress, the presence of Cupid. Lesbia comes to Catullus as if a virgin bride, and their lovemaking holds all the significance of their very first sexual encounters of *any* kind, not just between them as a couple.

60. Hyginus, *Fabulae* 103–4; Apollodorus, *Epitome* 3.30. C.68.107–8's mention of the *barathrum*, which means "Hades" as well as "drainage pit," probably alludes to her suicide.

61. Some have pointed to the sinister quality of Laodamia's love—the overpowering magnitude of it that (possibly) leads her to neglect sacrifice to the gods and thus dooms her marriage—as a direct point of comparison to the dove's weirdly sadistic, hungry desire. (For a review of the literature on the controversy over the degree of Laodamia's guilt, or innocence, see Shipton 1987.) But that tenuous parallel does not explain away the fact that Catullus elaborates on her passion using motives that cannot, by any stretch of the imagination, fit her situation—love for a child who redeems a house, and the love of a woman who desires more than one man. These motives look to Lesbia, *not* Laodamia.

62. On the general inappropriateness of the final similes, see Sarkissian 1983, 31ff., with previous bibliography.

63. Thomson does not capitalize "cupido."

64. On parental imagery as providing a persistent metaphorical framework for the Catullus-Lesbia affair, see Vinson 1989.

6. Some Final Reflections

1. "For Once, Then, Something" (Lathem 1969, 225). Frost's poem is in hendecasyllables, which R. Poirier sees as "Frost's affectionate nod to Catullus" (Poirier 1977, 252). See also R. Brower (Brower 1963, 138); and for an extensive discussion of Catullus' importance to Frost, M. C. J. Putnam (Putnam 1983, esp. 243n1) for further useful discussion of, and bibliography on, Catullus and Frost.

2. "Civilization and Its Discontents," *SE* 21:70.

Bibliography

Adler, E. 1981. *Catullan Self-Revelation*. New York.

André, J.-M. 1966. *L'Otium dans la vie morale et intellectuelle romaine*. Paris.

Baehrens, E. 1877. "Die Laodameiasage und Catullus 68s Gedicht." *NJb class Philol* 115:409–15.

———. 1885. *Catulli Veronensis Liber*. Leipzig. 2 vols.

———. (= Baehrens-Schulze). 1893. *Catulli Veronensis Liber*. Revised K. P. Schulze. Leipzig.

Baker, S. 1960. "Lesbia's Foot." *CPh* 55:171–73.

———. 1981. "Propertius' Monobiblos and Catullus 51." *RhM* 124:312–24.

Balsdon, J. P. V. D. 1960. "*Auctoritas, Dignitas, Otium*." *CQ* 10:43–50.

Barthes, R. 1974. *S/Z*. Trans. R. Miller. New York.

Barwick, K. 1947. "Catulls c. 68 und eine Kompositionsform der römischen Elegie und Epigrammatik." *WJA* 2:1–15.

———. 1958. "Zyklen bei Martial und den kleinen Gedichten des Catull." *Philologus* 102:312–14.

Bayet, J., et al. 1953. *L'influence grecque sur la poésie latine de Catulle à Ovide* (*Entretiens sur l'Antiquité classique*, t.2). Geneva.

Benveniste, E. 1971. *Problems in General Linguistics*. Trans. M. E. Meek. Coral Gables, FL.

Bing, P. 1988. *The Well-Read Muse*. Göttingen.

Birt, Th. 1890. *De Catulli ad Mallium epistula*. Marburg.

———. 1895. *Commentariolus Catullianus Tertius*. Marburg.

Blodgett, E. D., and R. M. Nielsen (= Blodgett-Nielsen). 1986. "Mask and Figure in Catullus, Carmen 11." *RBPh* 64:22–31.

Borch-Jacobsen, M. 1991. *Lacan: The Absolute Master*. Stanford, CA.

Borzsak, I. 1956. "*Otium Catullianum*." *AAntHung* 4:211–19.

Bowie, M. 1991. *Lacan*. Cambridge, MA.

Bramble, J. C. 1970. "Structure and Ambiguity in Catullus LXIV." *PCPhS* 16:22–41.

Braunlich, A. F. 1923. "Against Curtailing Catullus' Passer." *AJP* 44:349–52.

183

Brenk, F. E. 1987. *"Arguta solea* on the Threshhold: The Literary Precedents of Catullus 68, 68–72." *QUCC* 55:121–27.

Bright, D. F. 1976a. *"Non bona dicta:* Catullus' Poetry of Separation." *QUCC* 21:105–19.

————. 1976b. *"Confectum carmine munus:* Catullus 68." *ICS* 1:86–112.

Bröge, V. 1976. "The Generation Gap in Catullus and the Lyric Poetry of Horace." *The Conflict of Generations in Ancient Greece and Rome.* Ed. S. Bertman. Amsterdam. 171–203.

Brooks, P. 1979. "Fictions of the Wolfman." *Diacritics* 9:72–83.

————. 1984. *Reading for the Plot.* New York.

Brower, R. 1963. *The Poetry of Robert Frost: Constellations of Intention.* New York.

Brunt, P. A. 1965. " 'Amicitia' in the Late Roman Republic." *PCPhS,* n.s. 11, 191:1–20.

————. 1988. *The Fall of the Roman Republic.* Oxford.

Cairns, F. 1984. "The Nereids of Catullus 64.12–23b." *GB* 11:95–101.

Cantarella, E. 1988. *Secondo natura: La bisessualità nel mondo antico.* Rome.

Carson, A. 1986. *Eros the Bittersweet.* Princeton.

Charlton, W. 1988. "Socrates and Plato." *Weakness of Will.* Oxford. 13–33.

Cherniss, H. W. 1943. "The Biographical Fashion in Literary Criticism" *Uni.Cal.Publ.Class Phil.* 12:279–92 (= *Critical Essays in Roman Literature: Elegy and Lyric.* Ed. J. P. Sullivan. London, 1962. 15–30).

Clarke, M. L. 1976. "Latin Love Poets and the Biographical Approach." *G&R* 23:132–39.

Clausen, W. 1964. "Callimachus and Latin Poetry." *GRBS* 5:181–96.

————. 1976. *"Catulli veronensis liber."* *CPh* 71:37–43.

Clayman, D. 1982. "Hellenistic Poetry at Alexandria." *Ancient Writers.* Ed. T. James Luce. New York. 1.449–82.

Cochrane, C. N. 1944. *Christianity and Classical Culture.* 2d ed. Oxford.

Colaclides, P. 1981. *"Odi et Amo:* Une lecture linguistique du c.LXXXV de Catulle." *Contemporary Literary Hermeneutics and Interpretation of Classical Texts.* Ed. S. Kresic. Ottawa. 227–33.

Commager, S. 1965. "Notes on Some Poems of Catullus." *HSCP* 70:83–110.

Copley, F. O. 1949. "Emotional Conflict and Its Significance in the Lesbia Poems." *AJP* 70:22–40.

————. 1957. "The Unity of Catullus 68: A Further View." *CPh* 52:29–32.

————. 1974. "The Structure of Catullus C. 51 and the Problem of the *Otium-* Strophe." *GB* 2:25–37.

Coppel, B. 1973. *Das Alliusgedicht: Zur Redaktion des Catullcorpus.* Heidelberg.

Cramer, J. A. 1835, 1963. *Anecdota Graeca.* Reprint ed., 4 vols. in 2. Amsterdam.

Culham, P. 1987. "Ten Years after Pomeroy: Studies of the Image and Reality of Women in Antiquity." *Helios* 13:9–30.

Culler, J. 1980. *"Fabula* and *sjuzhet* in the Analysis of Narrative." *Poetics Today* 1:27–37.

Bibliography

Curran, L. C. 1969. "Catullus 64 and the Heroic Age." *YCS* 21:169–92.

Davis, J. T. 1971. "Poetic Counterpoint: Catullus 72." *AJP* 92:196–201.

Dee, J. H. 1982. "Catullus 64 and the Heroic Age: A Reply." *ICS* 7:98–109.

Della Corte, F. 1951. *Due Studi Catulliani*. Genoa.

Dettmer, H. 1984. "Catullus 2B from a Structural Perspective." *CW* 78:107–10.

———. 1988. "Design in the Catullan Corpus: A Preliminary Study." *CW* 81:371–81.

Diels, H. 1918. "Lukrezstudien I." *SPAW* 41:912–39.

Dornseiff, B. G. 1936. "Die Trümmer im Catullbuch." *Philologus* 91:346–49.

———. 1953. "Menophila von Sardes von Catulls *Passer* befreit." *Studies Presented to David Moore Robinson on His Seventieth Birthday*. Ed. G. E. Mylonas and D. Raymond. St. Louis, MO. 2.660–62.

Duban, J. 1980. "Verbal Links and Imagistic Undercurrent in Catullus 64." *Latomus* 39:777–802.

Duclos, G. S. 1976. "Catullus 11: Atque in perpetuum, Lesbia, ave atque vale." *Arethusa* 9:76–90.

Dyson, M. 1973. "Catullus 8 and 76." *CQ* 23:127–43.

Eisenhut, W. 1965. "Zu Catull c. 2a und der Trennung der Gedichte in den Handschriften." *Philologus* 109:301–5.

Elder, J. P. 1947. "Catullus' *Attis*." *AJP* 68:349–403.

———. 1951. "Notes on Some Conscious and Subconscious Elements in Catullus' Poetry." *HSCP* 60:101–36.

———. 1966a. "Catullus I, His Poetic Creed, and Nepos." *HSCP* 71:143–49.

———. 1966b. "The 'Figure of Grammar' in Catullus 51." *The Classical Tradition: Literary and Historical Studies in Honor of Harry Caplan*. Ed. L. Wallach. Ithaca, NY. 202–9.

Ellis, R. 1878. *Catulli Veronensis liber*. 2d ed. Oxford.

———. 1889. *A Commentary on Catullus*. 2d ed. Oxford.

Fedeli, P. 1972. *Il carme 61 di Catullo*. Fribourg.

Felman, S. 1987. *Jacques Lacan and the Adventure of Insight*. Cambridge, MA.

Fenichel, O. 1949. "The Symbolic Equation: Girl = Phallus." *Psychoanalytic Quarterly* 18:303–21.

Ferguson, J. 1970. "The Epigrams of Callimachus." *G&R* 17:64–80.

———. 1985. *Catullus*. Lawrence, KA.

Ferrari, G. R. F. 1987. *Listening to the Cicadas: A Study of Plato's Phaedrus*. Cambridge.

———. 1990. "*Akrasia* as Neurosis in Plato's *Protagoras*." *Proceedings of the Boston Area Colloquium in Ancient Philosophy*, Ed. John J. Cleary and Daniel C. Shartin. 6:115–150.

———. 1991. "Plato and Poetry." *The Cambridge History of Literary Criticism*. Ed. G. A. Kennedy. Cambridge. 1.92–148.

Ferrari, W. 1938. "Il carme 51 di Catullo." *ANSP*, 2d ser., 7:59–72.

Ferrero, L. 1955. *Interpretazione di Catullo*. Turin.

Bibliography

Finamore, J. 1984. "Catullus 50 and 51: Friendship, Love, and *Otium*." *CW* 78:11–19.

Fish, S. 1970. "Literature in the Reader: Affective Stylistics." *New Literary History* 2:123–62 (= Tompkins 1980. 70–100).

Fitzgerald, W. 1992. "Catullus and the Reader: The Erotics of Poetry." *Arethusa* 25:419–43.

———. Forthcoming. *Catullan Positions*.

Fontaine, J. 1966. Rev. of *L'Otium dans la vie morale et intellectuelle romaine*, by J.-M. André. *Latomus* 25:855–60.

Forcellini, E. 1771. *Totius latinitatis lexicon*. Padua.

Fordyce, C. J. 1961. *Catullus: A Commentary*. Oxford.

Forsyth, P. Y. 1975. "Catullus 64: the Descent of Man." *Antichthon* 9:41–51.

———. 1976. "Catullus: The Mythic Persona." *Latomus* 35:555–66.

———. 1980. "Catullus 64: Dionysus Reconsidered." *Studies in Latin Literature and Roman History*. Ed. C. Deroux. Brussels. 2.98–105.

———. 1987. "*Muneraque et Musarum hinc petis et Veneris:* Catullus 68A.10." *CW* 80:177–80.

Fortenbaugh, W. W. 1966. "Plato's *Phaedrus* 235c3." *CPh* 61:108–9.

Frank, R. I. 1968. "Catullus 51: *Otium* vs. *Virtus*." *TAPA* 99:233–39.

Fränkel, E. 1961. "Two Poems of Catullus." *JRS* 51:46–53.

———. 1962. Review of *Catullus: A Commentary*, by C. J. Fordyce. *Gnomon* 34:253–63.

Fredericksmeyer, E. A. 1965. "On the Unity of Catullus 51." *TAPA* 96:153–63.

———. 1970. "Observations on Catullus 5." *AJP* 91:431–45.

———. 1983. "The Beginning and End of Catullus' *Longus Amor*." *SO* 58:63–88.

Freud, S. 1940–68. *Gesammelte Werke* (= *GW*). 18 vols. Vols. 1–17: London. Vol. 18: Frankfurt am Main.

———. 1953–73. *The Standard Edition of the Complete Psychological Works of Sigmund Freud* (= *SE*). Ed. James Strachey. 24 vols. London.

Friedrich, G. 1908. *Catulli Veronensis Liber*. Leipzig.

Gallavotti, C. 1929. "Il carme secondo di Catullo." *BFC* 36:187–90.

Genette, G. 1980. *Narrative Discourse: An Essay in Method*. Trans. J. Lewin. Ithaca, NY.

Genovese, E. N. 1974. "Symbolism in the *Passer* Poems." *Maia* 26:121–25.

Ghiselli, A. 1953. "A proposito di una recente interpretazione del 'Passer' catulliano." *A&R* 3:111–15.

Giangrande, G. 1972. "Das Epyllion Catulls im Lichte der hellenistischen Epik." *AC* 41:123–47.

———. 1975. "Catullus' Lyrics on the *Passer*." *MPhL* 1:137–46.

Giardina, G. C. 1974. "La composizione del liber e l'itinerario poetico di Catullo." *Philologus* 118:224–35.

Giddens, A. 1979. *Central Problems in Social Theory*. Berkeley, CA.

Bibliography

Giri, G. 1894. *De locis qui sunt aut habentur corrupti in Catulli carminibus.* Turin.

Glare, P. G. W., ed. 1982. *Oxford Latin Dictionary.* Oxford.

Goold, G. P. 1974. "O Patrona Virgo". *Polis and Imperium: Studies in Honour of Edward Togo Salmon.* Ed. J. A. S. Evans. Toronto. 253–64.

———. 1981. "Two Notes on Catullus 1." *LCM* 6:233–38.

Granarolo, J. 1983. "Agitation des flots et mouvements de l'âme dans la metaphorique catullienne." *REL* 61:145–62.

Guarini, A. 1520. *Expositiones in C. V. Catullum Veronensem per Baptistam patrem emendatum.* Venice.

Gugel, H. 1967. "Catull, Carmen 8." *Athenaeum,* n.s., 45:278–93.

———. 1968. "Die Einheit von Catulls erstem Passergedicht." *Latomus* 27:810–22.

Hallett, J. 1988. "Catullus on Composition." *CW* 81:395–401.

———. 1989. "Women as *Same* and *Other* in Classical Roman Elite." *Helios* 16:59–78.

Hallett, J., A. Richlin, and M. Skinner, eds. (= Hallett et al.). Forthcoming. *Roman Sexuality.*

Halperin, D. 1985. "Platonic *Erōs* and What Men Call Love." *Ancient Philosophy* 5:161–204.

———. 1990. *One Hundred Years of Homosexuality.* New York.

Harkins, P. W. 1959. "Autoallegory in Catullus 63 and 64." *TAPA* 90:102–116.

Harmon, D. P. 1970. "Catullus 72.3–4." *CJ* 65:321–22.

———. 1973. "Nostalgia for the Age of Heroes in Catullus 64." *Latomus* 32:311–31.

Havelock, E. 1939. *The Lyric Genius of Catullus.* Oxford.

Heath, J. R. 1989. "Catullus 11: Along for the Ride." *Studies in Latin Literature and Roman History.* Ed. C. Deroux. Brussels. 98–116.

Hillard, T. 1989. "Republican Politics, Women, and the Evidence." *Helios* 16:165–82.

Hooper, R. 1985. "In Defence of Catullus' Dirty Sparrow." *G&R* 32:162–78.

Hubbard, T. K. 1983. "The Catullan Libellus." *Philologus* 127:218–37.

———. 1984. "Catullus 68: The Text as Self-Demystification." *Arethusa* 17:29–49.

Hutchinson, G. O. 1988. *Hellenistic Poetry.* Oxford.

Itzkowitz, J. B. 1983. "On the Last Stanza of Catullus 51." *Latomus* 42:129–34.

Jachmann, G. 1925. Rev. of *C. Valerius Catullus,* ed. W. Kroll. *Gnomon* 1:200–214.

Jacobson, H. 1974. *Ovid's Heroides.* Princeton, NJ.

Jakobson, R. 1956. *Fundamentals of Language.* The Hague.

Janan, M. 1991. Rev. of *100 Years of Homosexuality,* by D. Halperin. *Women's Classical Caucus Newsletter* 17:40–43.

Jauss, H. R. 1969. "Paradigmawechsel in der Literaturwissenschaft." *Linguistische Berichte* 3:44–56.

Jensen, R. C. 1967. "Otium Catulle tibi molestum est." *CJ* 62:363–65.

Jocelyn, H. D. 1980. "On Some Unnecessarily Indecent Interpretations of Catullus 2 and 3." *AJP* 101:421–41.

Jus, L. 1927. "De duodeseptuagesimo carmine Catulli, I." *Eos* 30:77–92.

Kenney, E. J. 1970. "*Doctus Lucretius.*" *Mnemosyne*, 4th ser., 23:366–92 (= *Probleme der Lukrezforschung.* Ed. C. J. Classen. 1986. Hildesheim. 237–65).

Kenny, A. 1973. "Mental Health in Plato's Republic." *The Anatomy of the Soul: Historical Essays in the Philosophy of Mind.* Oxford. 1–27.

Kent, R. 1923. "Addendum on Catullus' Passer." *AJP* 44:353–54.

Khan, H. A. 1968. "Style and Meaning in Catullus's Eighth Poem." *Latomus* 27:555–74.

Kiessling, A. 1877. *Analecta Catulliana.* Greifswald.

Kinsey, T. E. 1965a. "Catullus 11." *Latomus* 24:537–44.

———. 1965b. "Irony and Structure in Catullus 64." *Latomus* 24:911–31.

———. 1967. "Some Problems in Catullus 68." *Latomus* 26:35–53.

———. 1974. "Catullus 51." *Latomus* 33:372–78.

Klingner, F. 1956. "Catulls Peleus-Epos" *SBAW* 6:1–92 (= *Studien zu griechischen und römischen Literatur.* 1964. Zurich. 156–224).

———. 1961. *Römische Geisteswelt.* Munich.

Knopp, S. E. 1976. "Catullus 64 and the Conflict between *Amores* and *Virtutes.*" *CPh* 71:207–13.

Knox, P. 1984. "Sappho, fr. 31 LP and Catullus 51: A Suggestion." *QUCC* 46:97–102.

Konstan, D. 1972. "Two Kinds of Love in Catullus." *CJ* 68:102–6.

———. 1977. *Catullus' Indictment of Rome: The Meaning of Catullus 64.* Amsterdam.

Korzeniewski, D. 1978/79. "Elemente hymnischer Parodie in der Lyrik Catulls." *Helikon* 18/19:228–57.

Kroll, W. 1929. *C. Valerius Catullus.* 2d ed. Leipzig.

Kubiak, D. 1986. "Time and Traditional Diction in Catullus 72." *Studies in Latin Literature and Roman History.* Ed. Carl Deroux. Brussels. 259–64.

Lacan, J. 1957–58. *Séminaire V: Les formations de l'inconscient.* Unpublished.

———. 1960–61. *Séminaire VIII: Le transfert.* Unpublished.

———. 1962–63. *Séminaire X: L'angoisse.* Unpublished.

———. 1966. *Écrits.* Paris. (Selected essays translated as *Ecrits: A Selection.* 1977. Trans. Alan Sheridan. New York.)

———. 1966–67. *Séminaire XIV: La logique du fantasme.* Unpublished.

———. 1973. *Séminaire XI: Les quatres concepts fondamentaux de la psychanalyse.* Paris.

———. 1974–75. *Séminaire XXII: R.S.I. Ornicar?* 2 (1975) 87–105; 3 (1975) 95–110; 4 (1975) 91–106; 5 (1975) 15–66. Ed. J.-A. Miller.

———. 1975a. *Séminaire I: Les écrits techniques de Freud.* Paris. (Translated as *Book*

Bibliography

I: Freud's papers on Technique, 1953–54. 1988. Trans. John Forrester. New York.)

———. 1975b. *Séminaire XX: Encore.* Paris.

———. 1976–77. *Séminaire XXIV: L'insu-que-sait de l'Une-bévue s'aile à mourre. Ornicar?* 12/13 (1977):4–16; 14 (1978):5–9; 16 (1978):7–13; 17/18 (1979):7–23. Ed. J.-A. Miller.

———. 1978. *Séminaire II: Le moi dans la théorie de Freud et dans la technique de la psychanalyse.* Paris. (Translated as *Book II: The Ego in Freud's Theory and in the Technique of Psychoanalysis,* 1988. Trans. Sylvana Tomaselli. New York.)

———. 1981. *Séminaire III: Les psychoses.* Paris.

———. 1986. *Séminaire VII: L'éthique de la psychanalyse.* Paris.

Lachmann, K. 1829, 1874. *Q. Valerii Catulli Veronensis Liber.* 3d ed. Berlin.

Laidlaw, W. A. 1968. "*Otium.*" *G&R* 15:42–52.

Laplanche, J., and J.-B. Pontalis (= Laplanche-Pontalis). 1973. *The Language of Psychoanalysis.* Trans. D. Nicholson-Smith. New York.

Lateiner, D. 1977. "Obscenity in Catullus." *Ramus* 6:15–32.

Lathem, E. C., ed. 1969. *The Poetry of Robert Frost.* New York.

Lattimore, R. 1944. "Sappho 2 and Catullus 51." *CPh* 39:184–87.

Laurens, P. 1965. "A propos d'une image catullienne (c.70.4)." *Latomus* 24:545–50.

Leicester, H. M., Jr. 1990. *The Disenchanted Self: Representing the Subject in the Canterbury Tales.* Berkeley, CA.

Lejnieks, V. 1968. "*Otium Catullianum* Reconsidered." *CJ* 63:262–64.

Lenchantin de Gubernatis, M. 1928. *Il Libro di Catullo.* Turin.

Lesser, R. 1975. *Rilke: between Roots.* Princeton, NJ.

Levine, P. 1976. "Catullus C. 68: A New Perspective." *CSCA* 9:61–88.

Levitan, W. 1985. "'Dancing at the End of the Rope': Optatian Porfyry and the Field of Roman Verse." *TAPA* 115:245–70.

Licht, H. 1926. *Sittengeschichte Griechenlands.* Dresden.

Lieberg, G. 1962. *Puella divina.* Amsterdam.

Lobel, E., and D. Page, eds. (= Lobel-Page and LP). 1955. *Poetarum Lesbiorum Fragmenta.* Oxford.

Loraux, N. 1990. "Herakles: The Super-Male and the Feminine." *Before Sexuality.* Ed. D. Halperin et al. Princeton, NJ. 21–52.

Macey, D. 1988. *Lacan in Contexts.* London.

McClure, R. 1974. "The Structure of Catullus 68." *CSCA* 7:215–29.

McKay, K. J. 1962. *The Poet at Play.* Leiden.

Macleod, C. W. 1974. "A Use of Myth in Ancient Poetry." *CQ* 24:82–93.

Magnus, H. 1875. "Die Einheit von Catulls Gedicht 68." *NJb class. Philol.* 111:849–54.

Marquardt, J. 1886. *Das Privatleben der Römer.* Leipzig.

Martin, C. 1992. *Catullus.* New Haven.

Bibliography

Mayer, R. 1982. "On Catullus 1.9, Again." *LCM* 7:73–74.

———. 1983. "Catullus' Divorce." *CQ* 33:297–98.

Merrill, E. T. 1893. *Catullus*. Boston.

Milanese, G. 1988. "*Non possum reticere* (Catullo 68A, 4)." *Aevum(ant)* 1:261–64.

Miller, J.-A. 1984. "Another Lacan." Ed. Helena Schulz-Keil. *Lacan Study Notes* 1:1–3.

Miller, P. A. 1988. "Catullus 70: A Poem and Its Hypothesis." *Helios* 15:127–32.

Mitchell, J., and J. Rose, eds. 1982. *Feminine Sexuality: Jacques Lacan and the école freudienne*. New York.

Moorhouse, A. C. 1963. "Two Adjectives in Catullus 7." *AJP* 84:417–18.

Most, G. W. 1981. "On the Arrangement of Catullus' *Carmina Maiora*." *Philologus* 125:109–25.

Most, G. W., and W. W. Stowe (= Most-Stowe). 1983. *The Poetics of Murder*. San Diego.

Mulroy, D. 1977/78. "An Interpretation of Catullus 11." *CW* 71:237–47.

Muret, M.-A. 1554. *Catullus et in eum commentarius M.A.M.* Venice.

Mynors, R. A. B. 1958. *C. Valerii Catulli Carmina*. Oxford.

Nadeau, Y. 1980. "O passer nequam (Catullus 2,3)." *Latomus* 39:879–80.

Nauck, A. 1889. *Tragicorum Graecorum Fragmenta*. 2d ed. Leipzig.

Newman, J. K. 1983. "Comic Elements in Catullus 51." *ICS* 8:33–36.

Nussbaum, M. 1986. *The Fragility of Goodness*. Cambridge.

———. 1989. "Beyond Obsession and Disgust: Lucretius' Genealogy of Love." *Apeiron* 22:1–59.

Offermann, H. 1977. "Zu Catulls Gedichtcorpus." *RhM* 120:269–302.

Oksala, P. 1965. *Adnotationes criticae ad Catulli carmina*. Helsinki.

Oksala, T. 1962. "Catulls Attis-Ballade: Über den Stil der Dichtung und ihr Verhältnis zur Persönlichkeit des Dichters." *Arctos* 3:199–213.

Padel, R. 1983. "Women: Model for Possession by Greek Daemons." *Images of Women in Antiquity*. Ed. A. Cameron and A. Kuhrt. Detroit. 3–19.

Page, D. 1968. *Lyrica graeca selecta*. Oxford.

Parke, H. W. (= Parke-McGing). 1988. *Sibyls and Sibylline Prophecy in Classical Antiquity*. Ed. B. C. McGing. London.

Parker, D. 1936. *Not So Deep as a Well: Collected Poems*. New York.

Pasquali, G. 1920. "Il Carme 64 di Catullo." *SIFC*, n.s., 1:1–23.

Pearcy, L. T. 1980. "Catullus 2B—Or Not 2B?" *Mnemosyne* 33:152–62.

Pedrick, V. 1986. "*Qui potis est?* Audience Roles in Catullus." *Arethusa* 19:187–209.

Pennisi, G. 1959. "Il carme 68 di Catullo." *Emerita* 27:89–109, 213–38.

Perrotta, G. 1927. "L'elegia di Catullo ad Allio." *A&R*, 2d ser., 8:134–51.

Pfeiffer, R. (= Pf.). 1949–53. *Callimachus*. 2 vols. Oxford.

Phillips, J. E. 1976. "The Pattern of Images in Catullus 68.51–52." *AJP* 97:340–43.

Pietquin, P. 1986. "Analyse du Poème 76 de Catulle." *LEC* 54:351–66.

Pitcher, R. A. 1982. "*Passer Catulli:* The Evidence of Martial." *Antichthon* 16:97–103.

Plato. 1979. *Platonis Opera.* Ed. John Burnet. Oxford.

Poirier, R. 1977. *Robert Frost: The Work of Knowing.* New York.

Politian (Angelo Poliziano). 1489. *Miscellanea.* Florence.

Prescott, H. W. 1940. "The Unity of Catullus LXVIII." *TAPA* 71:473–500.

Preus, A. 1982/83. "Socratic Psychotherapy." *University of Dayton Review* 16:15–23.

Price, A. W. 1989. *Love and Friendship in Plato and Aristotle.* Oxford.

———. 1990. "Plato and Freud." *The Person and the Human Mind: Issues in Ancient and Modern Philosophy.* Ed. C. Gill. Oxford. 247–78.

Proust, M. 1970. *Swann's Way.* Trans. G. K. Scott Moncrieff. New York.

Pucci, P. 1961. "Il carme 50 di Catullo." *Maia* 13:249–256.

Putnam, M. C. J. 1961. "The Art of Catullus 64." *HSCP* 65:165–205.

———. 1974. "Catullus 11: The Ironies of Integrity." *Ramus* 3:70–86.

———. 1983. "The Future of Catullus." *TAPA* 113:243–62.

Quinn, K. 1959. *The Catullan Revolution.* Melbourne.

———. 1972. "Making Sense of Roman Poetry." *Ramus* 1:91–101.

———. 1973a. *Catullus: An Interpretation.* London.

———. 1973b. *Catullus: The Poems.* New York.

Ragland-Sullivan, E. 1986. *Lacan and the Philosophy of Psychoanalysis.* Urbana, IL.

———. 1991. "Beyond the Phallus." *Lacan and the Subject of Language.* Ed. Ragland-Sullivan-Bracher. New York. 267–308.

Ragland-Sullivan, E., and M. Bracher, eds. 1991. (= Ragland-Sullivan-Bracher). *Lacan and the Subject of Language.* New York.

Ramminger, A. 1937. "Motivgeschichtliche Studien zu Catulls Basiagedichten." Diss. Tübingen. Würzburg.

Rankin, H. D. 1972. "The Progress of Pessimism in Catullus, Poems 2–11." *Latomus* 31:744–51.

Realinus, B. 1551. *In nuptias Pelei et Thetidis Catullianas commentarius.* Bologna.

Richlin, A. 1983. *The Garden of Priapus.* New Haven, CT.

———. 1992a. *The Garden of Priapus.* 2d ed., with new Introduction. Oxford.

———. 1992b. "Julia's Jokes, Galla Placidia, and the Roman Use of Women as Political Icons." *Stereotypes of Women in Power: Historical Perspectives and Revisionist Views.* Ed. P. Allen, S. Dixon, and B. Garlick. Westport, CT. 65–91.

———. 1993. "Not Before Homosexuality: The Materiality of the *Cinaedus* and the Roman Law against Love between Men." *The Journal of the History of Sexuality* 3:523–73. (Also in Hallett et al. Forthcoming.)

Richmond, J. A. 1970. "Horace's Mottoes and Catullus 51." *RhM* 113:197–204.

Riese, A. 1884. *Die Gedichte Catulls.* Leipzig.

Roscher, W. H. (= Roscher, *Lex*). 1894–. *Ausführliches Lexikon der griechischen und römischen Mythologie.* Leipzig.

Rosenmeyer, T. G. 1969. *The Green Cabinet: Theocritus and the European Pastoral Lyric.* Berkeley, CA.

Ross, D. O. 1969. *Style and Tradition in Catullus.* Cambridge, MA.

———. 1975. *Backgrounds to Augustan Poetry.* Cambridge.

Rubino, C. 1974. "Myth and Mediation in the Attis Poem of Catullus." *Ramus* 3:152–75.

Rudd, N. 1964. "The Style and the Man." *Phoenix* 18:216–31.

———. 1976. *Lines of Enquiry.* Cambridge.

Russell, S. 1986. "Studies in Sappho (Fragment 31 L–P) and Catullus (Poems 11, 50, and 51)." Diss. New York University. New York, NY.

Salvatore, A. 1953. "Rapporti tra nugae e carmina docta nel canzoniere catulliano." *Latomus* 12:418–31.

Sandy, G. N. 1968. "The Imagery of Catullus 63." *TAPA* 99:389–99.

Sannazaro, J. 1535. *Epigrammaton liber primus ad Pulicianum.* (See his *Opera omnia latina scripta nuper edita.* Venice.)

Santas, G. 1988. *Plato and Freud: Two Theories of Love.* Oxford.

Sarkissian, J. 1983. *Catullus 68: An Interpretation.* Leiden.

Saussure, F. de. 1966. *Course in General Linguistics.* Ed. C. Bally and A. Sechehaye. Trans. W. Baskin. New York.

Scaliger, J. 1577. *Catulli, Tibulli, Propertii nova editio. J. S. . . . recensuit, eiusdem in eodem castigationum liber.* Paris.

Schäfer, E. 1966. *Das Verhältnis von Erlebnis und Kunstgestalt bei Catull.* Wiesbaden.

Schmidt, B. 1914. "Die Lebenszeit Catulls und die Herausgabe seiner Gedichte." *RhM* 69:275–83.

Schmidt, E. A. 1973a. "Catulls Anordnung seiner Gedichte." *Philologus* 117:215–42.

———. 1973b. "Zwei Liebesgedichte (c. 7 und 51)." *WS*, n.F., 7:91–104.

———. 1979. "Das Problem des Catullbuches." *Philologus* 123:216–31.

Schöll, F. 1880. "Zu Catullus." *NJb class Philol* 121:471–96.

Schuster, M. (= Schuster-Eisenhut). 1958. *Catullus.* 3d ed. Revised W. Eisenhut. Leipzig.

Schwabe, L. 1862. *Quaestionum Catullianarum liber unus.* Giessen.

Scott, R. 1983. "On Catullus 11." *CPh* 78:39–45.

Scott, W. C. 1969. "Catullus and Calvus." *CPh* 64:169–73.

Seager, R. 1974. "*Venustus, lepidus, bellus, salsus:* Notes on the Language of Catullus." *Latomus* 33:891–94.

Segal, C. 1968a. "Catullus 5 and 7: A Study in Complementarities." *AJP* 89:284–301.

———. 1968b. "The Order of Catullus Poems 2–11." *Latomus* 27:305–21.

Bibliography

——. 1970. "Catullan *Otiosi:* The Lover and the Poet." *G&R* 17:25–31.

——. 1974. "More Alexandrianism in Catullus VII?" *Mnemosyne* 27:139–43.

Shipton, K. M. W. 1980. "Catullus 51: Just Another Love Poem?" *LCM* 5:73–76.

——. 1987. "No Alternative to Ceremonial Negligence: Catullus 68.73ff." *SO* 62:51–68.

Simon, B. 1978. *Mind and Madness in Ancient Greece.* Ithaca, NY.

Sissa, G. 1990. *Greek Virginity.* Trans. Arthur Goldhammer. Cambridge, MA.

Skinner, M. 1971. "Catullus 8: The Comic *Amator* as *Eiron.* "*CJ* 66:298–309.

——. 1972. "The Unity of Catullus 68: The Structure of 68A." *TAPA* 103:495–512.

——. 1980. "Parasites and Strange Bedfellows: A Study in Catullus' Political Imagery." *Ramus* 8:137–52.

——. 1981. *Catullus' Passer: The Arrangement of the Book of Polymetric Poems.* New York.

——. 1987a. "Cornelius Nepos and Xenomedes of Ceos: A Callimachean Allusion in Catullus 1." *LCM* 12:22.

——. 1987b. "Disease Imagery in Catullus 76.17–26." *CPh* 82:230–33.

——. 1993. "*Ego Mulier:* The Construction of Male Sexuality in Catullus." Forthcoming in *Helios* 20.2. (Also in Hallett et al. Forthcoming.)

Skutsch, F. 1892. "Zum 68. Gedicht Catulls." *RhM* 47:138–51.

Skutsch, O. 1982. "Catullus, 1.9, and Vergil, *Aen.* 6.394." *LCM* 7:90.

Snell, B. 1971. *Tragicorum graecorum fragmenta.* 4 vols. Göttingen.

Solmsen, F. 1975. "Catullus' Artistry in C. 68: A Pre–Augustan 'Subjective' Love-Elegy." *Monumentum Chilioniense: Studien Zur Augusteischen Zeit. Kieler Festschrift für Erich Burck zum 70. Geburtstag.* Amsterdam. 260–76.

Sorci, A. 1980/81. "Il carme 68 di Catullo." *ALGP* 17–18:153–80.

Stark, R. 1957. "Sapphoreminiszenzen." *Hermes* 85:325–36.

Suleiman, S., and I. Crosman (= Suleiman-Crosman). 1980. *The Reader in the Text.* Princeton, NJ.

Swanson, R. A. 1963. "The Humor of Catullus 8. " *CJ* 58:193–96.

Sweet, D. R. 1987. "Catullus 11: A Study in Perspective." *Latomus* 46:510–26.

Syme, R. 1956. "Piso and Veranius in Catullus." *C&M* 17:129–34.

Tani, S. 1984. *The Doomed Detective.* Carbondale, IL.

Tennyson, Alfred, Lord. 1969. *The Poems of Tennyson.* Ed. C. Ricks. London.

Teresa of Avila, St. 1980. *The Collected Works of St. Teresa of Avila.* 3 vols. Trans. K. Kavanaugh and O. Rodriguez. Washington, DC.

Thomson, D. F. S. 1967. "Catullus and Cicero: Poetry and the Criticism of Poetry." *CW* 60:225–30.

——. 1978. *Catullus: A Critical Edition.* Chapel Hill, NC.

Todorov, T. 1971a. "Les transformations narratives." *Poétique de la prose.* Paris. 225–40.

——. 1971b. "The Two Principles of Narrative." *Diacritics:* 1:37–44.

————. 1973. *The Fantastic: A Structural Approach to a Literary Genre*. Trans. R. Howard. Cleveland.

————. 1977. *Poetics of Prose*. Trans. R. Howard. Oxford.

Tompkins, J. 1980. *Reader-Response Criticism*. Baltimore.

Tuplin, C. J. 1981. "Catullus 68." *CQ* 31:113–39.

Ullman, B. L. 1955. *Studies in the Italian Renaissance*. Rome.

Vahlen, J. 1902. "Über Catulls Elegie an M'Allius." *SPAW* 44:1024–43.

Venuto, D. de. 1966. "Il carme 70 di Catullo e *Anth. Pal.* 5,8 di Meleagro." *RCCM* 8:215–19.

Vlastos, G. 1973. *Platonic Studies*. Princeton, NJ.

Vinson, M. 1989/90. "And Baby Makes Three? Parental Imagery in the Lesbia-Poems of Catullus." *CJ* 85:47–53.

Vollmer, F. 1919. "Lesungen und Deutungen, X: Catull 68." *SBAW* 5:4–8.

Voss, J. H. (Vossius). 1684. *Catullus cum eruditissimo Is. Vossii commentario*. London.

Vretska, K. 1966. "Das Problem der Einheit von Catullus c. 68." *WS* 79:313–30.

Wagenvoort, H. 1935. "*Ludus Poeticus.*" *LEC* 4:108–20 (= *Studies in Roman Literature, Culture, and Religion*. Leiden, 1956. 30–42).

————. 1940. "De Catulli carmine secundo." *Mnemosyne* 8:294–98.

Weber, C. 1983. "Two Chronological Contradictions in Catullus 64." *TAPA* 113:263–71.

Weston, A. H. 1919/20. "The Lesbia of Catullus." *CJ* 15:501.

Westphal, R. 1870. *Catulls Gedichte in ihrem geschichtlichen Zusammmenhange übersetzt und erläutert*. 2d ed. Breslau.

Wheeler, A. L. 1934, 1964. *Catullus and the Traditions of Ancient Poetry*. Reprint ed. Berkeley, CA.

Wilamowitz-Möllendorf, U. 1879. "Die Galliamben des Kallimachos und Catullus." *Hermes* 14:194–201, 479.

————. 1913. *Sappho und Simonides*. 2 vols. Berlin.

————. 1924. *Hellenistische Dichtung in der Zeit des Kallimachos*. Berlin.

Wilkinson, L. P. 1974. "Ancient and Modern: Catullus 51 Again." *G&R* 21:82–85.

Williams, G. 1968. *Tradition and Originality in Roman Poetry*. Oxford.

Wills, G. 1967. "Sappho 31 and Catullus 51." *GRBS* 8:167–97.

Winkler, J. J. 1985. *Auctor & Actor: A Narratological Reading of Apuleius' "The Golden Ass."* Berkeley, CA.

————. 1990. *The Constraints of Desire*. New York.

Winter, T. N. 1973. "Catullus Purified: A Brief History of C. 16." *Arethusa* 6:257–65.

Wirshbo, E. 1980. " 'Lesbia': A Mock Hypocorism?" *CPh* 75:70.

Wirth, T. 1986. "Catull c. 2.: *Passer* und *Malum* als Zeichen der Liebe." *RhM* 129:36–53.

Wiseman, T. P. 1969. *Catullan Questions*. Leicester.

———. 1974. *Cinna the Poet*. Leicester.

———. 1979. *Clio's Cosmetics*. Leicester.

———. 1985. *Catullus and His World*. Cambridge.

Witke, C. 1968. *Ennaratio Catulliana*. Leiden.

Wood, N. 1988. *Cicero's Social and Political Thought*. Oxford.

Woodman, A. J. 1966. "Some Implications of *Otium* in Catullus 51.13–16." *Latomus* 25:217–26.

———. 1978. "Catullus 11 and 51." *LCM* 3:77–79.

Wormell, D. E. W. 1966. "Catullus as Translator (C. 51)." *The Classical Tradition: Literary and Historical Studies in Honor of Harry Caplan*. Ed. L. Wallach. Ithaca, NY. 187–201.

Yardley, J. C. 1981. "Catullus 11: The End of a Friendship." *SO* 56:63–69.

Zetzel, J. E. G. 1983. "Catullus, Ennius and the Poetics of Allusion." *ICS* 8:251–66.

Žižek, S. 1989. *The Sublime Object of Ideology*. London.

Index

197

Index

Hutchinson, G. O., 159n31

Identity: confusion of, in c.68, 126–29, 130, 131, 136–42; defined, 20, 102; and the Desire of the Other, 79, 88, 90–91, 95, 97; and difference, 121; as an Imaginary function, 18, 19, 102–3; and interpretation, 20, 79, 114, 124; and knowledge, 68, 85; and subjectivity, 19–20, 102–3, 124; as subject-object relation, 124

Imaginary, the 18–20, 22, 23, 24, 28; and identity, 18, 19, 102–3; and interpretation, in the epigrams, 85, 95; and intersubjective division, 18–19, 48. *See also* Real, the; Symbolic, the

Immortality and poetry, 40, 117–19, 127, 135

Imperialism and sexuality, 63–64, 65

Irony as dissimulating the subject, 44–45, 51. *See also* Callimachus: poetics of; Callimachus: poetics of, as influence on Catullus

Itzkowitz, J. B., 168n29

Jachmann, G., 102, 151n25

Jocelyn, H. D., 157n22

John of the Cross, St., 29. *See also* Lacan: on gender; Lacan: on mysticism

Jokes (wit), 48–49, 50, 51, 52, 53–54; Freud on, 49; and Law, 53–54

Jouissance: defined, 30; and dissolution of the self, 31, 54, 67, 74, 105–17; and the divine, 30–31, 103, 105–7; and gender subversion, 31, 55, 105–7; of the idiot, 68, 76; *jouissance phallique* and *jouissance féminine* distinguished, 30; and knowledge, 31, 75–76, 68–71, 141–42; and *otium*, 52, 54, 55, 74–75; and repetition, 30, 67, 72, 142; and skepticism, xi,

76; and the Symbolic, 30, 32, 54, 55, 56, 76, 105; and Woman, 30–32, 67–69, 71, 75–76, 105, 107. See also *Mania* ("divine madness")

Kenney, E. J., 167n21

Kent, R., 162n51

Kinsey, T. E., 176n26, 177n26, 179n42

Klingner, F., 173n19

Knowledge: and gender, 28–30, 32, 68–71, 75–76, 79–80, 85, 87–88, 90–91, 141–42; and identity, 68, 85; and *jouissance*, 31, 75–76, 68–71, 141–42; and narrative, 78; Plato on, 7, 9, 28–29, 32, 42, 68, 70–71; and the subject as divided, in Catullus, 78–79; unconscious, x, 7–9, 12

Kojève, Alexandre, 18

Konstan, D., 94, 173n19

Kroll, W., 169n23, 176n26

Kubiak, D., 169n22

Lacan, J.: on desire's connection to art, 7; distinguishes repetition from neurosis, 24–25; on the divided/lacking subject, 7–8, 16–20, 22–24, 27–28, 60, 67, 78–79, 97; on the drive (*Trieb*), 27, 57–58; extends Freud's psychoanalytic inquiries, 15–16, 19, 21–25; and the *fort/da* game, 22–24; on gender, 28–31, 67–69, 168n3; on language, 19, 20–21, 21–26, 57–58, 68, 86; on mysticism, 29–31, 68–69; and Plato, x–xi, 7–8, 9–10, 16–17, 25–26, 28–29, 32, 33, 42–43, 60, 62, 67–71, 80–81, 97–99, 103, 111, 117–18, 141; on the Other, 21, 23, 30, 79; on the phallus, 21, 26, 28–29, 48, 68, 153n61; on the three orders (Real Symbolic, and Imaginary), 16–21

200

MICAELA JANAN received her Ph.D. degree from Princeton University in 1988. She is assistant professor of classical studies at Duke University in Durham, North Carolina, where she teaches courses in classical and comparative literature and literary theory. She specializes in the literature of Late Republican and early Augustan Rome. Her work has appeared in *Ramus, Arethusa,* and other journals.